PETER FITZSIMONS was raised on a farm at Peats Ridge, eight kilometres north of Sydney, Australia. Throughout the 1980s he concentrated on freelance writing and playing rugby, which included seven test matches for Australia as well as club rugby in Italy and France.

FitzSimons now works as a journalist with the *Sydney Morning Herald*, also writing columns for the *Daily Telegraph*. He is the author of nine other books: *Basking in Beirut*; *Little Theories of Life*; *Nick Farr-Jones, The Authorised Biography*; *Hitchhiking for Ugly People*; *Rugby Stories*; *The Rugby War*; *Everybody But Phar Lap*; *Beazley, A Biography*; and *Everyone And Phar Lap*.

He lives in Sydney with his wife, Lisa, and their three young children.

NANCY WAKE

The inspiring story of one of the war's greatest heroines

PETER FITZSIMONS

HarperCollins*Entertainment*
An Imprint of HarperCollins*Publishers*

HarperCollins*Entertainment*
An Imprint of HarperCollins*Publishers*
77–85 Fulham Palace Road,
Hammersmith, London W6 8JB

www.fireandwater.com

This paperback edition 2002
1 3 5 7 9 8 6 4 2

First published in Australia by
HarperCollins*Publishers* 2001

Lines from *Sheik of Araby* (Smith/Snyder/Wheeler) © reproduced
with kind permission by J. Albert & Son Pty Ltd.

ISBN 0 00 714401 6

Set in Sabon

Printed and bound in Great Britain by
Omnia Books Limited, Glasgow

*To my late parents, who proudly served Australia in the Second
World War, as Lieutenant Peter McCloy FitzSimons, 2nd/4th Light
Anti Aircraft of the Ninth Division, AIF (North Africa [El
Alamein], New Guinea [Finchaven and Dumpu]) and Lieutenant
Beatrice Helen Booth OAM (AIF Physiotherapist in Darwin
and Bougainville). And to all the brave men and women
who served with them. We dips our lids.*

ACKNOWLEDGEMENTS

First, my warm thanks to Nancy herself for: the endless hours she has accorded me in answering my interminable questions; for the trust she displayed by telling me things of which she had never spoken previously; for the many wonderful meals she made for me in her apartment while I kept *tap-tap-tapping* away and rolling tape.

Let me also express gratitude for the many hundreds of hours she had already put into writing her autobiography, *The White Mouse*, which was a valuable resource for me when I started to tell her story from a different perspective. Ditto my warm acknowledgement of Russell Braddon, a wonderful writer long dead who also conducted many hours of interviews with Nancy in the 1950s, and was the first one to map out her war years on which so much subsequent writing has followed. His book, *Nancy Wake: The Story of a Very Brave Woman*, was equally an invaluable resource for me. So too, the many other books I called upon, particularly, *They Fought Alone: The Story of British Agents in France* by Colonel Maurice Buckmaster; *The Resistance, World War II* by Russell Miller; *They Came From the Sky* by E.H. Cookridge; and *SOE, An Outline History of the Special Operations Executive 1940–46* by M.R.D. Foot. Other books used are noted in the bibliography.

I particularly thank my friend, Kate Irvine, of Sydney's Mitchell Library for her help in tracking down some of the more obscure books.

Inevitably, when researching stories the bulk of which happened sixty years ago—and some nearly ninety years ago—I was hampered by the fact that so many of the key protagonists, apart from Nancy, are long gone. I was nevertheless delighted to find some still living, and I thank those all hereafter quoted. Another factor with researching events of so long ago was that there have been differing accounts of much the same action, and differing memories of what *precisely* occurred. When such clashes proved insoluble, I have gone with Nancy's memory.

To my principal researcher, Kevin Brumpton, my deep appreciation as always. In terms of ferreting out even the most minor details of military actions long ago, he was as always without peer. If it was somewhere on the public record, Kevin could find it and get it to me. Ditto, Jo Morris in New Zealand, who was a great help putting together the New Zealand part of Nancy's story. Thank you, Jo. Harriet Veitch, my friend, colleague and fellow Francophile at the *Sydney Morning Herald* was also a wonderful help, both in terms of general advice and her work in helping sort out tangled sentences, grammar and the like. I am also indebted to Greg Pemberton, a Senior Lecturer in Politics at Maquarie University—and a noted military historian—for his enormous efforts to verify historical accuracy of the text.

As to my wife, Lisa, I didn't marry her because when we met she was already recognised as one of this country's best editors, but in terms of our subsequent lives together, it certainly hasn't hurt. She edited this manuscript from first to last, gave me endless advice as to its structure and form and, as she has always managed to do, vastly improved it.

To my editor at HarperCollins, Belinda Lee, my thanks and professional respect as always.

CONTENTS

PREFACE

One hour of life, crowded to the full with glorious
action, and filled with noble risks, is worth whole
years of those mean observances of paltry decorum.

WALTER SCOTT

During the mid–1980s, while living and playing rugby in
la France profonde—at the tiny village of Donzenac, in *la
Corrèze*—I often used to have a drink at Madame Salesse's café
with my aged friend Martin, the local garage proprietor. A fairly
meek and mild bloke he might have been when I knew him, but
not during World War II. Then, his *nom de guerre* had been
'Tin-Tin' and, as one of the most ferocious fighters of the local
Resistance movement, he had been the scourge of the Germans.

'*Et l'Australienne, Nonc-eeeee Wake, Peterrrr,*' he asked me
once, early in our friendship. '*Tu la connais?*'

No, I didn't know Nancy Wake, or at least I had never met her.
But Martin knew a lot about her. She was a legend, he said, one of
the hardest fighters the partisans had ever had, a leader, a great
organiser, fearless, fantastic. And also '*trés belle*', he mentioned
with a twinkle, even all those years on. He had not fought with
her side-by-side, he said, as she was with the partisans in the
neighbouring region of Auvergne, but her fame knew no borders,
and he had been very proud to meet her once at a 'safe house' in
Aurillac, about one hundred kilometres away.

From time to time over the next four years, I would hear her
name from the old ones—this amazing Australian woman who, to
the locals, went by her own *nom de guerre* of 'Madame Andrée'.
She had been in this region four decades before me and had

covered herself in so much glory, that I would always walk a little taller that my countrywoman had acquitted herself so well and was remembered so fondly. Yet, even when working back in Australia as a journalist for the *Sydney Morning Herald,* I never came across her, though I do remember hearing somewhere that she was living quietly up in Port Macquarie on the New South Wales north coast. One day, I thought, I'd really like to meet her if the opportunity ever presented itself ...

More than a decade passed. Then, a phone call to me at the *Herald* out of the blue from my old rugby coach, Peter Fenton— the coach, incidentally, of the Sydney team with whom I first landed in France in 1984. Did I remember Bob Cowley, he wanted to know, who once scored a famous intercept try against Northern Suburbs for Parramatta?

'No.'

Oh, well anyway, Bob had a brother called Jim who lived in Port Macquarie and he was a very close friend and keen supporter of Nancy Wake, the most decorated heroine of the Second World War. Jim wanted to know if I would give him a call, because he wanted to talk to me about Nancy, and about a possible story for my newspaper. On my way, chief!

I indeed met the woman in question in her Port Macquarie apartment, and conducted the interview for a *Herald* story for Anzac Day. But that was not all ... so impressed had I been when I met her, so riveted by even the barest rudiments of her life story, that even as I was about to embark from Port Macquarie airport that afternoon for the last flight to Sydney I called my commissioning editor at HarperCollins, Alison Urquhart, and said: 'I'm going to write a book on Nancy, and you're going to publish it'.

I did, they did, and here it is ... At its conclusion, my chief hope is that I have done her story justice.

CHAPTER ONE

A Cry in the Night ...

The good stars met in your horoscope,
Made you of spirit and fire and dew.

ROBERT BROWNING
Quoted on the title page of Nancy Wake's favourite book,
Anne of Green Gables, by Lucy Maud Montgomery.

In a dingy little room at the back of a modest weatherboard home in the suburb of Roseneath, the air was thick with exhaustion, the sheets and floor nearby lightly spattered with blood and wetness. On the bed, a woman was just starting to recover from the searing waves of pain that had been washing over her during the supreme effort of giving birth. Even though this was her sixth child—yet her first for eight years—it never seemed to get any easier, only ever made her progressively more tired. In the gusty heights of windy Wellington, on the thirtieth day of August 1912, the timeless scene of human birth had just taken place and Ella Wake lay back exhausted, totally spent. A woman hovered close—a *tapuhi*, the Maori word for midwife—and she was positively beaming with happiness. Cradling the baby's head in the crook of her bountiful arms, she pointed to the thin veil of skin which covered the top part of the infant's head, known in English as 'a caul'.

'This,' she said softly tracing a gentle finger across the fold of extra membrane, 'is what we call a *kahu* and it means your baby will always be lucky. Wherever she goes, whatever she does, the gods will look after her.'

The mother groaned and lay back in the bed.

If so, so be it. At that particular time Ella was simply too tired to care and had room only for relief that her exhausting effort was over—though she would at least tell her daughter the story of the Maori midwife's predictions many times for years afterwards.

Ella Rosieur Wake came from an interesting ethnic mix, her genetic pool bubbling with material from the Huguenots, the French Protestants who had famously fled France so they could pursue their religion freely, and Maori, as her English great-grandmother had been a Maori maiden by the name of Pourewa. She had been the first of her race to marry a white man, in the person of Nancy's English great-grandfather Charles Cossell, and they were wed by the Reverend William Williams at Waimate Mission Station on 26 October, 1836. Legend has it that the great Maori chieftain, Hone Hoke, had loved Pourewa himself, and had sworn death to them both, but had been killed in the Maori Wars before fulfilling his threat.

In sum, Ella's people went a long, long way back in New Zealand, and physically she was like the land itself, rustically beautiful. As to personality though, the least that can be said is that she seemed to have inherited very little of the famous French *joie de vivre*—or perhaps it had simply been drained out of her over the long, hard years of child-raising. Rather, she always seemed to project a kind of long-suffering religious rectitude, a dowdy air that life was duty and duty was hard; hard was her lot and lots of children made it harder still.

Young Nancy's father, Charles, however, was of solid English stock and was an entirely different sort of person. An extremely good-looking, tall man of easy, extroverted charisma and enormous warmth, he was a journalist/editor by trade, then working on a Wellington newspaper. He was a dapper dresser who never seemed to have a worry in the world, and there must have been some wonder from others how such a different pair as he and Ella could have managed to marry and make it, but their large brood seemed testament to the commitment they had to each other.

True, Nancy cannot remember her parents ever showing affection for each other, but that may well have been because she could simply never see past the affection her father showed *her*. In her young life, she loved nothing better than sitting on her father's lap in his big easy chair, with him either reading stories to her, or dancing around the room to the sound of an ancient gramophone, or just cuddling and chatting gaily. In her memory at least, the two would laugh and joke and carry on for hours on end, and just as she instinctively felt that she was her father's favourite, she also had a vague sense that her other brothers and sisters, not to mention her own mother, resented her for it. Not to worry, life was too good to care.

With Charles Wake's journalistic career going so well he was receiving offers of employment from far afield, the whole family moved from the heights of Wellington to the lower North Shore of Sydney and—at an age when Nancy was still a toddler—established themselves in a rambling solid-brick residence in High Street, North Sydney. It was a house quite large enough to accommodate the equally rambling Wake family, with a sixteen year age range separating the first-born Gladys, down through Charles, Hazel, Stanley and Ruby to the youngest by a breezy country mile, Nancy.

Sydney pleased all of them. One of the jewels of the South Pacific, it may have been right on the edges of the British Empire, but as a town of 750,000 people—and three times the size of Wellington—none of them could get over the sheer *size* of it, the number of people crowding on the streets on a busy day. It might have started out as a convict colony, with people brought there in chains against their will, but something about it had drawn an awful lot of people there ever since.

The Wakes settled in quickly, even mother Ella, who had been initially very reluctant to leave her large extended family in New Zealand. Every day, father Charles went off to work, catching the ferry from Milsons Point across the harbour to his job in the city, and every afternoon Nancy—specifically Nancy—would be waiting for him at the gate when he returned home, simply because as she says, 'He was lovely to me and I loved him . . . we adored each other.'

* * *

But then one day he didn't come home. Not that night. Nor the next day. Nor even the one after that. He just didn't come home. He'd gone on a trip, Nancy's mother told her. To America, she said. Was trying to get something going in this new thing everyone was talking about called 'the movies'. He'd gone there with an idea to make a movie about the Maori culture in his native New Zealand and he would be back in about three months. Nancy patiently waited. And waited some more. But still he didn't come home, and still she received no word, no letter, no postcard, nothing. Where was Daddy?

Where indeed. One day, Nancy noticed that her parents' wedding photo which used to stand on her mother's dresser was not there any more, and that was that. Typically, it was not discussed—a fact that deepened the youngest child's confusion and sense of abandonment over her father. Never in her whole life would Nancy be quite sure of what had happened to him, but it was obvious that wherever he was, whatever he was doing, he simply would never again come waltzing Matilda up the garden path like he used to do. She would never sit in his lap again. He would never more read her stories. He really *wasn't* coming back. Perhaps her mother had received a letter to this effect, or even had known it all along, for although she never definitively told the children that their father had deserted them, nor did she ever give any indication that she feared for his safety.

The clearest sign that something *definitive* had changed, and that they were not going back to New Zealand as had been briefly discussed, was that just a few months after he disappeared they had to move to the adjoining suburb of Neutral Bay to a far less spacious residence. The reason—she would later find out—was that her beloved father had more or less sold the North Sydney house out from under them. Their 'new' house, the one that would subsequently be the one of Nancy's childhood, was the second on the left up leafy Holdsworth Street running roughly parallel to Ben Boyd Road with its backyard running all the way through to Spruson Street. It was a weathered weatherboard house set on the classic Australian 'quarter-acre block', just a stone's throw from one of the little sparkling fingers of Sydney Harbour that pushed deeply into the suburb. Typical of the times, it came complete with an outside 'dunny', and a clothing line of ropes strung between two posts dominating the backyard. As to the house proper, it had a large verandah, a whole rabbit-warren of bedrooms, a tiny kitchen and a ramshackle living room.

Without Nancy's father there as the breadwinner, things were a lot tighter financially for the whole Wake brood, though with the help of Nancy's older siblings, who were now earning a wage, and the rent paid by a long-term lodger from Tasmania, the family were just able to make ends meet. There were no second helpings of apple pie, but at least there were plenty of potatoes; no new clothes to speak of for Nancy, but lots of hand-me-downs that served their purpose; no room of your own, but everyone got a bed of some sort, with Nancy quickly taking over the abandoned spot left in the marital bed by her departed father (which would remain her sleeping place for the next ten years of her life). This increased physical closeness with her mother did not transform itself into any kind of emotional closeness. 'There was barely a kiss goodnight,' says Nancy flatly, 'though I at least remember that for some reason she liked to read to me in bed, which I loved.'

Of the siblings, far and away the biggest contributor to the family's finances was Nancy's brother Stanley, good ol' Stanley! Whatever part of a young girl's soul that needed a father-like figure to love and cherish had, in all probability, transferred its affections from Nancy's absent father to this warm-hearted and generous man—placing Stanley in her memory as a secular saint—and she loved him like no other.

'Charles,' she says of her oldest brother, 'was a scoundrel who would come to a bad end, and I would never really get on with the rest of them, but Stanley was always wonderful to me. He was in the navy ...'

This latter part of the 1910–1920 decade was a proud time for anyone to be in military service, at least for those who survived the Great War, as Stanley had. Even though he had seen only a small slice of action, it was still the family's pride that he had

served—and one of Nancy's first compelling memories was tied up
with it. She was six years old, and dressed in the very best hand-
me-downs she could muster. As she remembers the episode, the
sun had just barely come up and yet there were lots of people
gathered in Sydney's Martin Place with their heads bowed, lots of
soldiers standing up ram-rod straight with the butts of their
gleaming rifles positioned right by their shining boots, and a
minister of the church was intoning something ... Something
about ... *Gallipoli* ... and how ... *all those men who there gave
their lives so that we might live in freedom* ... and that ... *they
will never be forgotten.* Now let us pray ...

There was a lot more praying, and hymn singing, and sometimes
someone standing out the front of those soldiers would start
shouting and then all the men in their uniforms would start
twirling their rifles around at once before clunking them all down
at once and then the man would shout some more and then they
would do it again ... And the whole thing was ever so exciting!

And sad. For even through her amazement at so much colour
and movement all at once, she knew enough to realise that
something terrible had happened just a little while before, some
kind of army action where as many as ten thousand Australian and
New Zealand soldiers had died in some place called 'Gliply' or
something. Well, she was both an Australian *and* a New Zealander,
so it all seemed doubly important. And anyway they had sacrificed
their lives for the good of their nations and everyone still living
should always give thanks on this day that they had done so.
Nancy's family certainly did.

Having attended the first dawn Anzac Ceremony at Martin
Place, the family attended every one thereafter, always giving
thanks that those men had so bravely given their lives, and more
particularly that the life of her own beloved brother Stan had been
spared. Year by year, as the growing Nancy stood smack-bang in
the middle of the sometimes weeping crowd, she would come to
learn and understand more about Gallipoli; appreciate just why so
very many floral wreaths were being laid; and be enormously
impressed by such bravery and sacrifice for the country.

Never did it occur to young Nancy, nor to her friends, nor to the adult world around her, that they might question why so many young Australians and New Zealanders should have died in a foreign land essentially to serve the interests of faraway Britain. That was just the way things were back then. As a matter of fact, during that first Anzac Day ceremony that Nancy had attended, the Governor of New South Wales had read a message from the King, which had created quite a stir. (The King himself! Sending us a message!)

'Tell my people of Australia,' the Governor had intoned through the morning mist, 'that today I am joining with them in their solemn tribute to the memorial of their heroes who died in Gallipoli.

'They gave their lives for a supreme cause in gallant comradeship with the rest of my sailors and soldiers who fought and died with them. Their value and fortitude have shed fresh lustre on the British coat of arms. May those who mourn their loss find comfort in the conviction that they did not die in vain, but that their sacrifice has drawn our peoples more closely together, and added strength and glory to the Empire.'[1]

Before the Great War in which those men had died, the soon-to-be Australian Prime Minister Andrew Fisher had declared that Australia would fight on Britain's side 'to the last man and the last shilling', and had been widely acclaimed for it. Britain was the mother country, Australia and New Zealand her proud and strapping sons ready to do their bit to defend her.

'That,' says Nancy, 'was simply the way it was. I was brought up in a family where, although we were from New Zealand and living in Australia, we were "of" Great Britain, and we were loyal to whoever was on the throne. It was never something you questioned.'

Back in Holdsworth Street, life went on. Nancy's older siblings never seemed to talk about the absence of their father one way or another, and simply got on with their lives. Their mother, meanwhile, would never quite recover from the humiliation of her husband leaving her—it is possible she had some kind of nervous breakdown at one point under the terrible strain of it all—but at least she seemed to draw great strength from devoting tremendous energy to reading her Bible. Ever and always. When Nancy got up in the morning, her mother would be sitting there in the corner reading and reciting passages. At noon the same. In the late afternoon she'd still be at it and on into the evening. Even when Ella Wake wasn't reading her Bible, she was quoting vast slabs from memory, back and forth, forth and back. 'And Moses said come forth', always with an admonitory finger to show what God had in store for those who did not follow His way, by which, it often seemed to her youngest, she meant specifically *Nancy*.

Perhaps it was merely childhood perception, but it always seemed to Nancy that just as her father had always had a special place in his heart for her, her mother had no place at all and was always promising that the eternal damnation of God would come down upon her, and she would be cast into the flames of Hell.

'My mother used to tell me,' Nancy recalls, 'that God would punish me if I didn't pray to Him every night and fear Him, but I just couldn't bring myself to do it. She was never physically cruel to me or beat me or anything like that, but she gave me no affection, no affection at all. I am convinced she hated to even look at me, and I also suspect that I was an unwanted child by her—that my father came home late one night and had his way, but that she never wanted more children. She used to tell me that my eyebrows were too thick and too close together, that I was ugly, and that maybe that was part of God's punishment for me, but there would no doubt be a lot more punishment to come. I literally lived in fear of God and what he would do to me.' To her childish fancy, it seemed every crack of lightning, every roll of thunder was just a harbinger of what Hell had in store for her. Not for her next sister up, Ruby, or the one up again, Hazel, or any of the boys, just *her*. God—big as a steam train and coming right at her.

Partly in an effort to forestall this dreadful collision of God's will and her own manifest naughtiness and unworthiness, Nancy worked as hard as she could in the home.

'Even from an early age,' she says, 'I would cook, put the washing out before I went to school, bring it in after I came home, sweep the kitchen, the verandah, and make the beds. I did everything because my mother was useless and she told me God would get me if I didn't.'

Childish fancy or not, Nancy's perception of those very early days in Neutral Bay is that she had only three true friends—the galah, the cat and the dog.

'They were my friends and I used to talk to them,' she remembers. 'I couldn't really play with my sisters, because there was such a big age gap between me and them—and besides which most of my siblings had started to move out of home from when I was about six— so that was all I was left with.'

Clearly, not everyone in the world was so ill-used. *Some* people, she could see, were very well looked after. Like that nice Mrs King, living across the street in the house with all the jacaranda trees. She was getting very, very fat indeed, now that she was in something called 'the pudding club', going to have a baby, and there was always a lot of fuss made about her, everyone looking after her all the time and asking if there was anything they could do to help her. That looked very, very nice indeed.

'How are you this morning, Mrs King? Now you look after yourself...'

'Everything okay, Mrs King? Can I help you with your shopping bags?'

'Cheerio, Mrs King! You go inside now and have a nice cup of tea and a lie-down, okay?'

Okay. All of that looked very nice indeed and...

And on this morning the young Nancy pulled the thin woollen blanket up around her chin and declared that she wouldn't get up to go to school. Wouldn't. Wouldn't. *Wouldn't.* Told her mother she was simply too sick, felt absolutely terrible, and she simply must stay in bed until the doctor came. The doctor did come, kindly Dr Studdie. He turned up in his horse and cart, tethered the beast to the tree across the road, and was ushered to Nancy's bedside.

'Now, Nancy,' the doctor said, as he opened his bag and got out his stethoscope. 'What seems to be the problem?'

'Do you promise you won't tell Mummy?'

'That depends, but I promise you can trust me.'

'I'm going to have a baby,' she whispered gravely. With which, she pulled the bedclothes covering her torso downwards, to reveal the enormous lump on her belly, clearly visible beneath her jim-jams. The doctor paused, looked down at her, and gently proffered the next question.

'What makes you think you are going to have a baby, Nance?'

No answer.

'What makes you think you are going to have a baby, Nance?'

Still no answer. Gently, gently then, the doctor continued his examination of her distended belly, and quickly formed his considered professional diagnosis. She wasn't going to have a baby at all, but she did have a cushion tucked away beneath her pyjama top. This doctor of compassion, though he would certainly have had a right to some irritation for her having so wasted his time, simply laughed lightly and asked her why she had done such a thing.

'Well Mrs King's got a big tummy,' Nancy replied unhappily, 'and she's going to have a baby and everyone is nice to her, so I want one too. Please don't tell Mumma.'

Amazingly, Dr Studdie didn't—or at least Nancy never got into trouble from her mother for the ruse, which makes her think that he kept his promise. After the doctor told her that she shouldn't do such things and that he was sure things would turn out all right, he encouraged her to get up, get dressed, and he would drop her off to school himself. What he told Mrs Wake is unknown, but Nancy would ever afterwards appreciate the fact that he had never betrayed her.

'I think,' Nancy says, 'Dr Studdie knew that I was an unhappy little child and that all I needed was a little kindness.'

Others might have detected the same. In Holdsworth Street, the butcher used to come twice a week on Tuesday and Friday afternoons, also with a horse and cart, and he was always happy for Nancy to sit up beside him as he completed his rounds to his customers, chatting away as they went, allowing her to sometimes hold the reins and say *giddup, giddup,* to the plodding beast that made the gravel-crunching wheels of the cart slowly turn.

'I'd go all over Neutral Bay and sometimes have to walk a long way back,' Nancy remembers, 'but was happy just to do anything to get a ride with the horse and cart and be able to have a good talk with him. He was a lovely old bloke, Mr Van Den Burg, with a great big straw hat, and I'm sure we looked quite the pair. I got on with all the visiting tradespeople like that—the ice-man, milkos, rabbitohs and so on—and they were all lovely. They looked after me, they were absolutely wonderful to me.'

For all that, it was not as if Nancy grew up *entirely* without other children to rouse about with. Far from it. In her street she ran with a pack of five others—three boys and two girls—who would spend lots of time together playing such things as hop-scotch and marbles out and about on the footpaths and in each other's backyards. They would often congregate beneath the Beal's house which stood on stilts next to the Wake residence. This would happen most particularly during the summer holidays when it was hot and steamy outside. Under the house the cool earth and welcome shade provided not only great relief, but also a good hiding place from parents who all too often would be wanting them to do their chores.

'Then when we wanted to spend a penny,' Nancy says, 'we couldn't go to the lavatory because they'd see us, so we used to have a wee-wee down there, and then one of us, Adeline Beal, decided we'd have a peeing match and the boys won. Then I said "Oh it's not fair, you've got a little thing we don't have, you've got to take a handicap"; so we handicapped them—the boys having to stand further back behind the line in the sand—and they never won another time.'

Such activities, while fine fun for a time, are locked in Nancy's memory as no more than sometimes happy diversions from what was generally an unhappy time for her. Mostly, she says, she simply didn't feel a part of the family at all. Nor did she actually feel like she was meant to live and grow up in the archly conservative territory of the lower North Shore of Sydney. Lennie Lower wrote of the nearby suburb of Chatswood at around this time, as a place 'where respectability stalks abroad, adorned with starched linen and surrounded by mortgages'.[2]

There was, in short, a particularly hazy, lazy kind of lassitude in the air which, for whatever reason, was not pleasing to Nancy's natural spirit. All through her childhood, there seemed to be a pervasively stifling sense of stuffiness, at least for her. Others around her didn't necessarily feel it, but she did. As she recalls, it was a little like being in a small room on a summer's day with the windows closed, longing to be outside where the air was fresh, flowers of colour grew, and where she could *breathe*. Hell, she sometimes thought in a supremely unladylike fashion, that she'd actually rather be outside in a full-blown *storm* than inside where all was so damn still and unmoving.

In sum, from a very young age, the urge to be elsewhere was always very strong in Nancy Wake. Specifically, she wanted to go to New York, London and Paris, the three cities that seemed to be most often mentioned in the same breath as 'glamour'. Whenever she could, Nancy would bury herself in the magazines that her sisters sometimes left around, hoping to find articles or photos about these cities, as she conjured up what it would be like to one day make landfall in such places. Helping to sustain this fertile imagination was a great love of reading generally, and two books in particular:

'I loved *Anne of Green Gables*, and its sequel *Anne of the Island*,' Nancy recalls. 'Loved them, loved them, loved them. I wouldn't say those books were as big an influence on me as the Bible was on my mother, but in a way they were my own sort of Bible.'

The series of 'Anne' books was written in the early twentieth century by Lucy Maud Montgomery, and detailed the adventures of a fiery and adventurous red-haired orphan girl called Anne Shirley who ends up on Prince Edward Island off the east coast of Canada. She grows up in a house called Green Gables, and from there goes full tilt at everything to launch herself on the world!

Montgomery described her as 'a young girl who speaks her mind, often to her detriment'. Anne was forthright, feisty and fun, and though born into difficult circumstances which among other things included doing all the housework, went on to live a marvellous childhood. One of its features was that the adults in Anne's wonderful world—Marilla and Matthew who took her in—need her just as much as she needs them, and weren't remote omnipotent adults at all but deeply involved with her. Such bliss!

In *Anne of the Island,* the heroine flies entirely in the face of conventional behaviour for a young woman of her generation. Instead of immediately getting married and raising children, Anne leaves the home of her foster parents and goes away to university. Great romance follows, with wonderful times by the bucket-load. Which is more or less what Nancy always planned to do, though she was ever conscious that with a starting point as far away as Australia, her own ticket to ride was always going to cost a lot more than Anne's ever did. So, ever since she was a littlie, she'd set about saving it up. At the age of about eight, she started to look around for ways of raising capital.

One day while wandering past the local greengrocer, Creeneys up on Military Road, she noticed he was selling chokos, not at all unlike the chokos her mother grew on the fence in their own backyard.

'How much are the chokos?' she casually enquired of the grocer.

'Threepence.'

'My mother is very poor, and we have a choko vine, lovely chokos. If I bring you some will you give me a penny?'

The grocer looked her up and down, wondering if this young girl was on the up and up, but decided in the end that it didn't really matter—if she could deliver—and nodded assent. The next day, he had a bucket of chokos and Nancy could hear the delicious jingle of silver coins in her pocket for the first time. No more trying to live off brass razoos! This all worked extremely well for a few months, until one day when her mother was passing by the same grocery store and, noting the excellence of the chokos, commented on them to the proprietor.

'Yes,' replied the grocer, beaming. 'It's a dear little girl, her mother is very poor and she grows them in the backyard and brings them to us for extra money.'

And that, of course, was the end of Nancy's choko venture.

But by this time she had the bug. Encouraged by the success of this entrepreneurial venture, Nancy tried another one. Overhearing a conversation between her mother and her oldest sister Gladys to the effect that the eggs at the grocer's were often far from fresh, and it would be worth paying extra to get freshly laid ones, the sudden light of inspiration went on in Nancy's head. Shortly thereafter, she went to her mother and said she would be happy to organise the buying of the eggs from Mrs Breckenbridge who lived on the other side of Spruson Street, if her mother would give her the money. Her mother agreed, and gave her the money. That was one more chore for Nancy, one less for her, and that was fine. Nancy meanwhile went up to the grocer's, who by this time had become her friend, and carefully selected the eggs that still had feathers and chook poo attached to them—the ones that most *looked* like they were freshly laid. She bought them, took them back to her mother on the assurance that they were freshly laid from Mrs Breckenbridge's backyard, and pocketed the difference.

The scheme could only work of course on the reckoning that Mother Wake and Mrs Breckenbridge would never chat about the eggs and compare notes, but on that count Nancy had little doubt. Her mother didn't have a social bone in her body, and would have crossed the street to avoid having even minor pleasantries with a neighbour who was known to be not just a smoker, but also *(sniff)* to frequent public bars! Nancy knew that Mrs Breckenbridge may as well have spoken Swahili for all the chance that she would ever have a meaningful conversation with her mother.

'The whole thing,' Nancy says, 'taught me a lesson. Presentation is very important.'

Yet another way that Nancy found to raise regular money came via her sister—Hazel, she of the frizzy fair hair and even frizzier nature. Frequently, while Mrs Wake went off shopping or the like, Hazel would be given quasi baby-sitting duties over her young sister, with strict instructions not to let Nancy out of her sight. Hazel always had other ideas, wanting to use the time to be with her boyfriend on her own, while her mother was out of the picture.

'So,' Nancy remembers, 'Hazel would take me for a walk with her boyfriend and they would give me threepence to get rid of me because they wanted to be off courting together. She'd dump me anywhere and I'd go to the beach at Manly or somewhere, it didn't worry me. They could court—I didn't give a damn. It was threepence every time!'

Finally helping to extend her tiny income was money from another source ... 'I used to steal from my mother,' Nancy recalls without remorse. 'If she had given me threepence a week I would not have done it, but she didn't give me a cracker.'

All up, it started to add up to a tidy sum in her special Commonwealth Bank moneybox which she kept under her bed, getting close to the magical sum she was after—one pound. With one pound, she knew, she would be able to open a formal savings account at the Commonwealth Bank itself, attracting *interest* and everything! Once that account was opened, she felt she'd already have one foot on the gangplank leading onto one of those luxury liners she often spied on Sydney Harbour, one that would take her away to New York, London and Paris. On misty mornings when she might be sweeping the back verandah, she could even hear their massive foghorns blaring warning to each other or to passing ferries, and she would dream of the day when she would be on one, taking her leave. Certainly, she would have had the one pound a lot quicker had she not occasionally spent some of her money getting milkshakes and ice-creams from 'Tony the Greek', who ran the milk bar near the fire station. And then there were those amazing rides at passing travelling fairs—she loved those rides— but still, month by month, that ol' moneybox got heavier. Then, alas, disaster.

One Sunday, the whole family, bar the eldest brother Charles, went on a day trip on a big choofing steam train to the sparkling seaside town of Woy Woy. It was a rare treat for Nancy, and she remembers the unbridled joy with which she saw all the gum trees and water passing backwards in the sunshine. But when they got back that evening Nancy got a nasty, jolting surprise.

'My moneybox was empty,' she recalls, 'just lying there discarded on the floor!' Obviously, her brother Charles had simply helped himself to the money and had probably already spent it with his mates at the pub. Nancy can vaguely remember crying as if her heart would break, and more clearly recalls her blessed second eldest brother Stanley Herbert Kitchener Wake furiously fighting Charles in the backyard, either in an effort to punish him or to get him to give it back, she can't recollect.

'But I do remember,' she says, 'feeling very glad that Stan was sticking up for me, and sorry that I wasn't strong enough to have a whack myself, because I was very, very angry.'

If that frustrating feeling of powerlessness in the face of injustice was one she would come to know again at a later point in life, so too would another episode have echoes in another age. It occurred while she was in Year 4 at Neutral Bay Intermediate, her primary school, which was up the hill on the corner of Ben Boyd Road and Yeo Street.

Jenny, one of her best friends, told her a rhyme that made her nearly split her sides with laughter, the essence of which was: 'Isn't it funny to see a little bunny/ waiting for her Mummy to come and wipe her bummy'. Nancy wrote it down, the better to memorise it, and left it in the pocket of the same school tunic that her mother came across that night. When Mrs Wake discovered the ribald rhyme she informed the ten-year-old Nancy that she was more certain than ever that she'd be going straight to Hell, and did something else besides. That is, she took Nancy by the ear the following morning to her teacher and *demanded* that she be roundly punished. The teacher set out to do just that, and in the face of such twin fury from parent and teacher, Nancy panicked and crumpled.

'I pointed at the dear friend who had taught me the poem in the first place and tried to deflect the blame on to her.'

The result was that both girls were punished severely. It put a serious strain on the friendship between the two—the other girl quite rightly feeling betrayed—and caused the completely devastated Nancy to make a vow to herself.

'I swore,' she recalls, 'that no matter what, *no matter what*, I would never dob anyone in again.'

And she meant it too. The look in the eyes of Jenny, the friend betrayed, would stay with Nancy for a long time to come.

Another friend from those days was Barbara Bowering, who lived just around in Cranbrook Avenue. The two often sat together in class, and played together in the playground. Even eighty years on, Barbara would remember Nancy well.

'She was a great and very loyal friend,' she says, 'who was very clever at everything. I think in some ways she was too clever for most people, but if I was ever up the front of the class with the teacher asking me questions Nancy always mouthed to me the answers. What I most remember about her was how protective she was. I was probably a lot smaller than most of the kids in my class, but Nancy was always there. She absolutely hated teasing and bullying, and she had no fear of boys *or* teachers.

'We had a teacher called Fanny Menlove, and I remember once when she was out of the room Nancy went up to the blackboard and wrote it backward—Menlove Fanny—and we all fell around laughing. She got into big trouble, but she didn't seem to mind. She had *no fear*.'

And this, as it happened, was a point of pride with Nancy. For if what had most appalled her about the dobbing-in Jenny episode was that she had lacked moral courage—even if at that age she didn't have the words to describe it—there was no doubt that the youngest of the Wake brood had ample physical courage. She always maintained that she was every bit as brave as the boys, and was always happy to prove it. On one occasion, when she was about seven, Stanley was back on leave from the navy and playfully dared her to jump off the roof, never thinking she actually would . . .

This time, the trip by Dr Studdie was worthwhile, because he actually had some genuine injuries to look at. Abrasions, bruises, an extremely sore little girl, but happily no broken leg. Why had Nancy jumped he had enquired.

'Because he *dared* me,' Nancy says simply, 'and I always took up a dare. I never allowed myself to dwell on the possible consequences of taking up a dare—because that way, I knew I might be scared off—so I usually just did it.'

From Neutral Bay Intermediate, Nancy went to her secondary education at North Sydney Girls Domestic Science School, also up the hill from where she lived. As a matter of fact, just about everything in her young life was 'up the hill', as her home on Holdsworth Street was situated at the bottom of a small natural valley. This at least made for the formation of very strong legs on her part. One or two of the other girls were lucky enough to get dropped off in cars, but the Wakes didn't even know anyone who had a car, let alone dream of having one themselves.

A high-spirited girl such as young Nancy attending such a rigorously disciplined establishment was not necessarily a match made in heaven. For this was a school which did not aim merely to turn out educated adults, as some did, nor simply young *ladies*, as did some other girls' schools. This school was *specifically* devoted to turning out wives and mothers of conspicuous excellence, young women trained up to a sophisticated subservience to their men which would see such men prosper throughout their lives. Together with the standard subjects of mathematics, English and science, there was also a whole slew of special subjects including cooking, home decorating and needlework. It simply wasn't Nancy's cup of tea—tea which, incidentally, should be made by pouring the boiling water into a pot that had been pre-heated, and served with the jug of milk and sugar always moving around the table *together*. Remember girls, because it's important.

Whatever. Nancy knew she was never going to turn into one of those rich married women who really cared about such things, but her preferences were irrelevant. As with so many other things, she felt she had no choice in the matter. Until school was over, she simply had to put up with it. In the meantime she at least took pleasure in subjects such as English and geography, where she could pursue both her passion for reading and for dreaming about other parts of the world that she felt sure she would one day visit.

If her thoughts were often far away as she fantasised about adventures in distant lands, she was not, in herself, one who escaped attention, for the scrawny black-stockinged tomboy schoolgirl who had been such a familiar figure around Neutral Bay—the same one who had been gravely informed by her mother that she was ugly as a punishment from God (for sins unknown)—had by the time of her mid-teens blossomed into an extremely beautiful young woman. With a perfectly symmetrical oval face set off by long brunette hair, and a handsomely curvaceous silhouette from there, she may not have been at all well-versed in the ways of the opposite sex, yet she was aware that they were attracted to her ...

'I knew,' she says, 'by the way they would hover around and try to get me talking, but I was very naïve about all that sort of stuff, and really had no interest.'

Besides which, at the absolute insistence of her mother who had always taken her to church every Sabbath, at the age of fourteen she had become a Sunday school teacher at St Augustine, Neutral Bay, and it was conduct unbecoming to be running around with boys like that, as had her sisters.

Admittedly, she wasn't a *great* Sunday school teacher, but she found she at least loved singing hymns with the kids, such as 'Jesus Loves Me This I Know' and 'Onward Christian Soldiers'. Nor was she a particularly great teller of parables and stories from the Bible, as she was meant to be, far preferring to tell the kids stories from films she might have seen the night before at the Cremorne Orpheum. But one way or another, neither she nor Reverend Mr Pearce could help noticing that her classes became very popular, meaning he was happy and so was she!

'The film that affected me most back then,' she says, 'was *The Sheik of Araby* with Ramon Novarro, and I used to absolutely love the song of that name, which I would often sing to myself and even the Sunday school kids: "Well I'm the Sheik of Araby/ Your love belongs to me/ Well at night when you're asleep,/ Into your tent

I'll creep./ The stars that shine above/ Will light our way to love./ You'll rule this world with me,/ I'm the Sheik of Araby."'

While Nancy's Sunday school involvement pleased her mother, it remained about the only thing that did, for just about everything else Nancy did seemed to irritate Mrs Wake, and to avoid the constant clashing on the weekend, the young woman would let her independent spirit have its head and leave the house as often as possible to find amusement elsewhere in the city. Anything, *anything* to get out of a house that her mother liked to keep with the windows closed, the blinds drawn and the lace curtains pulled together—a house that often seemed to be suffocating for lack of air. No matter how hard and often Nancy cleaned the place, it always seemed to have the stale smell of boiled cabbage about it, of dirty laundry, of air that for too long had not seen sunlight.

Often she would walk the couple of miles it took to go down to the scenic North Sydney baths nestled right on Sydney Harbour and do a few laps, just as she would also occasionally get the ferry from Neutral Bay wharf across to Rose Bay and then make her way to Bondi Beach, where she would participate in the new rage of body-surfing. Sometimes she would go with friends, sometimes alone, it didn't really matter. She just loved the thrill of swimming hard with a wave and then that wonderful *whooooooosh* as it broke beneath her and swept her to the shore.

When she felt like sticking closer to home, she would make a trip to Taronga Park Zoo in the nearby suburb of Mosman, where she always found herself drawn to the sleek powerful tigers, or go down to the delightful Balmoral Beach, where she could sashay along the Esplanade, or sit 'neath the shade of the huge Moreton Bay figs and watch others do the same. Hers was not a classically happy childhood by any means—the early abandonment by her father and ongoing cold relationship with her mother always meant it was out of kilter—but it was manageable, and she was able to get through by nourishing the constant hope that things would get better for her. Just as Anne of Green Gables had discovered, Nancy sensed that there was a world beyond her immediate experience, a wonderful world just waiting to be discovered.

CHAPTER TWO

Bon Voyage

> Out of the night that covers me, black as the pitch from
> pole to pole,
> I thank whatever Gods may be, for my unconquerable soul.
>
> W.E. HENLEY

And at last it happened. At around the age of fifteen, Nancy achieved her dearest wish of travelling overseas when just she and her mother travelled on a big boat past Taronga Park Zoo on the left, Rose Bay on the right, through Sydney Heads, and kept going all the way to New Zealand! The wind in her hair, the sun on her back, nothing could be finer, and she didn't even mind the fact that her mother spent most of the trip with her head buried in her Bible. They were going back on a six-week trip to see Nancy's maternal grandmother on her farm in the spectacular Kiwi country of Mangonui, in the deep north of the north island of New Zealand. It was a revelation. Not just for the fact that New Zealand proved to be very much to her liking—full of friendly people, it seemed, for whom she was slightly exotic because of her 'Australianness'—but also because 'Grannie Rosieur', as she called her, was so warm and loving in her own right. It scarcely seemed credible that her mother's mother could be so extraordinarily different from Nancy's own mother, but there it was.

'She was lovely,' Nancy recalls, 'and we got on wonderfully well right from the moment she greeted me in the farmhouse kitchen with a huge hug.'

This stark contrast with Ella Wake didn't just come down to Grannie Rosieur's affectionate nature or her far more bountiful form. For Grannie Rosieur also liked Nancy to eat and have those around her eat! (Maybe, Nancy thought at one point, Granpa Rosieur had gone to an early grave because he had simply burst?) Morning, noon and night, Grannie plied young Nancy with wonderful meals from the New Zealand fare that abounded in the rich agricultural region, meals that were so very different from the bland bangers-and-mash with cabbage that had the life boiled out of it that the young girl was used to.

In the company of some of her newly-met cousins, with whom she got on well, Nancy soon got so into the rhythm of it that she was even able to manage some extracurricular eating as well ...

'At one point,' Nancy says, 'I went out into the barn and hanging up there were twelve Christmas puddings. Oh boy! So I get up there and I get one down and I eat the bloody lot. And then of course I've got to do something about it—so I fill it up with mud and stones and put it back up there, nice and fat. Unfortunately I made it too fat and when they went out on Christmas morning to choose the pudding they chose mine—and they put it in the water. And what happened? The whole ruse was explained. My mother wanted to give me a hiding, but Grannie wouldn't let her ...'

Grannie was a good stick all right, and she would live long in her youngest granddaughter's affection. Generally, this good New Zealand woman was such a happy soul it was a pleasure to be around her, not that she hadn't had her fair share of unhappiness. One of these unhappinesses, Nancy found out, was when Grannie's eldest daughter Hinamoa had run off with a whaling captain who was already married. This was pretty much the first that Nancy had heard of it as her mother had never mentioned this older sister or what she had done. Fascinated, Nancy tried to get as many details as she could about her wayward aunt, but with little success. Neither her mother nor grandmother seemed to want to talk about it, though one of her mother's other sisters who was still quietly in contact with Hinamoa was at least able to fill out the sketch a little. Always the wild-child of the family, Hinamoa had simply followed her heart without ever considering the consequences. She was, apparently, one who always lived for the moment, for whom the moral mores of the day were nought but nonsense.

Again, the contrast with Nancy's own mother on such matters couldn't have been greater. Still, it was funny for the teenager to see her mother like this, back in her natural habitat as it were. After a few weeks she even seemed a little more natural—as she relaxed just that little bit and was even able to *laugh* from time to time—and Nancy reflected how hard it must have been for her mother to have been abandoned by a husband to whom she had borne six children and to have been forced to bring the youngest of them up on her own. As it happened, Nancy thought less and less of her father these days, in the sense of both frequency *and* affection. From being the sun around which her life had revolved, he was now no more than a distant planet and a very cold, lifeless one at that.

The whole New Zealand exercise had been a pleasant sojourn for Nancy—and she would ever afterwards keep in touch with her grandmother. It was also the first dipping of her toe into overseas travel and she returned to school impatient for her studies to be over. More than ever she wanted to get out into the big wide world on her own, to make her own way, and *go* her own way. Finally then, it was with a mixture of relief and at least some trepidation that she left the halls of her high school for the last time. Relief because she felt she had been a square peg in a round hole for quite long enough; trepidation because she wasn't quite sure just where the 'square hole' that she could fit into was anyway, or even if such a thing existed. And there was the rub.

'I just had *no* idea what I was intended for,' she remembers. 'I didn't quite know which way to head. I still had my ambition to go overseas, but of course I didn't have the money necessary to do it, and would need to get a job to get that money together ...'

But what job? What was she really cut out for? Some of her friends from school had decided on clerical careers, others had already secured jobs in shops, one was going on to university, another to study physiotherapy, but Nancy didn't have a clue. As a matter of fact she didn't even know where to start looking, and so just continued to live at home listening to the constant *tick-tock tick-tock* of the old clock on the mantelpiece while waiting for something to break.

Something did break. Her relationship with her mother. Now sixteen years old, Nancy had fought a running battle with her mother all through her childhood and teenage years on a dozen different fronts at once, their momentary *rapprochement* in New Zealand notwithstanding. The younger woman was strong-willed, tempestuous, flighty, and didn't mind a scrap—while the older woman had very clear ideas about the proper subservience that should be displayed by daughters towards their mothers, and what's more she knew she had God on her side. It was a situation tailor-made for a climactic moment one way or another, and on a hot December day in 1928 that moment came.

Nancy, red in the face with fury, stood toe-to-toe with her mother in the mingy, musty hallway of their home, telling her she was 'going out'. Her mother, equally resolute, and with Bible in hand for added authority, stood directly in front of the door and *strictly* forbade it, do you hear me, Nancy?!?!

'If you don't get out of the way,' Nancy returned, 'I will simply go out the window!'

Ella Wake stood her ground, bristling with righteous anger. Nancy went out the window. From the ledge, she vaulted over the garden bed and over the fence and was at last out into the open air. It felt good, felt *great*, not just for the physical fact that she had escaped the strictures of a house that for too long had pressed in on her, but more importantly she had escaped the strictures of her too-tight life as well.

'Somehow,' says Nancy, 'I knew instinctively that I had just crossed a line into another phase of my life, a phase where I would no longer have to answer to my mother, and would instead be in charge of my own destiny. I was leaving my mother, I was going out into the world and I was happy.'

As luck would have it, Nancy was no sooner on Ben Boyd Road than she ran into her sister-in-law Lily, now the widow of her brother Charles, a woman who Nancy had always got along well with despite her association with *that bastard*. Charles, after all, had put Lily in 'the pudding club' when they had just started going out, and in those days there really wasn't much else you could do but marry in that situation, and that is what they had done. That Charles had subsequently come to a sorry death—either jumping or being pushed from a window in the city, it was never clear— only heightened the affection that Nancy had always felt for Lily.

That day, noticing Nancy's obvious distress, Lily had enquired if everything was all right, and Nancy had let her have it. All of it. How she simply couldn't stand being at home any more; how her mother was driving her up the wall; how she had just five minutes ago climbed out the window with the solemn promise that she was never going to return; how she actually had no idea what she was going to do now ... Her sister-in-law, taking pity on her, made a snap decision.

'Well,' she said carefully, 'you can come back to my house if you like, and stay under the house during the day in case they come looking for you, and then up into the house to sleep when it's all safe at night.'

Nancy could have kissed her.

'It was just such a wonderful thing for her to have done,' she recalls. 'She could see how distressed I was and wanted to help, even though because I was still under eighteen she must have known that the police would shortly be looking for me.'

And that is exactly what happened. That afternoon, the police did indeed come looking for Nancy at many houses in the neighbourhood—particularly those where Nancy had some acquaintance, like the Beals and the Kings—but when they turned up at her sister-in-law's, she was safely under the stilted house. She could even see their blue uniformed legs on approach, hear the conversation above, hear the tramp of booted feet on the floorboards, and then see those same blue legs receding down the garden path. Not long afterwards, either by coincidence or otherwise, she also saw the legs of her mother, heard her familiar step on the floorboards above, the low rumble of her voice, and then she too receded.

What a wonderful thing, she remembers reflecting at the time, to have a place of refuge when you were in trouble. Several days later when it came time to leave, when things had calmed down somewhat—through an intermediary she had at least been able to communicate to her mother that she was quite all right but that she wasn't coming home—she couldn't thank her sister-in-law enough for her kindness.

But it was time to make plans to leave. Taking the car-punt across the harbour into the city—because it only cost twopence and that was all she had, as opposed to threepence for the ferry—she went to an employment agency in Pitt Street. There, at last, things went right for her. Given that she had no interest in any of the retail trades, nursing was an obvious starting point—her sister Hazel by this time was a fully qualified nurse at Kogarah. There was the problem, though, that one of the conditions of being a nurse in Sydney was that one had to start with newly purchased uniforms and she simply didn't have the money to buy them.

'So I agreed,' Nancy remembers, 'to start with another scheme where you would be a nurse in the country somewhere and then they would supply your uniforms and you could pay it back as you went along.'

And actually, there was one other problem. That was, she couldn't use her real name of Nancy Wake because the police were still looking for her, and she had to give the employment agency a false name. That, at least, was easy as she came up with 'Shirley Anne Kennedy' on the spot. 'Kennedy' was the name of a woman who had once been kind to her, while 'Anne Shirley' was of course the full name of the heroine of *Anne of Green Gables*— Nancy's own heroine, who had often daydreamed about bravely nursing people through dangerous illnesses—so it was perfect! Yes, it was a bit weird to be using false names while having the authorities looking for her, but, hey, at least she knew that all of that was just a once-off, that it wasn't as if she was going to be making a life out of that kind of caper ...

The main thing was that she got the job, or at least the promise of the job. With still three weeks to go before taking up her position as a nurse near Mudgee, she secured a brief domestic job at thirty-five shillings a week at a house in the Sydney suburb of Northbridge. This involved facing the round eternal of ironing, washing and housework and was conducive to making her realise that while that sort of stuff was okay to do before and after school, it was most definitely *not* something she wanted to do for a living.

Life. She learned a lot about it up Mudgee way. Away from her family, and left entirely to her own devices while still at the tender age of sixteen, she had her first serious job, smoked her first cigarette and got drunk for the first time. And she loved it all, even if the job wasn't quite what she had expected. Calling the premises a 'hospital' was probably going a bit far. Set on the edge of what was essentially a gold mining shanty town, it was really a glorified bungalow with a couple of wards for patients—usually miners who had had accidents—and a kitchen to cook some food for them. And apart from that, just about nothing. There was precious little specialised equipment, no doctors, no matron, just a nursing sister and two trainee nurses in Nancy and another girl called Claire.

'But we were happy,' says Nancy. 'Claire was a runaway like me, and for both of us the whole thing was a great adventure. We were earning enough to pay off our nice crisp white uniforms, plus have a little bit of spending money, and maybe even save a little every week too, so what more did you want at the age of sixteen or so?'

Not much. Nancy herself had always been a good mixer with people from all walks of life—most particularly with rag-tag men for some reason—and both she and Claire were delighted to find the miners friendly to a fault and fun to be around. Not only that, the two young women found the sister tolerable, and the work itself sometimes even interesting. Over the nearly two years they were there, Nancy and Claire learned how to set broken limbs, clean weeping wounds, put salve on burns so that the patient wasn't screaming in pain, and informed themselves on many other minor medical matters besides. All that, and the buxom duo got to go to the little cinema in the village every Saturday night for free!

Not that there weren't serious medical problems to contend with from time to time though. On one notable occasion, when the sister was away getting her hair done in town one Saturday afternoon, old Mr Smith just up and *died* on them, just like that.

'There was nothing we could do for him,' Nancy remembers, 'and it wasn't actually suprising because he was very old and very worn out, but for both of us so young it was still tremendously upsetting.'

At least they had sufficient experience to know what their first duty was. That was, without making too much of a fuss in front of the other patients—most of whom were having their afternoon nap anyway—to pull the sheet up over him. This was not only respect for the dead, but it also avoided having to look at those unseeing eyes. Then—following what was apparently a hallowed strand of tradition among young nurses at that time in dealing with such matters—they retired to the kitchen to drink themselves pie-eyed with whatever alcohol they could get their hands on. In this case all they could find were alcoholic hospital spirits, but they judged this sufficient for them to work up the Dutch courage they needed to do what had to be done next. For it was one thing of course simply to pull the sheet up over the head of a corpse without actually *touching* it, but it was something else again to manhandle the corpse onto a stretcher, take it out the door, down the corridor, through the exit, and then across the extremely muddy patch of ground to the mining-town morgue. Just the thought of it gave them both the *creeps*, so much so that when they had knocked off the remains of the first bottle of hospital spirits they quickly searched out another, figuring they didn't quite have the requisite amount of nerve yet. Luckily, sister still wasn't due back for another couple of hours, so they figured they had the time.

At last, at last, it was time. Mr Smith could wait no longer and other patients were just starting to stir from their afternoon nap. Swaying their way back down the corridor and into the ward, Nancy and Claire bumped heavily into the door jamb as they went, then they placed the stretcher beside the bed, slowly, slowly drew back the covers ... and nearly collapsed. What lay before them wasn't just the deathly pallor of a man now gone to God. It wasn't that one of the eyes they had closed seemed now to be staring back at them. For one of those things they were expecting and the other they still could maybe have coped with. What they simply couldn't get over was what was now emerging from the fly of Mr Smith's pyjamas. It was ... was ... was ...

'The biggest penis I have ever seen,' says Nancy flatly. 'Actually at that point it was the only [adult] penis I'd ever laid eyes on. And it was *totally* erect.'

It may have been that this curious erection was due to rigor mortis setting in after the death, but neither of them could quite get over how such a small man could possibly have such a large protuberance. Trying not to look and yet still being mesmerised in spite of themselves, they at least got him on to the stretcher, put a sheet over him—which promptly resembled a circus tent in the middle—and drunkenly lurched their way out the door. Nancy still thinks they might have made it, had it not been for the rain which had started to fall heavily, but ...

'But when we got out into the middle of the field that lay between the hospital and the morgue, we were not only too drunk to keep our balance, but the mud was incredibly slippery, and first me and then Claire kept slipping.'

The inevitable happened. Suddenly, they both slipped over together, and Mr Smith went flying, landing deep in the mud.

'You have never seen anything like it,' Nancy says with some certainty, 'this man lying with this great prick sticking up covered with mud. Well, there we were, the sister due back shortly, a dead body in the mud, both of us rolling drunk, and our uniforms covered in muck, as were we.'

They survived, just. They got Mr Smith into the morgue, and while Claire did her best to clean him up—including with great embarassment, she would later recount, his massive penis—Nancy took both their uniforms quickly into town to get laundered by their friendly Chinese laundryman, who had always done their laundry for free. 'And they never found out. They never found out,' Nancy chortles, some seventy years after the event.

* * *

In September of 1930, shortly after Nancy turned eighteen—meaning it was now safe to return to Sydney without any problems from the police—she said goodbye to Claire, to the mining town, the hospital, the life of a nurse, the lot.

'It had been wonderful,' she says, 'but I just knew it was time to get back.'

Alighting at Central Railway Station from the train which had brought her from near Mudgee, she took the tram to Circular Quay on the southern side of the harbour, and by chance looked out to the west when ... she saw it. At that point it was almost the most extraordinary thing she'd seen in her young life. This of course was the famous Sydney Harbour Bridge, the structure that they had been building when she left Sydney two years previously. Things had moved on amazingly since last she was here. The two massive spans had reached out to join each other in wonderful embrace!

All of which was in great contrast to Nancy's mother who was certainly not yearning to embrace her after such a long separation. Though the word soon spread that Nancy was back—after she popped in on friends and went to visit her brother Stanley—her mother never sent word that she wanted to see her. Nor did Nancy make any effort to make contact herself.

'That part of my life was over,' she says firmly, 'and I wasn't going back to it.'

She had left Sydney a girl, but had returned a woman, a woman who knew she could never even pretend to submit to her mother's rule again. Instead, she rented a room in Rushcutters Bay on the other side of the harbour, taking a lodging in one of the old tenement houses that abounded there, at a cost of sixteen shillings a week.

Although at this time Sydney town was nearing the heights of the Depression and the streets were filled with people down on their luck or looking for work in the big city—often between visits to soup kitchens—Nancy was fortunate enough to quickly secure a clerical job with a Dutch shipping company based in Bridge Street. With a salary just above the basic wage, she quickly settled down to being a tiny cog organising the movements of massive ships that came to Sydney bearing cargo and passengers from such places as Amsterdam and Java.

Even while Nancy organised the passage of ships back and forth to all parts of the world, her thoughts inevitably wandered to her own dreams of travelling, of discovering New York, London and Paris as she'd always promised herself she would. That would of course take a lot of money, and she still wasn't any closer to having any, but not to worry. For some reason she was never quite sure of, she always felt confident something would turn up ...

In the meantime there were plenty of pleasures to pursue, plenty of growing up to do, new things to thrill to. She revelled still in being free of her mother and being able to do anything she damn well pleased, and her passion of the moment was the famous American actress Tallulah Bankhead, whose films Nancy simply devoured. With Tallulah as a model, Nancy delighted in spending a large portion of her small salary each month on having her hair tinted platinum blonde and closely cut in what they called an Eton Crop, just like Tallulah had it. She also loved buying and wearing slightly mannish clothes and ties just like Tallulah, or imperiously smoking cigarettes in long holders just like ... yeah, Tallulah.

'When I imitated her,' Nancy says, 'I thought I was Christmas. It made me feel good, because I simply adored her.'

Nancy was, as a matter of fact, dressed just like her idol on the sparkling morning of 19 March, 1932, while on one of her company's Dutch ships heading beneath the just completed Sydney Harbour Bridge as part of the celebrations of its official opening. Above them at that very moment, Nancy and her friends and colleagues knew, the Premier of New South Wales, Jack Lang, and many other dignitaries were making speeches. Their gaily bedecked vessel was sitting in close behind a British ship that was leading the aquatic parade, when they suddenly heard an enormous commotion from above, shouts, screams, the lot ... What on *earth* was going on?!

They found out shortly afterwards when they docked. A Protestant Irishman, Captain Francis de Groot, of the paramilitary group the New Guard, had raced forward on his horse and with his sabre had slashed the blue ribbon that the Premier had been about to cut, declaring the bridge open in the name of 'the decent citizens of New South Wales!'.

Sydney was agog with it for days, weeks, afterwards, amazed at such a public act of civil disobedience. Nancy too.

'In my limited experience,' she says, 'things like that just didn't happen. The government was the government was the government, and that was that. You did what they said, and you most certainly didn't take matters into your own hands like de Groot had done, whatever you might have felt about it. I was quite shocked.'

It was around this time—appropriately enough, given her line of work—that her own ship came in, metaphorically at least. One evening after work, she arrived home to her Rushcutters Bay abode to find a letter redirected to her from her mother's place. It was a letter that would change her life. It was from her Auntie Hinamoa. This was, of course, the older sister of her mother who—just as Nancy had 'disgraced the family' by running away—had herself run off with the married captain of a whaling ship off the north coast of New Zealand.

Hinamoa had done well, and the upshot of the letter was that she advised Nancy she would shortly be telegraphing her the extraordinary sum of two hundred pounds to do with what she liked. *'I've been thinking of you always and I hope this can help you,'* the letter said, among other things. Nancy, stunned at her good fortune, was some time in believing that it had actually happened. Things like this happened only in novels, and she was never quite clear how her aunt had formed such an affection for her.

'I mean,' she says, 'this aunt was the shame of the family. Personally I would never listen to anything wrong about her, I was not a nasty person, but I think that she probably sympathised with me because she knew how my mother used to treat me.'

When the money actually came through—meaning the whole thing was not a cruel ruse as she had half suspected—she knew immediately what she wanted to do. She wanted to *move, move, move,* to get away from Sydney and her cloistered life there.

Within a week of receiving the money she had booked herself a first class passage on an outward bound ocean liner, at the princely price of one hundred pounds, still leaving her the other hundred pounds for spending money—a tiny portion of which she spent on a Tallulah Bankhead-type tie which she had long coveted from an expensive shop called Richard Hunt's in Sydney's Pitt Street.

'It cost me 17/6d,' she recalls, 'but it was worth every penny.'

If it was against the norm of the day for a young woman to turn her back on the prospect of marriage and babies and to set off on her own to discover the world then, as far as Nancy was concerned, that was just too damned bad. Anne of Green Gables had never followed convention, and neither did Nancy feel any compunction about breaking the mould. Perhaps in deference to the blessed Anne, Nancy's initial destination on that luxury liner— after brief stopovers in Auckland and Suva—was Vancouver, Canada, Anne's homeland.

There remained a problem, however, before Nancy could physically take her place on the liner. She was still under the legal age of twenty-one, the old passport she used to go to New Zealand was out of date, and there was no way known that her mother would ever sign the necessary documents to get her a new passport to get overseas. But there were other ways around that problem. (Nancy had learnt all through her life to date, that there were always ways around any problem.) In this case the pertinent point was that in the absence of a parent or legal guardian affirming that an applicant was twenty-one years old, it was acceptable for the family doctor to do so. So Nancy went to see her old friend Dr Studdie, presented the papers to him, saying that unfortunately her mother had gone away to the country for a month, and would he mind signing right here? The doctor, still kindly, and by then in the twilight of his career, looked at her a little puzzled and said 'Oh Nancy, I would have thought you were only eighteen!'.

'Doctor!' Nancy playfully replied, mock-shocked, 'I'm twenty-one!'

'Doesn't time pass!' the doctor replied with a laugh, and signed right where she'd indicated.

CHAPTER THREE

•⤳

An Innocent Abroad

> Career! That is all girls think of now, instead of being
> good wives and mothers and attending to their homes
> and doing what God intended. All they think of is
> gadding about and being fast, and ruining themselves
> body and soul. And the men are as bad to encourage
> them.
>
> MILES FRANKLIN, *My Brilliant Career*, 1901

It was a strangely surreal thing. For most of the previous nine months, the rest of Sydney had joyously celebrated the opening of their brand new Harbour Bridge which had at last joined the two halves of Sydney. Yet for young Nancy in that first hot breath of the summer of 1932 the finest sight in her young life was the vision of that same bridge falling away in the distance as she stood gazing backwards from the stern of the good ship *Aorangi II*. It was not that she had anything against the bridge per se, just that the fact that it was disappearing into the haze of the steam from the ship's boilers meant that she was leaving Sydney behind.

As the Heads of Sydney Harbour fell away, her thoughts turned to what lay ahead. Essentially, her rough plan was to make her way to England, via a meandering route across the North American continent, find some kind of work in London, and then see what turned up! In the back of her mind she was keen to get to the capital of world glamour and the dream-time destination of her childhood—Paris—but was not sure at that point how it would be possible. Below decks, securely tucked away in her luggage, she had her two favourite books in all the world, *Anne of Green Gables* and *Anne of the Island,* both with *Nancy Grace Augusta Wake* written in her childish script on the title pages, and just as things had always worked themselves out for Anne, Nancy really felt they would for her too. Besides, the Maori midwife had told Nancy's mother that her daughter was born to be lucky, and though there had been times over the last twenty years when she doubted that to be true, the fact that her aunt had sent her two hundred pounds out of the blue was, she felt, a sure sign that she was maybe coming good after all!

Shipboard life was wonderful. Though she was certainly the only unchaperoned young single woman heading out on the boat—it simply wasn't done in those days—the other young people on the boat admired her for her courage, and as a good mixer she also soon became friendly with many of the older established couples who were off on their own trip-of-a-lifetime. The atmosphere was euphoric, exuberant. Whatever problems and hassles any of them might have had in their lives at home, they were very clearly left behind now ... so let's *dance.*

'I had a wonderful time,' Nancy remembers fondly, 'and I was glad I'd decided to hang the expense and go first class. There was a terrific band on board, and every night we'd all dress for dinner, dine superbly, drink the finest wines, chat and laugh, and end up dancing the night away. The following day you'd sleep late, wander to lunch, have a swim, a drink, play some games and get ready to do it all again as the ocean slipped by. It was lovely. I was an innocent abroad and I was loving it.' Luxuriously fitted out with shining mahogany and gleaming metal abounding, the *Aorangi II* itself pleased her greatly. When it had been constructed and launched only eight years earlier, it had been the largest motor vessel constructed in the world, and also the fastest with its four six-cylinder diesel engines powering it through the water at a seemingly incredible top speed of eighteen knots! The ocean fell away behind them as the band played on ...

Vancouver, high on the west coast of the north American continent, was everything she had ever imagined it to be. With a beautiful harbour nestled between the open sea and the huge mountains it was a busy port just like Sydney, and yet retained a bit of a 'frontier feel' about it—underlined by the fact that when Nancy arrived, fully two-thirds of the city's streets consisted of nothing more than gravel. Downtown was a little more sophisticated, and around the area known as the 'Commercial Streets' there were even street-trolleys.

What made the experience special for Nancy was less the physical details of the surrounds and more the Canadian people that filled them. She found she received a wonderfully hospitable welcome wherever she went, notwithstanding the fact that because of the severely straitened financial times in Canada—as with the rest of the world—a lot of their hospitality didn't extend to actually spending a whole lot of money. On Saturdays, with some Vancouver natives she had made friends with on the boat—or with friends she met through them—she would often be taken for a promenade around English Bay, where they would picnic and go swimming or simply sunbathe. Occasionally, she would go to the Hotel Vancouver where with all the beautiful people she could swing to the sound of the famous big band 'Mart Kenney and His Western Gentlemen'. Many songs tried to counter the Depression of the decade with happy, pick-me-up tunes such as 'I've Got the World on a String'. Some just faced troubles head on, like 'I Can't Give You Anything But Love' or 'Brother, Can You Spare a Dime?' Still others had silly, meaningless lyrics, like 'The Flat Foot Floogie' or 'Three Little Fishies'.

From Vancouver, Nancy travelled by train to the stunning Lake Louise—she had never known that such natural beauty existed on heaven or earth—and thence New York, where she settled into the famous Willard Hotel, recommended to her by fellow travellers.

'I didn't have a room, I had a suite,' she recalls delightedly of the thrill of spending some more of dear Aunt Hinamoa's money in such a place. 'It was a freezing winter, and I only had a woollen coat that I bought in New Zealand, but after waltzing around Fifth Avenue and throwing snowballs in Central Park, I used to go back to the hotel and have a sherry to warm up and then get into the huge bath in my suite. I kept calling for more towels, so they must have thought I was kinky.'

Out and about, New York proved to be everything she imagined and more. In the company of Helen, an English girl she had met on the train and hooked up with again as soon as she arrived, Nancy began to explore the city and found a wild and rollicking town afloat on alcoholic excess, notwithstanding that in these early months of 1933, New York was nominally in the full grip of the wretchedly puritan Prohibition laws. Nancy and Helen explored the speakeasies and cavernous nightclubs, where grog could be found, and soon realised that the town was actually consuming alcohol like it was oxygen and they were living at high altitude.

'It was terrific,' remembers Nancy, 'not just for the alcohol, but for the fun everyone was having and the friends we were making. The alcohol helped though. There was *gallons* of the stuff, everywhere you looked. Everyone I knew was mixing the stuff up in bathtubs. I have never had so much grog in my life.'

So copious were the amounts imbibed by the young Australian, and so strong was some of it, that her voice noticeably hoarsened just in the three weeks she stayed there, partying endlessly. But start spreading the news. She's *leaving* today. *New York! New York!*

'I actually hated to leave,' she says, 'because I was loving it so much and felt I was learning so many things about life, but my money couldn't last forever and I knew I at least had to get to London before it ran out, or I was going to be stranded while still a long way from my destination.'

The trip on the luxury liner from New York across the Atlantic—thankfully going in the opposite direction and by a different route from *The Titanic* two decades earlier, Nancy thought with a shudder—was a good'un, chiefly memorable for a fight she got into with a wrestler ...

'His name was "Bull Montana",' Nancy recalls, 'and he was married to a famous actress, Esther Ralston. I remember he taught me a gambling game with cards. Anyway, I noticed he was always winning and then I caught him cheating! So I got up and tipped everything on his head and punched him. We were playing for money and he was *rooking* me. I was furious, absolutely livid. A game I didn't know, and he was cheating me, so I hit him.'

So she hit him.

If New York had been sparkling and awe-inspiring at first acquaintance—the Empire State Building, the Statue of Liberty and more—then clearly Liverpool, coming in via the infamous Merseyside docks, was something else again. Pulling into the port on a day as dank as it was dark, as the city itself was dirty, Nancy took an *instant* dislike to it, all the better to save time. She was a little like that at the best of times and even some seventy years later, could still summon a little boiling bile at the memory of the British port.

'It was foggy and awful and horribly cold from the first,' she remembers, 'and I just couldn't believe that people lived like that. Ghastly. I couldn't wait to get away, get to London, because I knew it had to be better than Liverpool.'

It was better, more or less, though certainly no warmer.

By this time Aunt Hinamoa's money was starting to run out and, unlike New York, London was also freezing *inside* the hotel.

'When I got to London it was all right and then I stayed in a cheap hotel in central London, all I know is that it was freezing. I didn't stay there very long.'

Soon she had secured a room in a suitably cheap and nasty boarding house in Cromwell Road, and enrolled at a place called Queens College for Journalism, just four doors down. Queens College was the same name as one of the educational establishments that Anne of Green Gables had attended—something which commended itself highly as a choice for Nancy—and it promised to teach her both typing and shorthand.

For Nancy, becoming a journalist was less a lifelong dream than the best means whereby her all-consuming wanderlust would have a chance to be fulfilled at someone *else's* expense. Vaguely, she had aspirations to plunge into serious action and write about it, maybe one day even be a war correspondent; but the main thing in the short-term was simply to get some skills that she could trade on and so afford to stay in Europe. Perhaps, too, there was the thought that the person she had been closest to in her young life, her father, had been a journalist—giving her a natural predilection for it.

'I was not positive what I was heading for by doing those courses,' she recalls, 'just that I thought they would be useful tools to have. The promise was that after eight months at the college they would have you typing perfectly at the rate of eighty words a minute and one hundred and twenty in shorthand without mistake.'

In the meantime, the experience of being an attractive young woman overseas was, she found, a rich and varied one, most particularly if you weren't too particular about getting much sleep. And in a way it was odd. For just as New York was in the throes of Prohibition and yet she had never drunk so much, London remained deep at the bottom of the Depression—at one point their unemployment rate had reached twenty-five per cent of their entire workforce—and yet she had never really felt so joyous. London nightlife still had a few strictures, with many establishments licensed to serve alcohol only to people who were 'dining patrons', but as always for Nancy there proved to be ways around that.

'We used to go to all these places,' Nancy recalls, 'where after eleven o'clock if you just had a sausage you could drink as much beer as you liked, and there'd be music and dancing, so what else could you want?'

The short answer was a certain worldly-wiseness that she had always admired in others she had met, but which to this point had still escaped her. This would come, though, by simple dint of wide experience if nothing else. On one of her nightly sojourns to these clubs, Nancy was sitting with a fellow from South Australia she'd recently met at the college by the name of Robert Guthrie, drinking and smoking and simply enjoying the gloriously decadent feel of it all—thinking that her cropped blonde locks and her shirt with collar and tie had really set off the Tallulah Bankhead effect something special this night—when a waiter appeared and handed her a note. She carefully placed her deliciously long cigarette holder in the ashtray, and held it up to read it.

'*I think you are lovely and I would love to meet you,*' it said. Nancy looked over to see a rather statuesque blonde woman with a similar cut to her hair staring intently at her. Instinctively, she nodded that she understood and handed the message to her friend Robert sitting beside her, for whom the message was obviously intended. The waiter, hovering, shook his head to say, no, the message really was for Nancy, and only an instant later the statuesque woman emerged from the thick smoke and magically appeared by his side in the flesh.

'You are very beautiful,' she purred, looking Nancy directly in the eyes. 'Would you like to dance?'

Nancy was stunned. She might have danced around to music with girlfriends for fun in the past, but clearly this woman really wanted to dance *with* her! And probably a lot more besides, by the way she was looking at her.

'No ... I ... no ... no ... I ... uh ... no,' she finished rather lamely, for once at a loss for words, not quite sure where to look. The woman stormed off, leaving a still flabbergasted Nancy looking to Robert for an explanation.

'Well, Nancy,' he said gently, '*she's* a lesbian and *you* will wear ties, so what do you expect?'

Without a word, Nancy took off her tie, the very same one that had cost her 17/6d back in Sydney and gave it to him. And that was the end of her Tallulah Bankhead phase.

Life went on. Studies during the day—her typing and shorthand skills did indeed improve quickly, as advertised—and then gallivanting about with her friends at night. It was a lovely rhythm to live to. Letters to and from friends and family at home continued spasmodically, though at least enough for Nancy to know that still nothing had changed. Whereas *she*, by golly ...

'I felt I was growing, thriving in this new environment like never before,' she says. Then, as later, it was hard to define exactly what was so intoxicating about being in London, but it was something to do with a sense of *centred*-ness; that having been raised in the very outer provinces of the British empire, she was now in its very capital. Amazingly, that same King whose message she had thrilled to hear at the Anzac Day ceremony all those years ago, was right now, right on the other side of that wall somewhere, in that very palace! She loved seeing the changing of the guard at Buckingham Palace, window-shopping along Piccadilly, promenading around Hyde Park, hearing the sound of Big Ben in the distance. As a child she had adored singing the quasi-nursery rhyme, 'I am Big Ben/ Hear what I say/ All you other clocks/ Get out of my way', and now here she was hearing it for real! It all made her feel rather special, just as this town was special. London's history, she felt, made Sydney's look infantile by comparison, and so too did the range of possibilities of her existence here, make Sydney's look very narrow indeed. As it had always been for young people abroad for the first time, Nancy soon even felt a little *sniffy* when she gazed back upon the same tired old life she imagined her friends and family must be living back in Sydney. She simply did not miss them.

Whatever the joys of London calling though, the British capital wasn't the only one on the line. Paris was, of course, just across the English Channel, and about halfway through her course—having decided to be ludicrously extravagant—Nancy decided to fly there for the weekend on Imperial Airways.

'And it was amazing,' she remembers. 'That was the first time I had been on a plane, and it just seemed extraordinarily sophisticated to be flying into the French capital like that. I remember spending that whole weekend just wandering around in a kind of daze, soaking up the atmosphere, not quite believing I was there.'

And so, as Nancy happily lived out the dreams of her youth, this proved to be the first of many weekend trips to Paris during the rest of the year, each one of them delightful. The art galleries, the café society, the glorious monuments such as l'Arc de Triomphe, the colours of the Bois de Boulogne in spring, she loved it all. Conscious of her own French genealogy, it occurred to her that some atavistic urge was telling her she was now truly 'home', but she didn't care to analyse it too much. Joy was to be enjoyed, not dissected. What did you do over the weekend, Nancy, some of her friends might innocently ask her on a Monday morning as they attended their first classes.

'I went to Paris,' Nancy would reply pleasantly, and be amused at the staggered looks she got in reply. People simply didn't do that in those days. But Nancy did.

At year's end when she had completed all her typing and shorthand courses and received her diploma, it was time for the twenty-one-year-old Nancy to look for a job. Once again she had cause to think of the Maori midwife and her assertion that the infant babe in her arms would be lucky all her life, for after answering several advertisements in the newspapers, she was invited to a serious job interview with an editorial heavyweight from the famous William Randolph Hearst group of newspapers, based in New York, but looking to beef up its European bureaux.

The first part of the interview went well, and the fellow clearly not only liked the cut of her jib, but was also suitably impressed with the marks she had received at her college. Still though, he said, there were a couple of things they were specifically looking for in their new recruits, and he wondered if Nancy had ever been to or at least knew a lot about Egypt, as the Middle East was a growing area of interest at that time, and that would be a great boon if she did . . . It is not only in the field of arts, literature and science that great inspiration strikes. No sooner had her interviewer asked this question than Nancy had the answer!

'*Egypt*!?' she said, her voice incredulous at such a coincidence. 'I *love* Egypt! I've been there so many times, and studied so much about it, I can *write* in Egyptian!'

Staggered, the man couldn't believe his luck, but put her to the test by dictating to her from a book he picked up at random. For ten minutes he kept going while Nancy confidently trotted out what looked to him like hen-scratch on the paper, but was obviously making a lot of sense to her. On he went, and on she went, writing the most extraordinarily delicate squiggles, swirls and curls across the page from right to left. The man from Hearst watched, seemingly awe-struck, as she continued for line after line of hieroglyphics. Of course, modern Egyptian writing is in Arabic script and not hieroglyphics, but the executive appeared not to know that. When he had finished, she proceeded to read it back to him, word for word, perfectly, without a mistake. Just what had he stumbled across here?

In fact Nancy had never been to Egypt in her life, and had never so much as laid eyes on anything written in real Egyptian hieroglyphics. So what gave ...?

'I was simply doing Pitman's shorthand backwards,' she says, 'and this guy was an executive, not a journalist, so he didn't recognise it and really thought I was writing in Egyptian!'

Nor was she troubled by any namby-pamby notions that, while she was certainly showing high marks for resourcefulness here, others would give her low marks for honesty.

'I wanted the job,' she says simply. 'Gospel truth. I was so good at that kind of thing, I should have been a criminal.'

She was still to prove a capacity to write a coherent news story of course, but the fellow pronounced himself confident after looking at a collection of her completed assignments, that that would actually work itself out. She would be put on a modest retainer, together with her expenses taken care of, and then paid thereafter for every article of hers that their chain of papers published.

There remained just one problem, the fellow had said. The boss man, the American tycoon who owned the newspaper, despised all things British for some reason, so if he gave her the job on a six-month trial basis, there was no question of her remaining in London. She would have to move to Paris to work with their European bureau there, and use that as her base to move around Continental Europe and the Middle East ...

'Does this present a problem to you?' the man said, looking a little doubtfully at his freshly-found prize over the top of his glasses.

'No, I think it should be all right,' Nancy said quite calmly, considering that she was close to screaming with the ecstasy of it all. She got the job. PARIS! At someone else's *expense!* Someone get me a ... CABBIE!!!! The Maori midwife had been right.

CHAPTER FOUR

·

Paris

Bliss was it in that dawn to be alive
But to be young was very heaven ...

WILLIAM WORDSWORTH, *The Prelude*, 1850

Everyone, it is said, has a second country, a land where they feel immediately at home even when a long way from their actual birthplace. For Nancy, this country was France, and if she had half-surmised it from the first time she visited, it was doubly confirmed from the instant she returned there to live and work.

'See Paris in the 1930s and die,' she says flatly. 'It was the most thrilling place to be, and I simply couldn't believe how wonderful it was. I arrived there as a rather sensitive young Australian romantic, determined not to be uncouth, but I quickly felt at home, safe and very, very happy, I just loved it all. I loved the food, I loved their humour, I loved everything about it from the first.'

After staying for the first few days in the delightfully indulgent Hôtel Scribe in a particularly stylish nook on the Left Bank, it was time for her to go hunting for premises which she could actually afford on the Hearst group's meagre stipend. Eventually she settled on *un studio appartement* on the fifth and top level in the Rue Sainte-Anne, not far from l'Opera. It might have been fifth floor, but for Nancy it was closer still to seventh heaven, the first time she'd had a place to truly call her own. As it happened she was extremely lucky to get such choice lodgings at the reasonable price of the equivalent of eighty pounds a year. In getting it, however, she had a key advantage—the fact that she was from Australia.

'The concierge had fallen in love with an Australian soldier in the First World War,' Nancy explains, 'and had loved Australians ever since. After telling me what a good man that soldier had been and how brave and courageous he was, she said the flat was mine!'

This was not to be the last time that Nancy would thrill and walk a little taller to hear talk of the members of the Australian Imperial Force who had fought so bravely in the fields of France nearly two decades earlier. As the opportunity now arose to hear first-person accounts attesting to their bravery, she often sought out details of just what actions they had been involved in, and how they had performed.

'I felt a bond with them immediately,' Nancy says, 'and was very proud of the way our soldiers in France had gone in the First World War and I mean *very* proud.'

A small parenthesis here. In fact, the history of Australian soldiers in France to that point was a glorious, if notably bloody, one. The Australian Imperial Force had become heavily involved in the drive by the Allied war effort to break through German defenses around the Somme River in north-western France. In the town of Fromelles in late July, 1916, Australia suffered 5,533 casualties in just twenty-four hours. Over the next two years in France a staggering 60,000 of Australia's finest would be cut down in the fields of France, in famous battles such as Bullecourt and Messines. The Australians were widely regarded as fine fighters with a noted fierce refusal to submit even against superior numbers. In a crucial action at Villiers-Bretonneux, by way of example, a young Australian soldier in charge of a machine-gun company received instructions to hold the post at all costs. 'If the section cannot remain here alive, it will remain here dead,' he wrote in a diary which survived the subsequent carnage, 'but in any case it will remain'.[3] Close parenthesis.

But for Nancy in Paris, moving into the studio was a fairly simple matter, given that she didn't have a stick of furniture to bless herself with and there was barely room to put anything anyway.

But she did lash out early to buy one key item—a bath. As a studio it had no separate washing facilities, so the very kind concierge allowed her to set up a bath in the kitchen.

Now with her base secure, Nancy set about getting to work for the Hearst chain of papers and making herself at home in Paris. Socially, it hadn't taken too long to work out how things worked. In Vancouver people had congregated in each other's houses or promenaded in the park; in New York it had been apartments and speakeasies; in London it was 'I'll meet you down at the pub'; and in Paris the sun around which most social life revolved was the café. In only a very short time, Nancy's local café—half of which, she never ceased to marvel at, was out on the bloomin' footpath!— was practically her second home.

Bit by bit, she began to make friends with other people in her neighbourhood—from the butcher, baker and candlestick maker right through to the rich man, poor man, beggar man, thief—and she, herself, became a familiar figure, known as '*la demoiselle avec la bagne*', the girl with the bath, and was often hailed to come and sit down and have a wine.

From the beginning there was something about Nancy's exuberant knockabout charm that somehow fitted in well with that same part of the French character that gave its name to the whole notion of *joie de vivre*. (And maybe some of her mother's French genes really had survived the generational journey through to her, after all.) The locals seemed to appreciate the fact that she was up for anything, keen to have a go, and was not one of those infuriating *anglais* who came all the way to Paris only to sniff down their long noses at anything quintessentially French and who ended up hanging around with other *anglais* in their own English-speaking enclaves.

Speaking of which ... although Nancy had never studied French back at North Sydney Girls Domestic Science School she had at least arrived in France with a book called *French for Tourists* and a very basic idea of how the language was constructed—replete with perhaps fifty key words and phrases such as *grand, petit, prés, loin, un bière s'il vous plait*—and she went from there. There was something about the way the French pronounced her name, as *Nonc-eeeee*, that pleased her greatly, but oddly enough the part of the French language that pleased her most was their dirty words.

'I don't know why,' she says flatly, 'but I loved saying them, and they seemed to love hearing me say them.'

At first the French language was a thick and impenetrable fog of gobbledy-gook to Nancy, but bit by bit as she kept listening and talking, the mist started to clear, until she found that there were whole swathes of interchange she could understand perfectly well, and contribute to in kind.

'I never worried too much,' she says, 'about all that bloody feminine/masculine stuff, all the *le* this and *la* that—it would give you the shits—but it wasn't too long before I could communicate what I wanted to say, and I got better from there.'

Another factor, perhaps, in Nancy being so eagerly embraced by the Parisians, not to mention those in her own profession, was her sheer beauty. The gawky girl turned comely young teenager had now developed into a singularly stunning woman, with poise, presence, sexiness, the *lot*. Photos of her from the time show an elegant yet exuberant woman of refined dress, doubly generous bosom, and open expression. Not that this all came naturally.

'I had to *work* at it,' she laughs. 'I started copying the way the French women presented themselves, the way I used to copy Tallulah Bankhead.'

There was always a simple elegance about French women that amazed her. Whatever attributes nature might or might not have bestowed upon them, the duty of the Frenchwoman seemed to be to make the most of it with everything they had in them. Nancy followed suit.

'Trips to the hairdresser were no longer a luxury,' she says, 'they were a necessity. I put a lot more time into doing my face up, buying nice clothes like them, nice handbags, beautiful gloves and silk scarves. I'd wander for hours through shops up and down the Champs Elysées, trying to get just the right look.'

All up, the delights of Paris never seemed to end for Nancy. Some of her French friends would rave to her about how exciting

Paris had been in the decades before the Great War—the period known as *La Belle Epoque*—but Nancy could not imagine anything more wondrous than the period they were going through right now. If New York had seemed a quite masculine city to her, and London a particularly refined dowager, then Paris for her was all woman, and a young and beautiful one at that. Nancy felt at home there, *alive*, free to be quixotic, temperamental, fanciful— just as the city itself was—and to feel Paris's warm embrace around her.

Endlessly, gaily, she would wander the plane-tree lined boulevards in the early mornings through the delightful wafts of freshly baked croissants, stop at the cafés, gaze at the windows and on into the afternoon, discover the hidden parks, the back streets, the people of the pass-the-wine-please and the hip-hop hobos alike. All, all, *all*, she drank it all in, often sitting for hours at a particular café near the Eiffel Tower nursing several glasses of wine mixed with cassis—a drink called *kir*—and simply watching the world pass by. In the distance, the glorious spires of Notre Dame. Over there, the barges *chug-chug-chug*ging down the Seine on their ceaseless round in the lazy sunshine.

The other great thing about Paris was that there didn't appear to be any ridiculous moral strictures placed on young woman about the *correct* way to behave. In the Sydney she had left way behind, it was simply impermissible for a woman on her own to go for a drink at a bar without being thought of as a prostitute—and there were even similar views surviving in London and New York of all places—but there was no such unwritten law in Paris.

'You could go to these places and have fun and mix with the men,' she recalls, 'without them thinking you were "on the beat"! To be able to go into a place because you felt like it, and didn't have to go with a male as your moral protector, was a very good feeling indeed.'

Part of the joy was simply being away from her mother and being able to spread her wings without the fear of constant maternal pursed-lipped disapproval.

'My only thought was to have a good time. I was so thrilled to be in Paris, all these gorgeous Frenchmen chasing after you. I was the dizziest person there.'

Nancy did not exaggerate. There really were more than a few of these Frenchmen who pursued her, and less than a few who caught her, but none for long. Quite simply, she was having way too much fun and learning too many things to restrict herself in any heavy relationship that would involve committing herself.

'For the first time in my life,' she says, 'I was doing *exactly* what I wanted to do, and I was not going to give that up by being at someone else's beck and call. There would be time for that later, maybe, but I wasn't going to rush into anything. I had plenty of friends, and in a way when you're young and in a large group of happy friends, the very last thing you want to do is cut yourself off from the group so as to just be with one person.'

One as effervescent as Nancy simply could not live cheek by jowl by towel with the French without picking up some of their ways, and it was only a short time before, like them, she started having little more than a tiny strong coffee for breakfast, before she started buying ingredients for her meals immediately before cooking them, wearing scarves in a certain way around her neck in the classic European fashion, smoking way too many Gitanes until they burnt the back of her throat, and drinking cognac that had already been warmed up in the palm of her hand to produce more of that delicious vapour that was one of the key pleasures of drinking it. She learnt early, that on seeing any of her expanding coterie of French friends for the first time in the day, she did not simply nod and smile by way of greeting—as she had back in Australia—but instead kissed them on both cheeks. *Every day!* If they had become particularly close friends, then four or even six kisses was the go.

Then of course there were the dogs. Since arriving in *l'hexagone*, as she also learnt France was sometimes known to its inhabitants— in reference to its six-sided shape—Nancy simply couldn't help but notice that perhaps the key fashion accessory for every sophisticated Frenchwoman was a tiny little bow-wow that would mince around her at all times in all public places up to and including restaurants—where it was not uncommon for the dog, often a poodle, to sit up like Jacky on Madame's lap and be fed delicious mouthfuls from her own plate. Though initially a little put off at such spectacles—in the Australia she was from at that time, dogs were mostly useful for rounding up sheep in the country, barking at potential intruders in the city and sometimes to be given a kick up the backside when you had nothing better to do—she soon came around to the French way of thinking.

Which was why, after one morning spent taking her usual constitutional through the superb Tuileries gardens about fifteen minutes' brisk walk from her apartment, she was well-primed after crossing Rue de Rivoli to the shops, when she looked into a pet-shop window. A tiny puppy, a wire-haired terrier, was looking back at her. In a matter of minutes Nancy and 'Picon'—for that was what she named him shortly after, at the suggestion of her favourite barman—were on their way back to her own studio apartment, which appropriately enough was not much bigger than a kennel in its own right. A great and enduring relationship had just been formed. Only two weeks after bringing him into her life, she even went to the extent of having him 'baptised' at a bar with a group of her friends. A visiting American clergyman did the honours, and Nancy faithfully promised, amid high hilarity, to raise him as a fine God-fearing citizen.

As to her journalistic work, there was plenty of it, most appearing in some or all of the two dozen Hearst newspapers across America, including the *San Francisco Examiner* and the *Houston Chronicle*. She had arrived in France when the country was going through a very turbulent time. The great prosperity of the late 1920s had been split asunder by the Depression, and the result was that many hands from across the entire political spectrum were reaching for the steering wheel of power at the same time. This made for a wild ride, with governments and political movements crashing and clashing regularly, and it generated a lot of stories—which for Nancy at the time was the important thing. Politics had never been of enormous interest to her back in Australia, but she soon realised that it was the bread and butter of a lot of the journalistic work she was required to do. Thus, she attended protest rallies and reported on them, did the occasional interviews with key political figures, reported on nationwide strike actions, and recorded for the American readers the major machinations of French politics.

The journalism itself—in terms of the actual writing of such stories—did not develop into a great passion for her, but she enjoyed the kind of rouseabout life it encompassed.

Covering such a wide range of stories had brought Nancy into contact with many other expatriate journalists from newspapers such as the *New York Times*, *The Washington Post*, *The Times* and *The Continental Daily Mail* together with English-speaking journalists from French newspapers such as *Le Monde* and *Le Parisien*. She soon fell in with them, meeting most evenings after work at a well-oiled brasserie called Luigi's, just near l'Opera. Whatever else they were, these journos were born storytellers, and Nancy loved a good story more than most.

'I got on very well with them,' Nancy recalls, 'and they were so very good to me, the senior journalists helped me in lots of ways. They were very, very funny and I used to learn a lot from them. I used to hear stories about how the French always wanted to jump on top of you, and all this sort of business, but I never really found anything like that, I only found good men who helped me in my work and showed me how to get on. We were all friends. Most of those men were married with their wives in America or some place, but we were mostly just friends. Mostly.'

One particular wizened English journalist, coming up the five flights to fetch her one night to take her to the brasserie, found her still getting ready, and passed the time looking at the books in her tiny bookshelf. Picking up with an amazed look her battered tomes of *Anne of the Island* and *Anne of Green Gables* he came right out with it, in a voice that Nancy would never forget.

'Is *this* the sort of stuff you read, Nancy? Christ Almighty you'll have to learn a bit more than that to get along in the world.'

Well she never.

'I've never forgotten that,' Nancy says. 'And of course all of them always took the mickey out of me because whenever I went

away on any long journalistic trips, I always took my Anne books
with me!'

They'd get used to it. And so off to the café ...

This lifestyle of constantly going out was a little more expensive
than Nancy liked, but still she coped. Her journalist friends were
usually in the same straitened position.

'We stuck together,' Nancy says flatly. 'We were mates. If one of
us had something, we'd share it.' Financially, things were always at
their worst for Nancy every June and December when she had to
come up with the next six months rent, paid in advance—and
around that time she actually had to live very poor indeed—but
outside of that she coped. Besides, there were many ways to save
money if you were clever about it. One of these was to
manufacture your own necessities. Necessities like pastis. After
taking advice from a friend, and calling on her experience in New
York, Nancy was soon distilling gallons of the stuff in her own
kitchen, and inviting the journalists back to her apartment to drink
it. She and her journo mates caroused, talking on into the night.

While it was true, that some seventy years earlier, the great
German Chancellor Otto von Bismarck had famously said that 'the
great questions of the day will not be solved by speeches and
resolutions, but by blood and iron', this was different! As
journalists over a drink, their stock in trade was the first cousin
once removed of speeches and resolutions—that is, endless
conversation, specifically on those great questions of the day!
There were plenty of those great questions, and a lot of them
emanated from the nation Bismarck had been instrumental in
creating, Germany, where a man by the name of Adolf Hitler was
making a very big noise indeed at that time, a noise that the Hearst
chain of newspapers wanted their European correspondents to tell
them all about. So as the journalists drank, smoked, and chatted,
the name of Hitler would often come up, and Nancy was all ears
even more than usual, trying to get up to speed with what was
happening with the 'beast that sleeps on the other side of the
Rhine', as the French sometimes referred to Germany ...

Not that Hitler was the only story worth following, not by a long shot. Sometimes, pure happenstance placed Nancy in the middle of some very interesting news stories indeed. In October of 1934, Nancy Wake, journalist of Paris, boarded the Express at Austerlitz station, bound south, south for Marseille, via the Riviera. At the behest of her editors she was making her first visit to perhaps France's most famous Mediterranean city to report on a visit by King Aleksandar I of Yugoslavia.

From the moment of entering Marseille Nancy was entranced. With the famous boulevard, the Canebière, as its central thoroughfare leading up from the sparkling waters of the Mediterranean into the hills, the busy port city was not at all as she had expected. It had always had a reputation as a tough town, having grown up between wharves and warfare, and while that seemed true enough, no-one had warned her of the charm it possessed.

'Just being on the Mediterranean was wonderful,' she says. 'I hadn't fully realised before I got there how special a place the Riviera was, and Marseille had such an extraordinary history to it, I was completely overwhelmed.'

Yes, it had a seamy side too, particularly concentrated around the Vieux Port, the oldest part of the historical city, but even that was fascinating. Nancy wandered around the twisted and narrow streets and up the foul-smelling back alleys, past the many *tabacs*, soaking up the sights, smells, and scenes, delicately dodging the dog-droppings, gazing with compassion at the many ladies of the night who gravitated to the many dark doorways that so many foreign sailors were guaranteed to pass by. *'Ullo Cherie'*, they would smile and whisper to a chosen target in the passing parade, *'tu veux entrer?'* Around and about, the air was filled with the rich aroma of dozens of different dishes cooking in the tiny restaurants and bistros that abounded, particularly the bouillabaisse that was the local specialty.

But to work, and in the early afternoon of 9 October, 1934, Nancy was there, notebook in hand, among the milling crowds on the Canebière as King Aleksander I of Yugoslavia slowly made his way in his horse-drawn gilded carriage, up from the port where he'd landed, and through the cheering crowds, grandly waving his hand in classic monarchial fashion ... The 46-year-old King, she knew, was essentially a decent and competent ruler in an extremely difficult situation politically. His own restive kingdom had been formed and named by him as Yugoslavia out of a union of Serbs, Croats and Slovenians—but had been challenged from the beginning by, among other entities, The Croatian Peasants' Party, who wanted a separate Croatian state. In an effort to thwart such political dissension, the King had banned all political activities in 1929, but that did not quell the problem.

He had come to France to seek French support against the machinations of Benito Mussolini[4] and his overt support of Ante Pavelie, a native of Croatia who was an activist against the monarchy. Pavelie, with Mussolini's full support, had set up his terrorist headquarters in Fascist Italy where he worked to destroy the united state of Yugoslavia, so as to see his own dream of an independent Croatia set up—a state which would have been far more sympathetic to the Fascist goals of both Mussolini and Hitler, one of his other supporters. Then, amid all revelry and sense of wonder that a real live *royal* should be among them, came the clear sound of two shots.

'*Ils ont fusillé le Roi!*' a horrified shout rang out, 'They've shot the King!'

And they had indeed. At least someone had. There were screams, more shouts, and a sudden stampede of people away from the gunfire.

Nancy had no choice but to go with the tide of humanity away from the action. There was at least no question that she had a big story. It is a curiosity of the journalistic trade that even in the middle of the most extraordinary events, however upsetting they might be, there remains a sober, calm part of the mind weighing up just what sort of *newsworthiness* the event has. As she settled down in a bar about two kilometres away from the shooting, the answer here, clearly, was that it was a very big story indeed. The last time a royal personage had been gunned down in a public street in Europe had been in Sarajevo in June, 1914, when Gavrilo

Princip had shot and killed Archduke Franz Ferdinand, heir to the Austro-Hungarian throne, and his consort, Sophie, Duchess von Hohenberg—and the Great War had rumbled into being shortly afterwards. Who knew where this latest assassination would end?

'*Marseille. The King of Yugoslavia was shot yesterday,*' she began, in her careful shorthand. '*It is unknown how serious his injuries ...* '

She rang the story through to Paris on the first available telephone line, then resumed her position at the bar to see what would happen next.

She did not have to wait long ... there was shouting outside in the street, and in short order French policemen were swarming all over, wildly gesticulating and demanding to see people's papers—and Nancy was soon right in the sights of a particularly prickly policeman. What was *her* business in Marseille, he wanted to know with no little menace. She was, after all, a foreigner—an already suspicious status for many Frenchmen at that time. She told him, showed him her papers, and at least he seemed somewhat placated. The policeman was soon on his way, at which point Nancy was able to make some more enquiries as to just what the fate of the King was. It was not good. He was dead, shot through the lung, as was the French Foreign Minister, Barthou, who had been with him. An assassin unknown, though believed to be one of Pavelie's men, had approached the carriage and after shouting out loudly 'Long live the King!' had shot the same dead, before turning his gun on the Foreign Minister who had been so supportive of this same king. The assassin had in turn been instantly shot by the French police, and that was where things stood at the moment. One did not wish any of them their fate of course, but it really was a *great* story ...

Politically, it strengthened the growing grasp of Fascism on Europe. Only three months previously there had been another assassination, this of Englebert Dolfuss, the Austrian Chancellor who had resisted Adolf Hitler's first attempts at *Anschluss*, the incorporation of Austria into Germany. A small band of Austrian Nazis had forced their way into the Chancellery and shot him dead.

This rise of Fascism was of course the principal story of Nancy's time in Europe as a journalist, the one she was called on most often to write about for the Hearst chain of newspapers—specifically the rise of this same Adolf Hitler who she and her colleagues discussed endlessly. At this point, little was widely known of Hitler's background, other than that he'd fought in the Great War and been awarded medals for bravery; that he had launched a failed putsch in late 1923; that he had written a book called *Mein Kampf* (*My Struggle*) and that his own struggle had brought him an extraordinary rise to power.

Though born in Austria, Hitler had spent nearly all of his adulthood in Germany, and in February of 1932 he had formally become a German citizen—the month before he stood against Paul Ludwig Hans Anton Von Beneckendorf Und Von Hindenburg in the Presidential election. The results when they came out gave Hindenburg just under fifty per cent of the vote and Hitler just over thirty per cent with the rest divided among other candidates. Hindenburg's failure to win a clean majority, however, tipped the country into a second round of elections, in which Hindenburg achieved fifty-three per cent and Hitler thirty-seven per cent with a single other candidate getting the rest. In a stable democracy that would have been the end of it, but Germany at that time was not stable, and Hitler's Nazi party was not playing by the rules.

Just under a year later, on the night of 27 February, 1933, the German parliament, the Reichstag, was destroyed by fire, lit by persons unknown, but Hitler's deputies Goebbels and Göring were almost certainly the instigators, if not necessarily the ones holding the matches. In any case, the fire gave Hitler an excuse to blame the German communists in the Reichstag, to have them all arrested and thus heighten the instability on which he thrived. Most crucially, at the indomitable Hitler's behest, President Hindenburg issued a decree authorising Hitler's Nazi government to arrest and intern any person it deemed a threat to national security.

It was the beginning of the end, both for Hindenburg and Germany, for it was the end not only of free speech in Germany during that era—with extreme censorship laws quickly introduced—

but also the end of any serious resistance to Nazi rule. In March of 1933, the informal became formal, the convention became law when the Enabling Act was passed by a Reichstag which was in effect neutering itself, allowing Hitler's cabinet to assume legislative power for four years. Just four months later, Hitler and his cabinet outlawed all political parties in Germany other than the Nazi Party. Soon, even trade unions were banned, replaced by the Labour Front, a body under Nazi control. Churches came under extreme pressure to toe the Nazi line, with ministers who preached against the Nazis arrested by the Gestapo and taken to evil kinds of prisons called 'concentration camps'. Youth associations were banned bar one— the Hitler Youth.

If Nancy had had a reasonably good understanding of such events to this point—having always assiduously read newspapers and acutely listened to her fellow journalists —she now began to follow events with a professional eye, looking out for stories that she could write herself.

In August of 1934, President Hindenburg died and the last vestige of even ceremonial resistance to Hitler expired with him. Hitler's cabinet had already decided that when this occurred the Presidency and the Chancellorship would be merged into one all-powerful office, and that office of course fell to Hitler himself— titled *der Fuehrer und Reich Chancellor*. As such, the entire armed forces swore fealty to Hitler *personally*. Hitler's dictatorship was now complete. Not that the people appeared to complain. When a general vote was taken to ratify the moves already made, a resounding ninety per cent of the populace voted their support for a man who promised—among other things—that Germany could be great and powerful once again after he had freed them from the terrible humiliation imposed by the Versailles Treaty.

Tellingly, that election result did not include Jewish Germans— whose right to vote had been revoked—nor did it include those German citizens who had already fled the country. Many Germans who did not approve of Hitler, whatever he promised, had seen that things were ugly and getting uglier, and had already left. Increasingly, Paris witnessed a stream of German refugees through the city—people who had decided that their best option was simply to cut and run. The French capital was often their first port of call as they started to doorknock embassies desperately hoping for a visa to such far-flung places as Canada, Britain, America, or even Nancy's own native Australia.

Many of these unfortunates were Jewish—the main group that Hitler and the Nazis singled out for persecution. In 1935, the Nazis had passed the infamous Nuremburg Laws which explicitly stated that Jews were stripped of their German citizenship and which effectively made them non-persons with no legal rights, no right to hold public office or work in the civil service. Nor were they allowed to hold jobs in teaching, agriculture, the media or the stock exchange, leaving ... not much. *Juden Verboten,* 'Jews Forbidden', signs began to appear on shops and the rest of the German population were strongly encouraged to follow the Nazi line of unbridled hostility.

'All the Jews who could, were trying to get out,' Nancy remembers, 'and you could see them all the time, all with terrible stories. People coming through trying to get a transit visa either from there, or over to England, to get away.'

One night at the café—their regular table had expanded to accommodate some of the refugees—a particular fellow spoke of how the Nazi ideology could now easily be witnessed in Vienna, to where the politics of poison had already spread. On the spot, Nancy and some of her colleagues decided to go to see for themselves.

'From everything I had heard to this point,' she says, 'I simply couldn't understand how a government could do things like this to its own population, and that's why I wanted to go.'

Nancy's ongoing education continued.

CHAPTER FIVE

Vienna, Berlin, Marseille

'More fun than a Marseille shore leave.'

TRADITIONAL AMERICAN 'G.I. JOE' EXPRESSION

'So I set off on the train to Vienna with four of my male journalist friends,' Nancy recollects, 'not really knowing what to expect.'

What she saw there would subsequently motivate her beyond measure; for while the city itself was physically every bit as beautiful as she'd expected—with its boulevards, cobblestoned streets and classic soaring architecture—the human ugliness was staggering.

The poison of Hitler's Nazi party infiltrated the town, indeed the entire country, and everywhere she looked were huge strutting men of the *Sturmabteilung*, better known in English as storm troopers, Brown Shirts, or SA. This was the paramilitary organisation loyal to Hitler and Hitler only, which had essentially ridden shotgun for the Fuehrer's rise to power. Hitler had founded the SA more than a decade before, from remnant thugs left over from the Great War, had dressed them in brown uniforms (modelled on Mussolini's famous Fascist Blackshirts in Italy), and used them as violent muscle to protect Party meetings, march in Nazi rallies, and most crucially to physically assault all opponents of the Nazis. While they had started merely as a violent rabble, with Hitler's rise they had become a well organised, superbly resourced troop of still-violent thugs, who were essentially a law unto themselves.

Now in Vienna, they were everywhere and always violently intimidating those who were opponents of Nazi Party rule—first and foremost among these were the Jews.

'What I'll never forget,' Nancy says, 'is being in the main square of Vienna, and seeing these poor unfortunate Jews being tied to these massive wheels that were rolled along, with them being turned over and over as the wheels turned, and even as they went these huge fat Brown Shirts were beating them with whips! I couldn't believe, just *couldn't believe* what I was seeing! I mean, you wouldn't treat a cat like that.' Nancy was horrified and outraged in fairly equal measure, though it was perhaps the latter of the two emotions that held sway.

'Right there and then,' she says, 'I made up my mind that if ever I got the chance, I would do everything in my power to hurt them, to damage the Nazis and everything they stood for.'

This was not a vow made lightly, for it was often something she thought back upon in the years to come—her guiding star as it were. Back in Vienna, the final indignity was that the security forces confiscated their cameras and film as she and her equally appalled journalistic friends were leaving.

After they had witnessed such shocking examples of Nazi ideology at one of the outposts of its empire, it was a fairly natural progression for Nancy and her journalistic colleagues to go and view the very source of this river of vileness. With that in mind, only shortly after returning from Vienna, Nancy arranged to go to Berlin, again by the train. What she saw there, appalled her even more. It was not simply the ominous swastikas—a kind of twisted cross that had existed for many years but which now became the symbol of these wretched Nazis—nor even these same Brown Shirts who strutted everywhere. It was the very *atmosphere* of the place. All was fearful, divisive, militaristic, and the cult of Hitler worship was fully entrenched. His photo was omnipresent and the Nazi salute of the extended forearm and the shout of *Sieg Heil!* could be heard and seen everywhere they went. Again, amid all the general horror, a couple of particular episodes made an enormous impression on her.

One day she was walking along the *Kurfürstendamm*, when she saw an evil storm trooper in long leather boots strutting arrogantly along the street screaming imprecations at the Jewish storekeepers, as he lashed out at any of them not quick enough to get out of his way. In normal times, such a thug as this would likely be in prison or more likely an asylum for the criminally insane, but in the Germany of that time—so twisted was the Nazi system and what it stood for—not only was the brute not in trouble with the authorities, he *was* the authority. And there were plenty like him. Even as the man continued his tirade, striking hard and often with his whip, another storm trooper came behind, daubing the word *Juden* in huge red letters on the windows, while still other storm troopers gathered stock from the shops into piles and made huge bonfires out on the street. Nancy's blood boiled at the sight, everything in her wanting to do something to stop such senseless and wanton vandalistic brutality, but clearly it was useless. At least for the moment . . .

At least, at *least* she was a witness to it, and could write articles that would help warn the world of what the Nazis represented, but it was precious little salve for her sense of outrage.

'To that point I did not know I had such emotion in me,' she recalls, 'but I felt that if I'd been handed a gun I could have shot them dead on the spot. They were not human. This Nazi thing seemed to have just taken them over and turned them into something that I had not thought humanly possible. But I wanted it stopped, smashed, obliterated from the world.'

Who *was* this man Hitler who guided and nurtured such a terrible force to his own ends? Therein lay Nancy's other most powerful and enduring memory of the time. It came in the spring of 1935, and it was seeing him, Hitler, in the flesh addressing a huge rally just next to Berlin's Brandenburg Gate.

His entrance was in fact a long time in coming. Typically, a Hitler speech was engineered as the climax of extraordinary political theatre, and so it proved on this occasion. Nazi flags and banners were waved everywhere by people all dressed in their Nazi best of various stripes, ranks and affiliations. The crowds sang stirring martial songs, goose-stepping marchers passed as Wagnerian overtures sounded, and drums pounded a persistent beat that the man—*der Fuehrer*—was close!

Though Nancy cannot remember observing it on this occasion, one of the usual features of such rallies just prior to Hitler's arrival was 'the solemn consecration of the colours, in which new flags were touched to the *Blutfahne* (Blood Banner), a tattered standard said to have been steeped in the blood of those killed in Hitler's abortive Beer Hall Putsch of 1923', in which fifteen of Hitler's followers had died during his first attempt to seize power.

What she does remember is everyone suddenly jumping to their feet in a resounding ovation of cheering, saluting and shouting *Sieg Heil!* There he was! Standing on the stage perhaps only twenty-five metres from where Nancy sat, he presented a surprisingly small figure for one who generated such an extraordinarily large persona, not to mention such unequalled evil and loyalty. Just what he was saying, Nancy had no idea—her German not extending too much further than '*Jawohl*' and 'Berlin'—but the effect of his gutteral and staccato sentences was clear.

'Everyone around me,' Nancy remembers, 'was completely mesmerised, with their eyes glazing over, and their breathing seeming to stop. The longer he spoke the more the overall effect was simply hypnotic. He was shouting, his little moustache quivering, his hands punching the air as he jabbed away to make his points— and they loved it. He had what we probably would have called in Australia "the gift of the gab" but this was like nothing I'd ever seen before. When he finally finished, they all leapt to their feet and kept cheering him, before breaking into a whole new series of *Sieg Heils!* and salutes, which just seemed to go on and on.'

Her German trip complete, Nancy left Berlin and headed home to Paris in the vain hope that once she had got back into her bath for a long soak, she might be able to wash some of the dirtiness of the experience away. But she knew those images would never leave her.

* * *

Picon, Nancy's faithful little dog was, as always, waiting for her, having been cared for by neighbours while she was away. True to French form, Picon was never a stay-at-home dog, but was as incontrovertibly a part of Nancy's key accoutrements as her very stylish handbags and fashionable hats, and the two had become a common sight promenading together around the neighbourhood and farther afield.

On nights when Nancy was in a mood to go out to nightclubs, bars or restaurants—which was most nights and no mistake about it—the young Australian would say to her terrier, *'Picon, tu veux faire la bombe?'* always prompting the French-speaking Picon to rush to the door in preparation for another night on the town. To this day, Nancy maintains that her friends could judge at just what time she had got home the previous evening by how the terrier was faring. If he was drooping his way along behind her, or was fast asleep at her elegant feet, it meant that she had been out till the early hours. If instead Picon was bouncy and making the occasional yap, then Nancy had probably got home as early as eleven o'clock on the previous evening.

Nancy felt totally at home in Paris—Sydney and her life back there seemed far, far away, even though she still had the occasional exchange of letters with her friends and family. One of those letters, sadly, informed her that her sister Hazel had been one of the first people killed in a head-on traffic accident on the Sydney Harbour Bridge.

Nancy had now lived for well over two years in Paris but there was still time for this 23-year-old to go after *new* experiences! For nearly as long as she had been an adult, Nancy had been hearing about drugs and all the extraordinary feelings they could produce. Yes, she'd heard they could hurt you, yes they were illegal, but it didn't seem *right*, that so many people were talking about them, and yet she'd never tried them.

'It always rankled with me,' Nancy remembers, 'and I was determined that when the opportunity arose I would go after it.'

That opportunity arose a couple of years after Nancy arrived in Paris when she became very friendly with a Swiss girl called

Margo, who worked as a radiologist's secretary in Paris. As Easter of 1936 approached, the doctor decided he wished to visit his family in France's famous scent manufacturing town of Grasse for the holiday, and wanted Margo to stay in his apartment as security while he was away. Margo said she only would if the doctor could convince *Nonc-eeee* to come and stay with her as well.

'So he got in touch with me,' Nancy remembers, 'and I said "well listen to me Paul, on one condition—I want to know about drugs. I will come and Margo agrees with me, but you've got to leave some drugs there." He said "Okay".'

Done! Ready! At last cometh the day, the moment. At last she would discover just what it was that so many had been raving about.

On the evening of Good Friday, Nancy and Margo were indeed installed in the stylish apartment and, feeling deliciously wicked, decided that at long last they were ready to try some drugs.

'I will always remember it,' Nancy says. 'Both of us had a bath and put on clean nightdresses and then got out the white powder he had left for us. We got into bed before snorting it, because we didn't quite know what effect it would have on us.' At first ... nothing. And then ... still nothing! After half an hour solid of snorting the powder and then sneezing and coughing it out again, the net result was that both of them felt very foolish, but neither had got anything remotely approaching the promised 'high'.

'Finally I thought this is stupid,' says Nancy, 'and said "Oh Christ where's the cellar?" So we went down to the cellar and got two bottles of champagne and drank them and had a fine old time after all. When the doctor came back at the end of Easter I said, 'What's wrong with the drugs? They didn't do anything!' He said, "I'm not surprised, it was just mixed flour and salt".'

And that was the end of Nancy's drug career ...

Over the next few years in Paris, Nancy continued to live the life of a busy journalist by day, and Parisian party-girl by night. The same fingers that might be pounding furiously at a typewriter at 4 p.m., were just a few hours later heavily manicured and holding a cigarette, just as their mistress was holding court at one nightclub or another.

In the former role, she watched closely as in 1936 Hitler remilitarised the Rhineland—the same year he hosted the Berlin Olympics, a supposed festival of peace and humanity—with England barely raising a murmur. Meanwhile, Italy, led by the infernal Mussolini, stormed ashore in Abyssinia, as the Popular Front won the elections in France, and as the Spanish Civil War finally became a reality in July of that year. If Europe was not quite in flames at this point, it was at the very least smouldering heavily, with many spot fires breaking out. There were clearly enough stories to keep any serious journalist covering affairs on the continent very busy indeed.

And where was Britain in all this? Exactly. The short answer was that at this time Britain had particularly ineffectual leadership, paralysed by the desire to appease Hitler to avoid bloodshed, combined with the entirely opposite desire to punish him. And yet for all their huff and puff, threats and thundering condemnations, nothing actually happened. Nancy for one couldn't figure it out, but tended to endorse Winston Churchill's view that the British Prime Minister, Neville Chamberlain, was 'an old town clerk looking at European affairs through the wrong end of a municipal drainpipe'. He seemed to have absolutely no idea, and while he fiddle-faddled, a force was sweeping Europe, ugly and dangerous. The United States of America was similarly inactive, in the vain hope that by pursuing its isolationist policy, the whole thing might sort itself out without them . . .

And what was that Sir Isaac Newton line again, Nancy remembered from her days of studying physics? '*For every action there is an equal and opposite reaction . . .*' How true it was, and not just in the realms of physics. Just as most of Europe was sliding downwards, with an atmosphere of foreboding and lugubriousness, Paris itself was filling with gaiety as never before, awash with people who—perhaps sensing the doom that was almost upon them—were determined to have a good time, whatever the cost, whatever the future might hold.

The other part of the country experiencing great frivolity was the
French Riviera; Nancy had not lost her love of the Riviera since her
first trip three years earlier and she had found any excuse to return
since then. But she had never seen it so vibrant, so pulsating with
sheer joy as it was in that summer of 1936 when she went down there
to spend her holidays at the extremely popular casino and resort of
Juan les Pins, a place made famous by the patronage of such stellar
names as Coco Chanel, Somerset Maugham, Maurice Chevalier and
Charles Boyer ... As Nancy detailed in her autobiography:

'It was a mad, high-spirited resort which I was sure would suit
the mood I was in. I arrived there about eight in the morning. As
was usual at this time the streets were empty except for tradesmen,
workmen hosing the streets with perfumed water and the gardeners
tending the beautiful little parks and flower-beds.

'Some mornings a few stragglers in evening dress wending their
way back to the hotels would stand daringly in front of the hoses.
It was always taken in good part amidst peals of laughter. Then
suddenly the beaches would be covered with sunbathers dozing
and others swimming in the lovely blue sea. Late afternoon, as
soon as the warmth had gone out of the sun, the beach would
become deserted and it would be the turn of the bars and cafés to
be filled with light-hearted patrons consuming their apéritifs. Just
as suddenly as the beach had become deserted, so would the cafés
and bars as everyone wandered home to change for dinner, and
then the restaurants would be the scenes of activity.

'After coffee everyone would make a beeline for one of the two
nightclubs that existed in Juan ...'[5]

Juan les Pins was, in short, exactly her kind of place, and
therein, specifically in those two nightclubs, lay a tale ... Most
nights would find Nancy in one of those clubs dancing the night
away before, somewhere around midnight, a kind of conga line
would be formed and all the patrons of one club would join up and
drunkenly, with high hilarity, dance their way over to the other
club. One particular night Nancy was dancing cheek to cheek with
her companion of the moment—an American journalist originally
from the West Coast whom she had been seeing a lot of lately in

Paris, a man who'd come down to the resort to spend a fortnight with her—when she suddenly became conscious that someone was watching her intently.

And *tango* one, *tango* two, step one, step two, and *whirl*, and there he was ...

Standing tightly in the shadowy corner, a dimly perceived, though elegant, figure was indeed watching her and shortly afterwards when the lights went up, she recognised him as someone with whom she'd had a flirtatiously glancing acquaintance on her few trips to Marseille.

His name was Henri Fiocca, and in that town he was indeed a big wheel, she recalled, a local industrialist from one of the leading, and certainly richest, families in the town. Beyond that she knew little other than that he had something of a reputation as a playboy. Sure enough, there beside him was a supremely attractive blonde, at least momentarily miffed that she had lost Henri's attention. Shortly afterwards, the industrialist dropped by their table briefly to pay his respects, before disappearing on the arm of the blonde and that, Nancy thought, was the end of that ...

Mais non.

Over the next week, she ran into him several times, sometimes three times on the same night, and here was the thing: *every time* he was with a different woman. Even on the same night!

'He wasn't bad looking,' Nancy remembers, 'but I was more intrigued by his stamina. It *amazed* me.'

Nancy didn't think too much about it, until the following weekend when he was back at the resort, this time *sans* blonde, which worked out well because she was also without her American friend, who had since returned to Paris. Henri asked her to dance. And tango one, tango two, step one, step two, and *whirl* ... They seemed to move well together. For starters Nancy liked the distinguished, mannish but sensitive look of the bloke and she adored the fact that with all that he had a highly developed sense of fun. Finally, it was more than flesh and blood and curiosity and spirit could stand—let alone understand. She decided to tackle him at the end of a particular evening ...

'How on *earth* do you do it?' she asked.

'Do what?'

'Go out with so very many beautiful girls.'

In reply, Henri Fiocca waxed breezy. 'Because they ring me up,' he said lightly.

'*They* ring *you* up!?!'

'Yes,' he said, dropping down a couple of gears now before carefully navigating the next bit of terrain. 'Every girl rings me up, except the girl I truly want to ring me up ...'

The air was full of a portentous pause before Nancy drew herself up to her full height and retorted haughtily: '*I* do not ring men up. *They* ring me up. Otherwise they get nowhere.'

With which she stormed off, though perhaps with just a little more sway in her hips than usual. Needless to say, he rang her up ... and very soon thereafter they were seeing each other.

'I was madly attracted to him,' recalls Nancy. 'He was charming, he made me laugh all the time and he was dead sexy.'

Steady though. However sexy she might have found this thickset but suave Frenchman, and however clearly attracted to her he seemed to be, something rather curious happened in the first months of their courtship. He never made a serious physical move on her. Not once. Here she was thinking that he was a playboy to beat all playboys, obviously with the sexual stamina of a bull, and yet he always seemed to haul himself in after some particularly wondrous kissing! What was going on?

'And I really began to think,' Nancy says, 'that he might have a bit of a problem "down there". I had seen this film where the hero had been wounded and lost his balls, and as Henri had served for a few months in the Great War I thought the same might have happened to him and that's why he didn't make a move.'

Such thoughts were just consolidating in her mind as the weeks and then months passed, when one moonlit night in Cannes ...

'I found I had no need to worry on that account,' Nancy says delicately. 'He was just being extremely elegant with me, waiting for the right time.'

When a while later she mentioned her previous fears to one of

Henri's friends by the name of Louis, the fellow roared with laughter and said '*Nonc-eee, Nonc-eee*, it was simply because he *respected* you that he waited.'

So they were off, with Nancy Wake embarking on what was really the first serious relationship of her life. Of course she genuinely loved him, but there were many bonus pleasures that went with that love. After years and years of living poor in the day so she could at least pretend to live rich at night, it was an enormous pleasure to be with someone who automatically reached for even the heaviest of bills without raising the tiniest of sweats, and without making even the teensiest of dents in his very substantial wallet. Not that Nancy wanted things to move *too* fast and go *too* far with Henri, she maintains.

'It was marvellous when I saw him,' she says, 'but there was no question of me simply throwing away everything I had in Paris to be with him. I valued my life there too much.'

That said, she still agreed that whenever she was in the southern part of France she would go and stay with him. (Not always in his Marseille house—somewhere between a mansion and a *maison*—but often in a Cannes or Nice hotel.) She was as good as her word. From that point on, even the whiff of a story anywhere in the region was excuse enough for her to jump on the Marseille Express from Austerlitz station, settle down and then count the hours until she would see Henri again.

During this early part of their courtship along the Riviera, Nancy also met and became very friendly with one of Cannes society's leading ladies, Madame Andrée Digard. The two just clicked, and often in the lazy afternoons, if Henri was perhaps attending to a business matter in town, Nancy and Andrée and her 12-year-old daughter, Micheline, would laze around by the Digard's pool sipping tea or something stronger and chatting into the early evening until Henri's work was done. As Nancy confided to Andrée, while Micheline might still be gallivanting around in the water, she felt that even though Henri was a full fourteen years older than she—which was a lot older than anyone Nancy had ever been out with before—there was just something *about* him.

And unfortunately, about his father and sister, for, from the beginning, Fiocca Senior and his daughter did not like Nancy and she did not like them, and neither side made any particular effort to hide their antipathy. To them she was clearly an upstart gold-digging Protestant from (*sniff*) Australia, wherever that was, while for her they were people with pretensions to a high class they did not genuinely possess. Everyone said that Henri got his gentility and generosity, his charisma and character, from his late beloved mother, and Nancy could easily believe it, for it scarcely seemed possible that such a man as he could have sprung from such a man as his father. They were obviously close by genealogy, and in their common business—of breaking and brokering defunct ships—but a long way apart in spirit.

'Henri was a gentleman and gentle man,' Nancy says flatly, 'and his father was a mean arsehole.'

Never mind. Nancy knew she loved Henri, and that was good enough for her.

Fortunately, on greater acquaintance she also came to love Marseille even more than previously. The historic pearl of southern France, the city was a maze of cafés, restaurants, cathedrals, museums and buzzing bunches of people carousing late into the night. It even had a touch of Hollywood, for soon after she began spending time there with Henri, from early 1937 onwards, she discovered that the city was also a place where the great P & O liners taking the well-heeled cosmopolitans from all over the world on luxurious Mediterranean cruises would drop in to let off passengers—often to spend a few days before boarding the train to Paris and then across the Channel to London. This meant that it was not at all uncommon for Marseille nightclubs to boast international stars as patrons.

'And the best thing for them,' Nancy says, 'was that they could just enjoy our nightclubs without being hassled by the photographers or the press. They were able to have a nice old time relaxing with us, and not a worry in the world.'

And hello to you too, Gary Cooper! Lovely to meet you, Gloria Swanson! All up, it was a superb life and she could quite easily have settled into it forever.

But steady on; as she kept telling herself, it was important to keep her journalistic career in Paris going, and it simply wasn't on for her to stop her whole life there to go and live Henri's life in Marseille.

'*Alors, Henri, il faut que je m'en aille,*' she would whisper gently. I must go.

'*Pas encore, Nannie,*' he would reply, using his pet name for her. Not yet.

Many, many times, the two would have this exchange on the Marseille train platform, as they had one last kiss before the train pulled out for Paris with Nancy on it. Sometimes the kiss would last so long that it would in fact be the many thousands of horsepower being generated by the train's massive steam-engines that finally pulled their lips apart. But, just as Nancy was constantly finding journalistic reasons to visit Marseille, Henri too was adept at finding business reasons to go to Paris. It was, after all, the national capital, a centre of international finance, and a great place to do business ...

Luckily, Henri formed an instant affection for Picon, and luckily for the Frenchman, Picon seemed to return it. (Otherwise it would likely have gone very badly for Henri. More than one potential suitor of Nancy's had been sent on his way with the dog's unfriendly yips still ringing in his ears.) On his trips to Paris, Henri came to understand Nancy even better.

'I think it helped,' Nancy says, 'when Henri saw the way I lived my life, with this large group of male journalists who were my close friends but not my lovers. He told me he had been jealous but now that he saw the men, the way that we were all such great comrades together, he wasn't any more. And he became friendly with a lot of them too.'

By contrast, the backdrop of their burgeoning romance was one of ever more bad news about the direction in which Europe was heading; but instead of distracting their ardour, it simply helped put their relationship onto the fast-track.

'There was really a sense,' says Nancy, 'that Europe was going straight to Hell and that there was only limited time to enjoy what you wanted to do. Everyone was packing as much pleasure into every day as we could, because no-one knew what tomorrow would bring.'

For every action, an equal and opposite reaction.

The hatred that was bringing war might have been on a violent upsurge—Hitler's forces had already swallowed both Austria and Czechoslovakia, and now seemed to be looking voraciously at the rest of Europe, and a million people had now been killed in the Spanish Civil War—but plenty of people continued to react to it by heading off in entirely the opposite direction. That is, they made love, not war.

Early in 1939, while dining at their favourite restaurant in Marseille, 'Verduns', Henri suddenly seemed uncharacteristically nervous, and then came out with it. He was wondering ... would it be possible ... how does one say this ... Let him start again.

'The thing is, *une fois de plus, Nannie, est-ce que tu veux me marrier?*'

'*Oui.*'

In short order, Joseph, the delighted maitre d'hôtel, was serving them the house's best vintage of Krug champagne and their happiness was complete. Or almost, there were a couple of minor things to still work out, but that didn't take long. On the spot, Nancy told him she would not convert to Roman Catholicism. Wouldn't. Wouldn't. *Wouldn't.*

'Not a problem,' replied Henri with a smile. He had previously discussed with Nancy her absolute refusal to accept the principle of Immaculate Conception—*pshaw!*—and was not surprised by this stance. Nor would she observe the French tradition of the bride providing a substantial dowry, redeemable should the couple ever split. In the first place, she simply didn't have money like that and in the second, she didn't agree with the tradition of the bride providing a grateful thank you for the groom agreeing to take her down off the shelf. That too was okay, Nancy, so long as you don't mention anything to Papa. Henri in turn had a minor pecuniary problem, that his father had recently made a disastrous deal to buy an abandoned battleship at huge cost only to see the bottom fall out of both the market and the ship at the same time—meaning that the family's fortunes and the vessel were equally momentarily sunk—but that could be overcome. It had at least hastened Henri into taking over reins of the firm from his father, and if Nancy could see her way clear to waiting until, say, May of the following year for the nuptials, he felt confident that they could do it in true Fiocca style. Done! Knock the deal down to the man with the beaming smile.

'Timing was nothing to me,' Nancy says, 'I was just glad to be marrying such a man as Henri, and exactly when it happened was neither here nor there.'

It was set then. For the moment, Nancy continued to live and work in Paris, but her trips to Marseille to see her *fiancé*—she really liked that word, she decided—became ever more frequent. As did, coincidentally, the demands on her from her employers for clear copy on exactly what was going on in Europe. The spot fires were now starting to join up into serious approaching fire-fronts and each month brought waves of staggering news. But to a certain extent, now that she was engaged, the demands of her profession could wait.

The summer of 1939 saw the couple staying together in their favourite suite of their favourite hotel, the Martinez, in the true jewel of the Riviera, Cannes. From the balcony of their suite you could see both up and down the Cannes esplanade, and across to the yachts coming in and out of the marina. Where could be finer for two people in love to stay? Yes, it seemed all but certain a full-blown war involving France was coming and, yes, each day's papers brought news of new atrocities carried out in the name of Adolf Hitler, but once again it was equally clear that there was nothing they could do about it, and Nancy and Henri felt that they must enjoy each other while they could.

'It might have seemed frivolous to do what we were doing when we were doing it,' Nancy says, 'but we thought that it was not only probable that this was our last summer before the war, it might just be our last summer, full stop.'

Clearly, if war did break out Henri would have to go away to fight. He was fit, healthy, only just over forty years old, and a French patriot. If it came, he would go, they both knew.

Meanwhile they were living in the Martinez, and for two glorious months they dined, drank, danced, dallied, made love and frequently went to the casino. They went on day-trips to St Tropez, danced themselves to a standstill in the nightclubs of Monte Carlo, and hobnobbed with some of their friends on luxury cruisers, taking day-trips to picturesque seaside villages. Through it all, the newspapers and radios, as well as several of Nancy's journalist friends passing through, continued to beat the same drum—the war was coming and nothing was going to stop it.

When the summer in Cannes was nearing its end, one thing was clear to them both. They did not want to split and go their separate ways again, war or no war. If there was only a limited time left to them, they wanted to spend that time together and it was with that in mind that Nancy agreed that she would return to Paris only to resign from her job, pack, lease out the flat, and then come down to Marseille and move in with Henri.

One thing though. Nancy felt a strong compulsion to spend a little time in England before taking up her life in Marseille. Part of it was physical—all of that fine food and champagne had taken its toll—and she wanted to lose weight before she married and knew just the health resort in England for such a task. And maybe part of it was spiritual—the need to spend some time with English-speaking people before marrying into a life fully French.

Henri agreed, which was just as well for Nancy had *already* booked a whole month at one of England's most famous health resorts, Champneys,[6] in Tring, Hertfordshire, and shortly thereafter was packing her bags—all the while telling Picon that he would be quite fine with Henri while she was away, but that she would miss him *terribly*.

In that last week of August, 1939, the two had what they hoped would be their last long and languorous goodbye on the platform of Marseille station before Nancy got onto the Paris Express to take her back to her apartment and then onto England. The train was what to Nancy's Australian mind could only be called 'chock-a-block' with soldiers who had received papers demanding that they return from leave and head north immediately to reinforce

France's defensive lines on the German border from possible attack. As well, there were many Europeans from countries other than France, hurriedly and worriedly proceeding to Paris, before they changed trains to head to their own homelands. Paris was in uproar when she arrived. War was in the wind and the wind was gaining velocity by the hour. A fierce storm was setting in.

The very day Nancy arrived in the French capital, Hitler's forces had launched themselves on Poland, using their trademark *blitzkrieg*—literally 'lightning war'—of a heavy air attack, followed by overwhelming tank divisions and then swarming infantry after that. The news of the battle was spasmodic at best, but the thrust was as hard to miss as a division of panzers on the charge. Poland looked to be providing no greater resistance to the Nazis than Czechoslovakia and Austria had before it. In response, both France and Britain had issued ultimatums to Hitler to withdraw from Poland immediately, or face their combined might. Few had any confidence that Hitler would do so.

The tension in Paris was palpable. Hurry. Hustle. Hassle. People held onto each other in the streets and wept, before parting to go their separate ways. Children wandered around a little dazed, trying to comprehend just what all the fuss was about. Patrons huddled together in bars and bistros around radios, straining for news. Queues formed up in front of both banks and food stores. Cars loaded to the gunnels with people and furniture, headed out of town along the crowded, swirling boulevards. In the face of the coming war, many people were simply upping sticks and taking off. One such was Nancy's concierge who, as Nancy saw when she arrived, was packing before heading off to stay with her sister in the country. She burst into tears as she hugged Nancy goodbye and wished her all the best for the future. (Alas, Nancy learned that the concierge was killed shortly afterwards.)

The tension did not dissipate even away from the French capital. Once landed in London and installed in her suite at the Strand Palace Hotel—thank you, Henri—Nancy found the entire place full of refugees from Continental Europe, escaping from what they feared was about to happen.

And it did happen. On the morning of Sunday, 3 September 1939, to clear her head and get out of London, Nancy had gone off on a train to visit Micheline Digard—the daughter of her great friend from Cannes, Andrée Digard—who was now in the St Maur Convent at Weybridge in Surrey. She wanted to collect Micheline and bring her back to London for a lovely day, and the young girl was indeed delighted to see her ...

Now living in Paris, Micheline remembers, 'I always had a soft spot for Nancy because she was always so much fun to be with. I always remember one time we were going to go on a picnic, and it turned out to be pouring with rain. Nancy said not to worry, my mother and I should come to her apartment and we would get a surprise. When we got there Nancy had put leaves all over the floor, and flowers all around to make the whole thing look like a park, and we had our picnic inside. That was Nancy ...'

And here was Micheline now, all of sixteen years old and waiting for Nancy at the gates of the convent when she turned up there from the train station. Nancy could barely believe how much the dark-haired and strapping girl had grown in the three years since they'd first met, and the two of them headed back to London. But when they pulled in at Waterloo station, people were running everywhere, some shouting, others crying, men in uniform scurrying to catch trains, newspaper boys screaming. Read all about it! War had been declared.

It was true. While Nancy and Micheline had been gazing from the train, *clickety-clack, clickety-clack,* as the green and pleasant land fell behind them, and continuing to chat happily, the British Prime Minister Neville Chamberlain had addressed the nation over the radio from the Cabinet Room at 10 Downing Street, in singularly sombre tones ...

'This morning,' he said in a voice breaking with fatigue, 'the British Ambassador in Berlin handed the German Government a final note stating that unless we heard from them by eleven o'clock that they were prepared at once to withdraw their troops from Poland, a state of war would exist between us. I have to tell you now that no such undertaking has been received, and that consequently this country is at war with Germany ...

'At such a moment as this the assurances of support that we have received from the Empire are a source of profound encouragement to us ... Now may God bless you all and may He defend the right. For it is evil things that we shall be fighting against, brute force, bad faith, injustice, oppression and persecution. And against them I am certain that the right will prevail.'

Nancy immediately cancelled her stay at the health resort—'I thought it's no good going to Tring, I'll be starving anyway'—and looked at what to do next. The first and most obvious thing to do was to give Micheline as good a day as she possibly could under the circumstances before dropping the weeping girl back at the convent that night. They went promenading and sight-seeing, both being staggered to see these new fangled Zeppelin things on display above Hyde Park; but nothing could get their minds off the obvious for long. The war. What would happen to them? What would happen to their countries, their loved ones? In the end there was nothing for it but to take her back to her school.

'*Nonc-eeee, ne me laisse pas!*' Nancy don't leave me! the sobbing girl cried, just before the heavy convent doors closed on her.

'I was petrified,' Micheline recalls, 'that Nancy would go back to France without me, leaving me to rot in England while my mother was in danger at home in Cannes, but Nancy said there was nothing she could do right then, and I'd have to stay in the convent for the moment.'

The following day, Nancy turned up at recruiting offices to offer herself as a great candidate for one of the services in any frontline capacity. Upon the outbreak of war, she had immediately taken the attitude that her impending marriage to Henri would have to stay just that, impending, while she did her bit for King and Country. Of course she was still going to marry him, and wanted to spend the rest of her life with him, but clearly this matter had to be settled first, and she had to do her bit. In her mind's eye she saw them offering her a post somewhere important in either the army, navy or air force.

Alas, it was not to be. The recruiting officer—a particularly taciturn man who looked like the fact that war had been declared was the very least of his concerns on a day when his false teeth were just *killing him*—looked rigidly over his glasses, past the pointy end of his nose, and suggested that perhaps instead of serving in one of the armed forces, serving in the canteen might be more the go ...

And he was serious!

There and then Nancy decided to head straight back to France, to be with Henri, and to see what she could do there. At least she would be closer to the action, and at least she would be with him. But one thing she was *not* going to do, dammit, was stand behind a counter and serve out tea and bikkies to the real fighting men and women. She had more to offer than that, she felt sure. The following morning at the hotel, she received two messages. The first was from Henri, bless his cotton socks, insisting that she come home immediately where he had already been arranging to have their wedding brought forward. The second was from Micheline's mother, asking whether there was any chance that she could safely bring the girl across the English Channel with her, and then down to Cannes.

Nancy cabled back 'OUI!' and 'OUI', and set out to do just that.

'NO. You *cannot* take Micheline without written authorisation.'

The speaker was the Mother Superior of the convent where Micheline was studying—a severe woman's severe woman, if ever there was one—and she meant it. For one of the few times in her life, Nancy, sitting in front of the big oak desk of the Mother's dark and forbidding inner sanctum with crucifixes on the wall all around, accepted defeat. The worst of it was that the woman was being no more than reasonable. Outright stupidity Nancy could have argued against, but she was flat out floored by good sense. The Mother simply couldn't release one of her students into the hands of one who said she had the blessing of her parents, even when the said student said she *wanted* to go with her.

'Thank you, Mother, I will be back as soon as I can, with what you require,' Nancy said as she made her leave. And she was as good as her word. After many cables back and forth, at last Micheline's parents sent the authorisation in a form that satisfied the Mother Superior and they were away.

Or almost. For it was a sobering thing, indeed, to leave England under these circumstances; saying goodbye to the comparative stability of a nation that was at least semi-protected by the Channel from invasion, and then heading off to a country right next door to the beast. And it was made all the more sober by the English customs officer to whom they presented their passports. This worthy one, like the many officials Nancy had dealt with even to that point, tried to dissuade them from this clear path of madness. To her, as the adult, he was well-meaning but insistent, looking at her like she'd just announced she was going to eat his tie.

'You know France will soon likely be invaded, Miss?'

'Yes.'

'You know there's not even any guarantee you won't be sunk by a German torpedo 'alfway across the Channel?'

'Yes.'

'But you're still absolutely determined to go, even though you're not French yourself?'

'Yes.'

'Good luck. But I've got to tell you. If you go, you'll never come back, do you understand?'

Nancy nodded—by way of terminating the conversation rather than agreeing with his premise—took their papers and Micheline by the hand and boarded the boat, which was barely more than a car ferry. In this instance, it was simply a bigger version, Nancy mused in passing, of the old punt she used to catch from Milsons Point across Sydney Harbour to the city.

Not that you could see anything of it, after night fell. With the ship's captain rightly terrified of being blown out of the water by a torpedo, all lights were doused, and he meant *all* lights—right down to forbidding people to smoke on deck for fear of the glow their butts would cast. A similar regime had operated back in London, where a blackout applied overnight to help send awry the

German bombs that might shortly come raining down upon them. As the French coast approached, and submarine sirens sounded, Nancy really did have a fleeting moment of wonder about whether this was madness, to be taking a terrified young girl like Micheline back into a country which the Nazis would shortly be attacking. She held the girl close to her as the sirens continued to blare, and was not sure if the shudder that passed through them was the boat, the girl, or herself. Whatever, she felt extremely protective of her, and conscious of the tremendous responsibility she had to return Micheline home safely to her mother. The boat throbbed on, nosing forwards.

And then they saw it. Entering the harbour of Boulogne sur Mer it looked as if the French had not only left a light in the window by which all their returning countrymen could find their way home, they'd left *every* light in the city on! Cars careened around the streets with their headlights blazing, the lighthouse winked at them that this was *La France* all right, and the sounds of music from fully-lit nightclubs wafted across the water to them. The two travellers looked at each other before they burst out laughing together. After what they'd been through, they felt like butterflies coming out of the darkness to land on a blazing Christmas tree!

'*Voilà, La France!*' exulted Micheline. They were home. They laughed and laughed till the tears ran down their faces.

CHAPTER SIX

.⸌

'Cry "Havoc" and Let Slip the Dogs of War.'[7]

'What I have really loved in my life were infantry and love-making.'

MARSHAL HENRI PHILIPPE PÉTAIN

The wedding of Henri Edmond Fiocca and Nancy Grace Augusta Wake took place on 30 November, 1939, and went off a treat. Nancy had experienced no nervousness in the lead-up, only impatience for it to happen—so positive was she that this was the man for her—and it was a wonderful moment when Henri at last slipped the wedding band over her finger.

After the official nuptials were held in the Marseille Town Hall, *la Mairie*, the wedding breakfast was staged at the same Hôtel du Louvre et Paix which the two had often frequented during their courtship, and was attended by *la crème de la crème* of Marseille— it was after all the Marseille society wedding of the year—plus three surprise guests, in Nancy's closest trio of confidantes among the Paris journalists!

'Henri brought them down as a surprise for me,' Nancy recalls, 'and it was one of the nicest things he ever did for me.'

Her other journalist friends had sent gifts, with love.

Nancy, if she does say so herself, never looked finer than on that very day.

'My wedding dress was pure black silk,' she says. 'It was the most beautiful dress that you could imagine, with embroidered pink orchids in it. I bought it on the Canebière in the very famous haute couture boutique, George's. Black silk, with pink underneath, as the lining of the dress ...'

The only competition for her splendour was the meal of the wedding breakfast. Their chef of choice, Marius, had positively outdone himself in the three weeks leading up to the reception in securing delicacies for a gourmet meal in a country already beginning to suffer wartime privations, and the guests were so knocked out by the results that they gave him a standing ovation when the meal appeared. And for good reason. The first course set the tone, grilled fish *sans* backbone filled, as Nancy has previously described it, 'with the most delicate mousseline made with the flesh of *oursins* (sea urchins)'. Then, she continues, the sole were deep fried 'until they puffed up, light and airy like a soufflé. They would be accompanied by a rich, luscious sauce made with *oursins* among other ingredients. For the first meat course we decided to serve loin of a special lamb—*pré-salé*, which Marius ordered from Normandy. It has a unique flavour because the sheep graze on fields near salt water.'[8]

And so, no expense had been spared.

If there was one downside to the wedding reception for Nancy, at least initially, it was the presence among the one hundred guests of her now father-in-law and sister-in-law. Even this far down the track she still did not feel an ounce of warmth either *for* them or *from* them. Both Fiocca *père* and *soeur*, damn their *nouveau riche* hides, continued to make it clear that they were there under sufferance and did *not* approve of the nuptials. And yet, wouldn't you know it, by the end of the evening even they seemed to have loosened up a bit, and were cracking the odd smile.

Nancy would have loved to think that this was because they had been carried away simply by the euphoria of the evening, or by the love that she and Henri so clearly felt for each other ... but in fact she knew better.

'It was because we spiked their punch,' she says flatly. 'We put a lot of vodka in the punch, partly for the fun of it and partly to help loosen them up for one night. One way or another it worked to the extent that by midnight Henri's father and sister seemed to be dancing as if there was no tomorrow with everyone else and singing and carrying on! The whole thing, with everyone getting into the spirit, was just fantastic ...'

The war? Yes, it raged on, elsewhere, but it wasn't as if it had yet made a *real* impact on the lives of either the bride and groom or any of their guests. The Germans and the French had yet to really get to grips and it frankly didn't seem likely that the *Boches*—as the French often called their Teutonic neighbours—had much chance of over-running France any time soon. Their country had, the guests assured each other, the highly prized Maginot Line to protect them. Apart from the assured happiness of Henri and *Nonc-eeeee*, the key conversational subject at the reception was probably the fact that the Maginot Line had been a typical stroke of French genius!

And ladies and gentlemen, a toast to the French politician and Minister of War, Monsieur Andre Maginot, who had been the key champion of its construction. This long and bristling defensive line composed of forts, blockhouses and pillboxes connected by trenches and tunnels and minefields, extended for some 220 kilometres from the impenetrable Ardennes Forest in the north down to the equally impassable Alps of Switzerland, and from there again south all the way to the Mediterranean. With some foresight, it had been built between 1929 and 1939, specifically to keep the brutes of Germans on their side of the common border, and in the situation in which France currently found itself, the Maginot Line really was the toast of the nation—as were the 800,000 men then in France's army, judged by military experts to be the most powerful in Europe.

So dance! And drink! And dance and drink some more! And toast the bride and groom! Waiter, more of that *fabuleux* PUNCH! Perhaps the moment of highest hilarity during the whole reception was when Nancy and Micheline brought out the absurd gas masks they had brought with them from England and lots of the guests tried them on while everyone fell about laughing and the photographer took snaps. Ah, how they laughed. How they *screamed* with mirth when Nancy held up Picon with the gas mask attached to his little furry head! All up, the wedding was judged to be a complete success.

'It's the only night that Henri and I didn't make love,' Nancy recalls. 'We were too busy celebrating. When it got very late and most of the guests had gone home, Henri and I took the three journalists from Paris with us and went drinking and carrying on all night long. A mad life ...'

And a good life, the war be damned. They spent their honeymoon in Cannes, staying once again in their favourite suite in their favourite Hôtel Martinez on the main boulevard running along in front of the beach, and returned to Marseille to live the good life in a penthouse apartment Nancy had secured for them at Henri's behest at the top of the Canebière, just beneath the famous zoological gardens. From their windows and balcony they could see over the hazy red rooftops beneath to the old city and beyond that to the sparkling deep blue waters of the Mediterranean. Standing on tippy-toes Nancy could almost imagine that she could see the distant shoreline of Africa!

She loved it all from the first. If it was one thing to be known around Marseille as *la fiancée de Henri Fiocca*, it was quite something else again to be known as *Madame* Fiocca. The French accord a particularly reverential respect to those who have earned the title of 'Madame' and in that town when the name 'Fiocca' was attached to it, signifying her fully-fledged membership of the Marseille Millionaires Club, then that respect and reverence was total.

Lulled, like most of the rest of France, into the ongoing false comfort of the phony war—the belief that the 'war' was really only that in name only—Nancy let herself be carried along with it all. Discovering that she simply adored both caviar and champagne, and that she could now afford to buy them both, she ordered copious amounts. A typical day might see her waking at ten o'clock in the morning to ring for her maid Claire—one of a household staff of five—and have brought to her a breakfast of champagne and caviar, before gently arising to a freshly drawn hot bath. She would then have an hour or so to make herself boooot-iful before Henri arrived home for lunch, and in the afternoon she would

A studio shot of Nancy taken in Marseilles, circa 1936.

Above: Nancy's mother, Ella Wake, on the streets of Sydney, circa 1940.

Above right: Charles Wake, Nancy's father, who abandoned his family when Nancy was five years old.

Right: Nancy, aged four, on the steps of her new home in Australia, at North Sydney.

Above: This was a store in Rotorua, New Zealand, held by Nancy's father's family in the 1880s.

Below: The soldier on the right is Nancy's brother, Stanley Herbert Kitchener Wake, with a friend.

Nancy in London in the late 1930s just before she returned to Henri in Marseille.

Nancy, Henri, and friends just before the war began. Henri is front left, and Nancy is second from the left at the back.

Henri (right) with a friend in the late 1930s.

Henri just after the outbreak of the war.

Nancy during the war, pretending to relieve herself against a tree in the fashion of her dog, Picon, just out of the frame.

Micheline, sixteen years old, safely back in France after Nancy escorted her across the English Channel.

Above: Micheline with her Canadian husband, Thomas Kenny, in the late 1940s.

Below: Nancy and Micheline (seated in front) reunited in Paris in 1985.

Above: Tardivat with his daughter, and
Nancy's god-daughter, also named Nancy.

Below: Nancy and Colonel Maurice
Buckmaster in London, circa 1985.

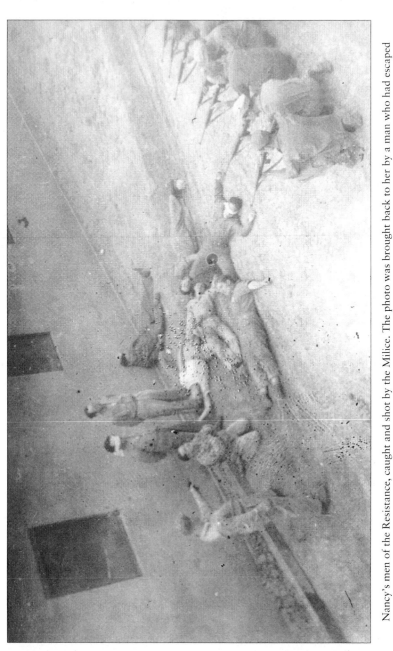

Nancy's men of the Resistance, caught and shot by the Milice. The photo was brought back to her by a man who had escaped and wanted proof of the Milice's atrocities. Nancy says 'the Milice were worse than the Germans'.

perhaps make a visit to the beauty parlour or a café with girlfriends to have a good gossip, before all of them would return home to ready themselves for the return of their husbands in the evening. Nancy and Henri ate out most nights, often taking in a concert or a film afterwards.

All up, though Nancy had the occasional wistful feeling of missing the hardworking days of privation in her tiny flat in Paris, and the wonderful nights with her fellow journalists at their brasserie, it now seemed long gone—as did her life long, long ago back in Australia. She continued to send and receive the odd letter from Sydney, but it was more from duty that she read and wrote them than anything else. *This* was her life now, *this* was what she was actually born for, not all the rest of it.

Her love for Henri continued to grow as well. She never ceased to marvel at his kindness to her, his preparedness to drive along the Riviera coastline in their shiny open-top two-seater Buick for as far as two hundred kilometres to take her to a wonderful restaurant he had heard about; his total refusal to cut corners on expense when it came to her needs being met; his true physical passion for her. She in turn, did everything she could to please him, including making sure that the house was run properly the way he wanted it— everything in its place and a place for everything—and if there was one thing she concentrated sustained effort on, it was her cooking. Through Henri she had met the greatest of all Marseille chefs, Pepe Caillat, and the master had taken her in hand and taught her *la cuisine Provençale* so well that it was her proud claim that when she once cooked at a dinner party for Maurice Chevalier, the great French singer simply couldn't believe that the bouillabaisse *à la Marseillaise* had not been made by someone to France born.

Henri professed himself—and seemed to be—delighted at how well she was fitting in and embracing their common married life together. True, she sometimes had a sense that his overwhelming Frenchness also meant a less than complete commitment to marital fidelity, but she more or less coped ...

'I remember one time visiting a friend in Nice,' Nancy remembers, 'and her saying to me "Nancy why didn't you call me when you were here last week?" I said "What on earth do you mean?" and she showed me a paragraph in the paper saying "Henri Fiocca and Madame Fiocca had checked into a Nice hotel", at a time when I knew he'd been there on a business trip. It was that sort of thing. I thought "you bastard", just like I did when I found photos of his previous girlfriends that he kept in various places—but of course I still loved him and he loved me.'

But of course. Whatever else he was mostly very discreet, she reasoned, and it must have been hard for him after all, to reduce from a diet of so many different women down simply to just one.

'I was not very experienced in the ways of the world,' she says delicately, 'and he was very experienced indeed.'

While Nancy was not the type to exact revenge by taking a lover of her own, there was no way she was going to let him off entirely. She quickly conceived a great passion for the famous French actor Charles Boyer and insisted on carrying his photo in her purse, as well as displaying a photo of him up on her bedroom wall. When Henri on occasion would ask if it might be time to take that photo down, she refused outright. And then there was the lovely satin underwear. Having been advised by her French girlfriends that *everyone* knew, including French men, that you had to have at least one such set to wear for when you were visiting either your lover or your gynaecologist, she bought some and came up with a plan.

'Henri always came home for lunch, would be home at midday to two o'clock, always had a drink first, wine, brandy—then lunch. And during lunch I'd say 'I'm going out with the girls to the cinema this afternoon'. And I'd always have my clothes laid out on the bed, my dress, my coat and my fancy sexy pants. He knew I wasn't going to see my gynaecologist, so *that* really gave him something to think about.'

If it was all a part of 'the games people play', still nothing changed the central fact.

'We loved each other,' Nancy says, 'we had a fabulous time together, we were soul-mates. As to the possibility of children, we didn't plan to have them but we didn't try not to have them ... they just didn't come.'

* * *

Just before Christmas of 1939, Henri received papers advising him that he would soon be required to present himself for service in the French army, just as he had done for a few months in the final stages of the Great War. Yes, Henri was an important businessman in Marseille but the rule remained: millionaire, miner or milliner, it made no difference. If you were called up, that was the end of it. Henri was happy to serve his country, made no protest, and prepared himself to leave.

Not to be outdone, Nancy made Henri promise that when hostilities truly began he would provide her with a truck which she could use as an ambulance to ferry the French wounded. Maybe she could make the experience of her Mudgee nursing days worth something in this life after all.

'Henri,' Nancy says, 'wasn't happy about me wanting to put myself in a position of danger, but I got him at a weak moment, and he did make the promise.'

With Henri granted at least some time to get his affairs in order, the two enjoyed a wonderful Christmas in the Alps with close friends, and late at night as the wine flowed and their spirits soared, it was quite possible to forget they were in a country at war. Of course it couldn't last.

Early in 1940, after the couple had attended a whole series of parties farewelling friends who were going off to fight at the front, Henri himself received some more papers, requiring him to report to receive his allocated uniform in preparation for training camp. He returned that afternoon with stuff which to Nancy's Australian mind looked like nothing so much as 'a dog's breakfast!'.

'Everything he had,' she said, 'was either too big or too small for him. He had a greatcoat that was too big for him. He had trousers that were way too small. Coats that were short in the arms. Some of the stuff, and I swear this is true, had been stockpiled in a French army warehouse since the 1890s! They explained they were short of uniforms and would have to make do until he got into camp, where he could exchange everything with other soldiers until he got his own right size. Well, we laughed so much and made so much noise that the neighbours came in to see why we were laughing. Then they started roaring with laughter too. We had a dinner party where Henri came out in his new uniform and everyone fell about. Fortunately for Henri, he had enough money that he could have his tailor make everything fit, but others were not so fortunate. It did not really bode well for France's state of preparedness for the war ...'

In March, Henri and Nancy finally said their tearful goodbyes. He, to march off to serve along the Maginot Line near Belfort, and she, to prepare to drive the makeshift ambulance—an old rustbucket from Henri's factory—if the Germans invaded.

'And I didn't have long to wait,' Nancy remembers.

She didn't, at that. From April 1940 the powerful German war machine rolled all but unchallenged through Denmark, then Norway, Luxembourg, the Netherlands and Belgium. Nancy, like the rest of France, followed the battle closely, devouring the morning newspapers for such information as there was and listening closely to the radio—hoping against hope for German reverses that never came. The obvious question was on everyone's lips: was France next? Would the Maginot Line really hold, or were they doomed to suffer the same humiliation as the rest of Europe?

In the meantime, Nancy didn't muck around. Having secured the promised truck from Henri's factory, she'd had it converted into a makeshift ambulance and had also given a whole new meaning to the term 'crash driving course' by having several of them as she learnt to drive it in a single day's instruction. In all her travels and experiences, Nancy had never held a driver's licence.

Now ready, she joined a voluntary ambulance corps and drove up near to the Belgian border in the far north of France, where she got to work. Frequently, Nancy would find that her vehicle was the only one heading north to Belgium and the front line, while all the refugee traffic was coming south, loaded to the gills and then some with people and material, nearly always with mattresses strapped on the top in the vain hope that they would offer some protection if they were strafed by the Luftwaffe's Stukas. And all too often again, Nancy would be heading back south with an ambulance full of the wounded and dying, standing as testament that very little indeed stopped those bullets. Her 'nursing' background at the Mudgee mining hospital was some help in trying to help stem the flow of blood, but it was little enough. So, too, the first-aid kit she'd been able to cobble together from materials she'd purchased in Marseille's pharmacies proved entirely inadequate to the task.

'It was a very difficult time for me,' Nancy remembers, 'as it was my first real experience of war, and though I did have some medical background, I'd never seen injuries like these. Often when I was driving along with the wounded and dying I'd be wondering about where Henri was, and hoping and praying he wasn't in the back of a similar ambulance somewhere, equally hurt. I didn't know where he was or what he was doing, but at least I was glad I wasn't just waiting at home for him and not doing anything while the real fighting was going on elsewhere.'

With an amalgam of other ambulances, she was engaged in this work when, on 10 May, 1940, Hitler's forces launched a lightning attack through what had been thought to be the 'impenetrable' Ardennes Forest in France's north. As it turned out, the forest wasn't so impenetrable at all, and the Germans made great headway, for the Maginot Line had not extended that far! What she saw around her in the coming weeks as the Germans continued their relentless forward march did not inspire her confidence in French military might. All around was disorganisation, lack of resources and total confusion. Most appallingly there seemed to be a common acceptance that nothing would stop the Germans.

Even as Nancy continued to ferry load after load of refugees south—often careening to the more natural and Australian left-hand side of the road in her stress—the entire French military structure in the north began to shake and then fall.

'And finally,' Nancy remembers, 'we decided it really was hopeless and that we had to get out while we still could, before the Germans over-ran our positions.' Nancy loaded up her ambulance with as many refugees as she could carry and headed south. Somewhere on one of those trips she heard that in Britain, the great pacifist prime minister and appeaser Neville Chamberlain had been so humiliated by the turn of events that he had resigned in favour of Winston Churchill. Good!

Nancy would later thrill to the famous words of Churchill replayed on the BBC, delivered in his famous 'Blood, sweat and tears' speech to the British Parliament:

'You ask, what is our policy? I say it is to wage war by land, sea and air. War with all our might and with all the strength God has given us, and to wage war against a monstrous tyranny never surpassed in the dark and lamentable catalogue of human crime. *That* is our policy.

'You ask what is our aim? I can answer in one word. It is victory. Victory at all costs—victory in spite of all terrors—victory however long and hard the road may be, for without victory there is no survival.'

Just a fortnight after Churchill delivered that speech, the emphasis fell on the fact that without survival there could be no later victory. Over on the north-western coast of France, in the tiny town of Dunkirk, the British themselves had reached similar conclusions to Nancy and her fellow ambulance drivers that the situation truly was hopeless and, deciding that discretion was the better part of valour, had begun pulling their troops out of France and back to the comparative safety of Britain—to regroup and live to fight another day. In an extraordinary British operation of enormous collective bravery and great ingenuity, no fewer than 364,000 troops were evacuated by a flotilla of British naval vessels together with literally hundreds of tiny civilian boats, while the Wehrmacht and Luftwaffe continued a series of raids to thwart them. British heroism and selflessness on a grand scale saw the complete success of the evacuation.

An editorial in the *New York Times* immediately afterwards reflected the overwhelming joy with which the success of the amazing operation was greeted, and the hope it generated:

> So long as the English tongue survives, the word Dunkirk will be spoken with reverence. For in that harbor, in such a

hell as never blazed on earth before, the rags and blemishes that have hidden the soul of democracy fell away.

There, beaten but unconquered in shining splendour she faced the enemy. They sent away the wounded first; men died that others might escape.

It was not so simple a thing as courage, which the Nazis had in plenty.

It was not so simple a thing as discipline which can be hammered into men by a drill sergeant.

It was not the result of careful planning, for there could have been little.

It was the common man of the free countries rising in all his glory from mill, office, mine, factory and shop and applying to war, the lessons learned when he went down the mine to release trapped comrades; when he hurled the lifeboat through the surf; when he endured hard work and poverty for his children's sake.

This shining thing in the souls of men Hitler cannot attain nor command nor conquer.

He has crushed it where he could from German hearts.

This is the great tradition of democracy.

This is the future.

This is victory.[9]

Yet if Operation Dynamo—for so was it named—was a stunning success that made the Allies' spirits soar, the short-term physical reality was that it denuded France of all but the last of its serious military resistance to Nazi rule. The consequences were inevitable. Nancy was still making her way home and—after walking the last twenty kilometres into Nîmes when her ambulance finally gave up the ghost—was in a tiny hotel in that town, when she heard the news: the Germans had occupied Paris. France had fallen.

'People were stunned, *stunned*,' she remembers. 'They simply couldn't believe that after everything they'd been told about how strong the Maginot Line was, how *Germany* was on the edge of defeat, it was all over so quickly.'

All of France's much vaunted military might—the so-called impregnable defences, the unbeatable army—had been summarily crushed by Hitler's mighty war machine in less than six weeks.

In Europe, Britain now stood alone against the might of Nazi Germany, both the USA and the USSR having declined to become involved at this point. France was, both literally and figuratively, shot to pieces. Nancy returned to a Marseille that in her absence had been bombed by the forces of Benito Mussolini, and found that there had been no word from Henri. She shut herself in her room for three days and cried. Of course, she was not alone in feeling such total devastation and alone-ness. France itself, felt much the same.

To whom could the nation turn in this time of terrible trauma? Who better than France's most famous hero from the Great War, Marshal Henri Philippe Pétain, the one who had led French forces with such distinction in the battle of Verdun. Pétain became the Prime Minister on 17 June 1940, and immediately addressed the nation in a quavering, yet portentous voice.

'I give to *La France*,' the now 84-year-old said, 'the gift of my person to alleviate her misfortunes ... With a heavy heart I tell you today that the fighting must stop.' Essentially, it was a plea for the French to make the best of a bad lot and reconcile themselves to German subjugation.

Nancy was appalled at this seeming subservience to the Nazis, and she wasn't alone. In a Cherbourg restaurant, for example, a group of French army officers had been sitting around a radio waiting for Pétain to speak, to see what he would say. When he had concluded, there was stunned silence. Then, the first to speak was Captain Pierre de Vomecourt.

'I do not accept this shameful surrender,' he said. 'I am going to England. Britain will continue to fight, and I shall go there to help free France!'[10]

De Vomecourt left on a boat bound for England that very night from the port of Cherbourg, while another French officer made the same trip, and for the same reasons from Bordeaux, though he travelled by air. This last was a haughty and classically imperious

Frenchman by the name of Charles de Gaulle, and in the inimitable words of Winston Churchill 'de Gaulle carried with him in that small aeroplane, the honour of France'.[11] De Gaulle had begun the war as a colonel, and just a couple of months before the German army had arrived had been made a Brigadier General. During the German invasion he won further note by leading the only successful counter-action against the German advance.

On his resumé was the fact that he had fought under Pétain at the famous battle of Verdun, and been promoted by Marshal Pétain in 1925 to the staff of the *Conseil Supérieur de la Guerre* (Supreme War Council). But this was where they most definitely parted company.

De Gaulle now flew to Britain and unilaterally formed what would soon become known as the Free French—essentially a French government in exile. At six o'clock on the evening of June 18, de Gaulle went into a BBC studio and broadcast to his fellow French.

'It is quite true that we were, and still are, overwhelmed by enemy mechanized forces both on the ground and in the air'... he said. 'Must we abandon hope? Is our defeat final and irremediable? To those questions I answer—*Non!*

'There still exists in the world everything we need to crush our enemies one day ... Whatever happens, the flame of French resistance must not and shall not be extinguished.'

It was inspiring rhetoric for those precious few who heard it, but even for those who didn't, a certain spontaneous reaction to the German subjugation was just beginning to take place. Henri's return about two weeks later—*hurrah! hurrah!*—was a case in point. He had not had a bad go of it, occupying a part of the Maginot Line that was never really tested by the Germans, but he was as horrified as Nancy with the fall of France, and eager to again see the day when she would be free.

'*La France* will be liberated again,' he told her, 'and we must help it.'

In the meantime, however, the country still had a bit more humiliation to endure. Shortly afterwards, Pétain signed a formal armistice with Germany in the same railway carriage where just over two decades earlier France's Marshal Foch had forced the defeated Germans to agree to punitive terms after their own defeat in 1918. This time the jackboot was on the other neck, as it were.

Under the terms of the armistice, two-thirds of France would be formally occupied and governed by the German Army while the two million French soldiers still under arms would be interned in mass prison camps. All of that would of course be very expensive, but no problem—Pétain agreed that France would make payment to Germany of four hundred million francs *per day* to pay for their own supreme humiliation. The only remotely positive result of the agreement was that while most of German-occupied France would remain under the firm control of the Nazi occupier, the bottom third of the country would remain nominally 'free' to be governed by Pétain's government out of the town of Vichy, some two hundred and fifty kilometres south of Paris. It would be a case of *'le wait and see'* though, as to just how free the Vichy government of the so-called 'Free Zone' would be.

Pétain formally met with Hitler at Montoire-sur-le-Loire in the first days of October, 1940, then reported again his thoughts to the nation.

'It is in a spirit of honour, and to maintain the unity of France,' Petain gravely announced, 'that I enter today upon the path of collaboration.'

Collaboration! Nancy, down in Marseille, could barely believe it.

'For me,' she says, 'there was never the slightest question of collaborating with the Germans. I had seen what they had done in Vienna, in Berlin; I had witnessed their handiwork in the back of my ambulance near Belgium, and I wanted to have nothing to do with anything other than trying to *stop* them.'

Again, she was not alone. Yes, figuratively at least, the lights that Nancy and Micheline had seen on returning to France had now gone out as the darkness of Nazi domination descended—just as they had gone out all over Europe. But even from the beginning of this darkness there remained a few scattered sparkles of *résistance* by the subjugated populations showing that they weren't simply going to submit to the Germans.

To begin with, it was not organised resistance in terms of roving bands of armed men striking at German convoys and the like before melting away, but it was resistance nevertheless. In the famously complicated Paris Metro underground railway, French travellers would make a point of giving false directions to any German enquiries as to how to get to a certain point—it was a point of honour to send them in the diametrically opposite direction. A blind beggar on the Champs Elysées would insist on playing the Marseillaise on his accordion, the better to infuriate passing German soldiers who particularly liked strutting down the famous boulevard.[12] Under cover of darkness all over France, graffiti artists moved up a gear and daubed the famous French symbol, the double-barred cross of Lorraine, in as many public places as they could get away with it. In Amsterdam, the native Dutch would simply up and leave cafés and bars when any German soldiers came in, and any Dutch businesses which were trying to curry business favour with the invaders by putting up signs announcing that they spoke German, soon found themselves ignored by the locals.

In Denmark, in one of the most celebrated acts of resistance of the war, the Danish King, King Christian X, chose a singularly wonderful way to react to the German edict that all Jews had to wear the Star of David on their sleeves, to make them more easily identifiable. The following morning, the King emerged from his palace and showed the way to his people—for he, too, was wearing a Star of David. 'From now on,' he is reputed to have said, 'we are *all* Jews.'

And Nancy, down in Marseille? She was essentially watching and waiting, not quite sure which way to turn. Conscious that she wanted to make a contribution to the fight against the Germans— and so honour the vow she had made back in Vienna in 1934—she was as yet unsure which form her fight would take. But she would be ready, when the first opportunity presented itself ...

Shortly after Pétain had concluded the armistice with the Germans, Henri and Nancy's wide social activities brought them into contact with an extremely charming but tough French army

officer by the name of Commander Busch, who was suitably
disgusted with what Pétain had done. Not only disgusted in fact,
but actively doing something to harm Germany and further France
along the road back to its former independent glory—just as both
his father and grandfather had fought to their last gasp against the
Germans in the last war. He could, he told them, have gone to
Britain to help de Gaulle organise the French fight-back from there,
but had been prevailed upon to stay on the ground in France and
help set up networks of like-minded men and women who would
strike when the time was right. He was part of, he said, something
called the Resistance.

Having ascertained that Henri and Nancy shared similar views
with him, he asked very casually would they mind taking a
'package' with them when they visited Cannes the following
weekend. He did not say what the package contained and they did
not ask. But it was equally clear that this was as important to their
cause as it would be dangerous if they were caught.

'And that's really how my involvement with the French
Resistance began,' says Nancy. 'We took that package with us to
Cannes, it was picked up without problem, and shortly afterwards
he asked me to take another thing somewhere else.'

Before she knew it, Nancy—for Henri was already more than
occupied with rebuilding his business—had become a courier for a
shadowy network of people operating undercover against the
interests of both the Vichy government and, more particularly,
Germany. More often than not, what she had secreted deep within
her handbag, or sewn into a fold of her coat, was part of a radio
transmitter. Though the resistance movement was still small and
scattered, it was forming up into something stronger and the
key tools in making it a genuinely powerful force were radio
transmitters with which those of a like-mind against the Germans
could keep in touch with each other, and even more importantly,
with London, where de Gaulle's Free French were based.

(Aux armes, citoyens! Formez … vos bataillons!) Those initial
sparks of resistance had served their purpose. Others were
encouraged by them—*the spirit of liberty still lives!*—and joined in

in their own fashion. In response, the occupying Germans were left with little choice but to punish those they caught, often with imprisonment, hardening further the subjugated population's resolve to show that they would not be cowed. Inevitably, the tiny little pinpricks of light in the darkness had started to join up, to shine together a little more brightly, and bit by bit, the resistance started to turn into something a lot grander, something wonderful called *la Résistance*. Where all resisters in Europe previously had been merely informal groupings of people against the Nazis, these groupings were starting to form into a loose liaison where they could communicate and work together towards a common goal.

For those now devoting and risking their lives to taking the Germans down, the material support of London was most crucial if their opposition was to be effective. While it was all very well to have a large group of *partisans* united in their hate, without guns, explosives and money they simply could not be an effective fighting force. From London's point of view, one of the key roles of the Resistance would be to thwart German attempts to get reinforcements to wherever it was that they were going to invade, although at this time that kind of thinking was still in its infancy.

From delivering parts of radios for others, it wasn't long before Nancy had a whole radio to herself to use while doing her courier work, a radio straight from the annals of *I Spy*. The receiver was roughly the size of a small saucer and was carefully secreted within the fabric of her handbag. From there, wires ran out of the bag, up her sleeves, along her back through her hair to two earpieces nestled all-but-invisibly in her ears. Thus, as she was sitting quietly on a train bound for Cannes, or perhaps taking coffee in a Nice café as she waited for a contact to turn up, Nancy could be listening to the BBC and following just what was happening with the war effort. The need for secrecy in such matters was paramount, for while Nancy and Henri were nominally in 'unoccupied France', ruled by their own Vichy government led by Marshall Pétain, there were clear laws passed by this government which forbade doing anything which would damage the German war effort, and those laws were enforced by Vichy gendarmes and other government officials constantly checking on the movement and actions of the Vichy population.

For those caught seriously *disobeying*, sometimes a quick death was the best they could hope for. Often, slow torture and subsequent 'disappearance' was their lot, with the Vichy forces not even bothering with some of the niceties of their now sham judicial system.

'One of our neighbours,' Nancy recalls, 'who was caught with an illegal cache of weapons in his basement was taken away, and no-one ever saw him again—though it was obvious enough to us all what had happened to him. The bastards shot him.'

Such arrests and subsequent disappearances, though initially quite rare in the more benign days of the early part of the war, became more frequent as the months passed. None of this panicked Nancy—she simply wasn't the panicking kind—but it did encourage her and Henri to take all sensible precautions. For example, when Nancy and Henri listened to BBC broadcasts at home in the evening, they had to be very careful indeed, given that a Vichy Commissaire was on the other side of their apartment wall.

'We got around it,' Nancy says, 'by turning the radio next to his wall on to a popular music station and turning it up loud, while we were on the other side of the apartment very quietly listening to the BBC French service. We'd always listen to the news then turn it to another station so that if we were raided in the middle of the night we could still deny everything. We had to be very careful.'

Her favourite in such sessions was clear.

'When I was in occupied France as a British agent during the war, it meant a firing squad to be caught listening to London,' she later noted to a Sydney newspaper. 'But I always tuned in to Winston Churchill, and his speeches were an inspiration.'[13]

Through these evening transmissions they were able to follow the progress of the war better than ever before. Clear, unfettered news at last came their way, rather than news that had come to them at the end of a long line of Chinese Whispers, or with the approval of the Vichy government as properly sanitised for public consumption. *'Ici Londres,'* the voice would come through every night, and proceed to tell them the day's events.

In the meantime, through everything and despite it all, Nancy continued to enjoy her married life with Henri enormously, and the fact that she had at least had the foresight before the war to fill their cellars and pantries to overflowing with food and wine. This meant that they often had visitors over for dinner—frequently neighbours and acquaintances who had not displayed similar foresight, and thus were starting to go hungry as the severe wartime rations came into effect—and before she knew it, their own dining room table was quite the regular social centre for their large group of friends. Inevitably these gatherings were made up of people who, like them, were outraged at the Vichy government's collaboration with the Nazis. But such views were not necessarily in the clear majority!

'From the moment that France fell,' Nancy remembers, 'everything changed with neighbours spying on neighbours, and everyone very careful what they said around whom until they knew for sure and certain which side you were on. I mean, put yourself in that kind of situation, with a foreign power having taken over your country. *Who can you trust?'*

In short, while it was very much a case of 'us' versus 'them', there was a very real problem in determining just who 'us' was. While all but insoluble in the early days of the war, over the months the answer gradually appeared as a shadowy network of the relentlessly anti-German emerged and carefully connected up with each other. This was not the aforementioned Resistance that was growing across France, but a much more modest version of it that appeared in local communities. It was not a formal body, simply a group of people with fellow-feeling who wanted to do what they could against the invaders.

A good starting point in determining where someone's loyalties lay, Nancy found, was to find out whether their father or grandfather had fought against the Germans in the last war—or better still, whether they had personally. If so, they could usually be counted on to be implacably anti-German in this one.

'My butcher's father for example,' Nancy says, 'had been in the First World War and his grandfather in the one before that. He knew I was Australian, although French by marriage, and knew he could trust me and I could trust him. The butcher would get me meat, he would charge me what he had to pay for it, not black-market [rates]. And it was the same thing with other people that over time you knew you could trust. They knew what I was doing, and they helped me and tipped me off, anytime anything got a bit suspicious. The man running the newspaper kiosk for example one day warned me to stop buying the Swiss newspapers I had been— the best ones to get information from, instead of the censored French press—because there had been enquiries from the authorities wanting to know the addresses of everybody who buys the Swiss papers. They'd thought that was the best way to find out just who were sympathisers to the Allied cause, so he tipped me off.'

Careful, though. Such people wanting to help her in her work and protect her were not universal.

'The Germans,' she says, 'were very clever putting Pétain in power, because he had a terrific backing among the French, who loved him. He was the saviour of France in the First World War, and his presence at the head of the government in the Second World War gave the people a reason to kid themselves it was okay to fall in with the Nazis now, that it would really be for the good of France.'

Helping to confuse the issue for the French of just who were the good guys and who were the bad guys in the whole affair was the Mers-el-Kebir affair which occurred in the Algerian port of that name on 3 July, 1940. A key part of the Vichy settlement that Marshal Pétain and Hitler had forged in their armistice was that the French navy would remain entirely neutral, and would not be put in the service of the Axis powers. Churchill, however, simply refused to take Hitler and Mussolini's word for it. With that in mind, the British Prime Minister instructed Vice-Admiral Sir James Somerville and his Royal Navy 'Force H' to go into Mers-el-Kebir port and either secure the French naval squadron for the Allies, or sink it outright.

The French Admiral Gensoul refused to hand his ships over to the British, and Somerville proceeded to follow his original instructions. Just before five o'clock that afternoon, the British ships opened fire and immediately the French battleship *Bretange* was sent to the bottom, with 977 lives lost. Shortly afterward, the *Dunkerque* took some direct hits and another two hundred French lives were extinguished by force of British fire. Other French ships were severely hit, with just one French battleship, *Strasbourg*, making it free to the open sea. It was eventually able to limp into Toulon.

When she first heard reports from outraged French friends of what had happened, Nancy simply refused to believe them. *Refused!* 'British forces firing on innocent French and killing them?' she remembers as her response. 'I knew it couldn't be true. Britain was France's best friend, and Britain *simply didn't do things like that.*'

Soon, though, there could be no denying it as many horribly wounded French sailors were delivered into the hospitals of Marseille, and Nancy could see with her own eyes, and hear with her own ears, what had been done. At the time it appalled her, and outraged many of her French friends, while the German propaganda machine went into overdrive.

Ultimately, in terms of winning French hearts and minds for the Allies, the episode was a complete disaster, but as Churchill would always maintain, it simply had to be done. Nancy and Henri—with some time in which to calm down—could finally understand this, as could their friends.

'But it was hard,' she says. 'We had to come to understand that in wartime, everything was different, everything was new. What had been the wrong thing was now the right thing, and the right thing the wrong thing. As terribly tragic as it was, the key factor, we realised, was that the French fleet would not be placed at the service of Hitler and Mussolini.'

And so it went. No-one who expressed any views sympathetic to Pétain lasted long at Henri's and Nancy's dinner table, and their apartment continued to be a magnet for those who thought like them.

It was through such gatherings that Nancy's young friend, Micheline—by then a very fetching nineteen going on twenty, and a constant visitor to their house from her parents' base in Cannes—met and shortly afterwards married a young Canadian by the name of Thomas Kenny who had been holidaying in the south of France, when the world had been turned upside down and he had been stranded.

'Micheline's mother was very angry that she had met this Canadian at my house only to fall in love at such a young age,' Nancy recalls, 'and she blamed me terribly, but there was nothing I could do. It was one of those things that from the first moment they clapped eyes on each other they just didn't want to be with anyone else. Besides which, Micheline was no longer the young girl she'd been when I met her and even [when I'd] brought her back to France; she was a fully grown woman old enough to make up her own mind.'

For her part, Micheline would never have any regrets, and as a grown woman in her own relationship by then, is able to give some perspective to Henri and Nancy's own marriage.

'They were very, very good together,' she says, 'and always liked to be physically close to each other. Henri was a gentleman, Nancy was an exuberant lady and they were always a lot of fun to be around. Everyone liked to be dining at their table.'

Sometimes, it seemed, there were too many, for as time went on and rationing became severe it became progressively more difficult to maintain this fine table—particularly in regard to providing fresh meat, the friendly butcher notwithstanding—and Nancy had no choice but to go to the black market. On one occasion she bought a pig, and assumed it would be delivered in tidy chunks of meat, but ... not a bit of it.

Nancy returned home the following day to find it tethered to her table in the kitchen! Beside it—and more to the point beside herself—Claire the maid was in tears. What to do? Nancy tried ringing the friendly butcher to see if he could come on over with a suitably murderous cleaver, only to find he was otherwise engaged. It looked like she would have to do the deed herself, and urgently at that, because the incessant squeals of the pig surely would soon alert the Vichy Commissaire next door that something was amiss. It was, after all, going to be very hard indeed to explain where she got that pig from, if not from the highly illegal black market.

Taking advice from another friend, she quickly came up with the right plan. That was to hit the pig on the head with an almighty hammer and then slit its throat. (Brilliant! Now why didn't she think of that?) As Nancy has already written:

'Claire hit the pig on the head, but not hard enough. I slit its throat, but not deep enough. The pig careered around the kitchen screaming. What pig wouldn't? We were covered in blood. There was blood on the floor, the walls and even the ceiling. Finally, I picked up the hammer, gave the pig a mighty wallop and knocked it out ... [Shortly afterwards, Henri arrived home,] and opened the kitchen door. His face was a picture as he looked at the mess. Then he looked at me and said with mock sadness, "Nannie, how is it that with all the women I could have married I chose you?"'[14]

On nights when the Fioccas were not at home, Nancy would often meet Henri down at Marseille's mighty Hôtel du Louvre et Paix, where they were on first-name terms with many of the staff. As perhaps the town's finest establishment, though, it regrettably also attracted the custom of the newest power in town, the German officers. Like an infernal rising damp, there had been more and more of them showing up in Marseille since the day that Paris fell, and though they were at least sensitive enough not to goose-step around in their uniforms—as they were nominally in 'free and unoccupied' territory—there was usually no mistaking it when you saw or heard them. Neither Nancy nor Henri could bear to be around them, Henri least of all because Nancy—particularly in the earlier days of the war—would *insist* on singing 'Rule Britannia' at the top of her voice.

So they gravitated to a back bar where they could be among their own kind and gossip with, among others, Antoine the Corsican barman who hated the Germans more than people who didn't tip—not that those two groups were mutually exclusive. One night when entering this back bar off the *Cour Belsunce* to wait for Henri,

Nancy noticed that her usual seat was taken by, of all things, a tall, blond bloke reading an English book! It was one thing, of course, for her to sing British songs now and again—as a woman she had a fair chance of getting away with it—but a military-age male publicly identifying himself with things English was a rarity at this time. But, *of course*. He was obviously a German, setting up a trap, Nancy felt sure as she took her seat well away and started quietly observing him. Clearly, he was waiting to see if someone—perhaps an Allied airman on the run—might see him reading the book and so identify himself as English also, at which point he would be taken into custody.

Antoine promised to investigate, offering him a drink on the house in the hope that he would be drawn into conversation, but he simply accepted it quietly and kept on reading—not even looking up as Henri came in. Subtlety in such matters was not Henri's strong point, and when apprised by Nancy of the situation he simply went over and asked the bloke, up-front, who he was and why he happened to be publicly reading an English book in a country that had just been invaded by the Germans? 'He is an Englander from Newcastle-on-Tyne,' Henri shortly reported back to Nancy and Antoine, 'and says he is an officer in the British army who is interned up at Fort Saint-Jean.'

Oh. Fort Saint-Jean was a curious place indeed. Part of the armistice agreement struck between Hitler and Pétain had required France to intern for the duration all Allied soldiers, sailors and airmen then on French soil, and this had been done. Places like Fort Saint-Jean were the result. A historic fort built at the entrance to Marseille harbour, it was now filled with British officers who had given their word as officers and gentlemen that they would not try to escape, and who were therefore free to leave the bounds of the fort during the day and early evening, so long as they returned to sleep. (It was the kind of benign and lenient culture that would be unthinkable in the latter days of the war.) Well, that sort of did make sense then. Nancy invited him over to their table and had Antoine working overtime keeping up a constant supply of drinks as she plied the fellow with questions. How many officers were there in the fort? (About two hundred.) Were their basic needs met? (Not quite.) What could she do to help them? (How long have you got ... ?) All up, they got on famously well and before the evening had drawn to a close, Nancy had solemnly promised that the full resources of Henri's wallet were open to them. She meant it! She would get them cigarettes by the bundle, food by the wheelbarrow, and very discreetly and most crucially ... a radio with which they could surreptitiously follow the war via the BBC.

It seemed like a good idea at the time. In the sober light of day, though, the couple wondered whether it really had been a trap after all and whether they had just positively identified themselves as two Marseille residents who were more than willing to bat for the British against the Germans. After all, what did they really know about this fellow other than what was learned in a few hours spent in his company where they all drank too much? Had they *really* promised, not only all that stuff, but also a meeting with him and his compatriots that very morning at a café in the Vieux Port where they would deliver it? They had. Whatever their fears of being betrayed, however, it was unthinkable that they should renege on their promise if the bloke was genuine, so they decided on a compromise. They would assemble the food, cigarettes and radio, but not actually take it all with them to the designated café. It would be much wiser, they decided, to get another good look at him now that they were awakened to the possibility of betrayal, and *then* decide how to proceed.

And sure enough. Nancy took one look at the fellow with his friends gathered outside the café at the appointed time and burst into peals of laughter. Everything was going to be all right after all. One of them had the sort of ludicrously large and bristling ginger moustache that only a Brit would ever dare to wear! There was no way known on heaven or earth that the owner of such a moustache could ever be a double agent and Nancy was shortly proved a hundred per cent right. Their companion from the night before introduced them all, and not only did they quickly pick up from where they had been left the night before, but the British also picked up the ciggies, food and radio.

It was the beginning of a very close relationship between Nancy, particularly, and the interned British at Fort Saint-Jean. So much so that even apart from her ongoing efforts acting as a courier for the French Resistance, she now also became progressively more involved with the British network of resistance that was forming in France. She and Henri opened their doors, their cellar and their pantry to a revolving raft of different British prisoners each evening. Henri as always opened his wallet and Nancy continued to procure whatever black market items they needed through her own contacts, including the things they sometimes needed to keep their clandestine radio going. It was an expensive business indeed for Henri to finance such things and yet he never quibbled.

'Never once,' Nancy recalls. 'He loved England, he admired the British, he'd done business with them and he respected their methods and their integrity, so he was very generous. He sometimes would say wistfully that he wished he could find me alone more often, as there always seemed to be men in the house, but that was the end of it.' Not the least of his generosity was the stipend in French francs—the rough equivalent of twenty-five pounds a day which he gave to Nancy—the vast majority of which he knew she spent on her undercover work.

The two were fully conscious of the risk they were taking by Nancy getting involved in this kind of work, but they joked about it. On one occasion around this time when Henri was suffering from a dreadful case of the flu—or *la grippe australienne*, as the French quite seriously called it—he was sitting uncommunicative in the corner near the fire, as Nancy playfully tried to cheer him up. 'Oh go on,' Nancy laughed, 'you'll talk all right when the Gestapo finally catches up with us.'[15]

'Yes, I suppose I will,' Henri replied thoughtfully.

CHAPTER SEVEN

Working Undercover

'We'll beat the bastards over the heads with
broomsticks if we have to.'

WINSTON CHURCHILL
His reported comment, immediately after he sat down in Parliament
to thunderous applause after making his famous
'We will fight them on the beaches' speech.

All precious things, discover'd late,

To those that seek them issue forth,

For Love in sequel works with Fate,

And draws the veil from hidden worth.

ALFRED, LORD TENNYSON
'The Day-dream', quoted on the opening page of *Anne of the Island*,
by Lucy Maud Montgomery.

Throughout 1940 and into 1941 Nancy continued her courier work for Commander Busch—though he had now taken on the *nom de guerre* of 'Xavier', and insisted he be addressed only in this fashion—and added yet one more string to her Resistance bow.

'Two of Xavier's comrades in the Resistance movement were in danger of being exposed and arrested,' she remembers, 'and he asked if we could help hide them. We said "of course", and spirited them away to the home of a doctor friend of ours living in the mountains, and then shortly afterwards they went to stay in the chalet near Nevache that Henri had given me as a wedding present.'

In short, in the space of only six months, Nancy had gone from being a lady of leisure to an ambulance driver, then to a significant operator for both the French and British anti-Nazi movements in France. That this occasioned significant danger for her went without saying—she could have been arrested and, at best, imprisoned at any moment—but she did what she could to keep up the front of Madame Fiocca, social butterfly. She continued to have conspicuous frivolous lunches in town with girlfriends, to attend functions at night, and promenade with Picon along the Canebière, dressed in her finery as if she had not a care in the world.

By this time, she had forged identity papers and a cover story for her undercover work, identifying her as 'Mademoiselle Lucienne Carlier', a secretary to a doctor. These false identity papers were essential, given that her old *carte d'identité* identified her as a British subject—which immediately aroused suspicion at every checkpoint—and it also meant that if ever she were arrested and were able to stand up to their interrogations, Henri had a fair chance of not being drawn into it all. She could simply refuse to divulge anything, she thought confidently to herself, and take whatever was coming to her. She might have ratted on Jenny, her friend back in fourth class at Neutral Bay Intermediate, but she knew she wouldn't do that to anyone else, whatever they did to her, least of all her beloved husband.

Always, but always, Nancy had to be vigilant on her undercover journeys, for there were constant roving patrols asking to see people's papers, just as there were checkpoint controls every time she crossed the border between Vichy-France and the German-occupied territories.

On one occasion, a particularly pedantic official was examining her papers and asking quite prying questions, including the extremely dangerous one of just how it was that a humble doctor's secretary on such a very low wage, as she undoubtedly was, nevertheless, to judge from the cut of her dress and her recent travelling record, seemed to travel far and wide in the very best of style? Hmmmmm, Mademoiselle, *hmmmmm?* Good question. *Extremely* good question. But having thought her way through exactly that possible question previously, and going over her options, Nancy felt she had the answer. Blushing demurely, she told the official that he had to understand that as secretaries went, she was a very *private* kind of secretary ... if *Monsieur le Gendarme* could, ahem, understand that. Monsieur the Gendarme could, as a matter of fact, seeming to appraise her appreciatively from a now entirely different perspective before waving her on her way with a laugh. Never let it be said that *he* would be the one getting in the way of another Frenchman's pleasures.

And there, in its essence, was one of the great advantages that Nancy enjoyed in all her wartime activities. Able-bodied men were always suspicious because they of course looked like 'the enemy' and might very well be just that, but for the particularly macho German men, attractive women didn't look like the enemy at all.

'I played the part of a giddy Frenchwoman who didn't give a bugger what happened in the war,' Nancy says frankly. 'I was a *good-time girl*. I used to give Germans a date sometimes, sometimes three or four times if I was away on a long trip and give them a little bit of hope. I played the part—I should have been an actress.'

The other advantage she had, and Nancy never quite understood how it worked, was that even in extreme situations when one wrong answer would likely land her in gaol or worse, she never faltered through fear.

'I really don't know why,' she says, 'but it never really gripped me like that. I always felt that one way or another, I would be all right.'

Alas, whatever her efforts in helping the Allied war effort at the time, she had to say it wasn't *obviously* showing up in terms of the way the war was running, at least in that first year. Frankly, the war was going very badly as Hitler's forces continued to dominate on all fronts, and she and Henri listened in despair to the BBC broadcasts every night.

Against this was one, and only one, bit of good news. It was the long-running action known as the Battle of Britain. In this sustained action, lasting from July to November of 1940, Hermann Göring's Luftwaffe went up against the Royal Air Force over the skies of Britain and the English Channel. The Luftwaffe's initial targets, in an effort to soften up Britain for a planned German amphibious invasion, were British shipping—as they hoped to destroy all of the island's naval defences. In August, the attacks substantially switched to airfields, particularly against planes on the ground and radar facilities. From September onwards the Luftwaffe focused on direct bombing of London and other cities, hoping to destroy British morale. In the famous 'Blitz', London was bombed on fifty-seven nights in succession, but through it all—and despite the fact that the RAF was outnumbered in planes and pilots by four to one—Churchill's nation was able to withstand and successfully beat off the attacks visiting terrible losses on the German planes.

Not for nothing would the British Prime Minister say in his famous stentorian tones: 'The gratitude of every home in our island, in our Empire, and indeed throughout the world except in the abodes of the guilty goes out to the British airmen who, undaunted by odds, unweakened by their constant challenge and mortal danger, are turning the tide of world war by their prowess and their devotion.

'Never in the field of human conflict was so much owed by so many to so few. All hearts go out to the fighter pilots, whose brilliant actions we see with our own eyes day after day . . .'

He was speaking Nancy's kind of language!

'That gave us the first ray of hope,' Nancy says flatly. 'When those young pilots in their Spitfires repulsed a superior Luftwaffe, I was in France listening, and I thought they were magnificent. Britain was wonderful during the war. The King and Queen were admirable. They didn't leave the country—if anything happened they went the next day and saw the people. Good gracious me, I would have died for them. I don't know why it is, but I'm like that.'

Nancy particularly loved, from the moment she heard it, the Queen of England's famous reason for why the Royal Family did not depart for the safety of Canada during the Blitz: 'The children will not leave unless I leave, I will not leave unless the King leaves, and the King will not leave.'

'That,' Nancy says, 'was the Royal Family all over.'

In April of 1941, she and Henri despaired at the news that Yugoslavia and Greece were both being invaded by the Germans— was there no end to their voraciousness?—but thrilled to the news, in May, that the pride of the German navy, the *Bismarck*, had been hunted down and sunk.

'That night,' Nancy remembers, 'we all got very drunk indeed as we celebrated.'

There was plenty of bad news to follow, however, for all of loyal France was stunned when on 22 June, 1941, the BBC announcer gravely informed them that Germany had not only invaded the Soviet Union but appeared to be advancing without trouble ...

'We were staggered by this news,' recalls Nancy. 'Just how many of these buggers were there, that they could invade all these countries at once!? But, strangely enough, a lot of the French took heart from it. Many referred back to the time when Napoleon had also invaded Russia and been brought low by it. A lot of people thought the same must happen to Germany, that they were now stretching themselves impossibly thinly.'

Further stacking the odds against an ultimate Nazi victory was when, on 'a day that will live in infamy',[16] 7 December, 1941, the Japanese airforce bombed ships of the American navy in Pearl Harbor, Hawaii. America promptly declared war on Japan, and Germany replied by declaring war on America. Over to President Roosevelt, who four days later sent this message to the American Congress:

'On the morning of December 11, the government of Germany, pursuing its course of world conquest, declared war against the United States. The long-known and the long-expected has thus taken place. The forces endeavoring to enslave the entire world now are moving toward this hemisphere. Never before has there been a greater challenge to life, liberty and civilization. Delay invites great danger. Rapid and united effort by all of the peoples of the world who are determined to remain free will insure a world victory of the forces of justice and of righteousness over the forces of savagery and of barbarism. Italy also has declared war against the United States.

'I therefore request the Congress to recognize a state of war between the United States and Germany, and between the United States and Italy.'

'It was easily the best thing that happened that year,' Nancy says. 'At last Britain was not on its own any more and Henri and I felt that now it might be more like a fair fight!'

Meanwhile, they continued their lives, she with her undercover work, he with rebuilding his business. One night, a new man appeared at their dinner table, a Scottish officer by the name of Ian Garrow who had been interned at Fort Saint-Jean for quite 'long enough', to quote his opening remark to Nancy at the time. From the beginning, Nancy liked Garrow very much.

'He was very impressive, tall, well-built like an athlete, good-looking and [a] charming gentleman,' she remembers. 'And he wasn't married in those days.'

Garrow, as he explained to Nancy and Henri, was even then in the process of setting up an escape network of 'safe houses' in a series of converging lines across France, all leading to the Pyrenees—not just for the men at Fort Saint-Jean, but more particularly for the many Allied servicemen who had been left behind at Dunkirk. In this way, the nascent networks that were forming all across the country could assist all those needing to escape the Germans and the Vichy police, passing them along the line to the base of the Pyrenees near Perpignan, where guides could take them across the mountains to nominally neutral Spain and get them to Britain from there.[17]

Nancy—as Garrow had of course hoped—offered her own services and that of Henri's, particularly his factory on the outskirts of Marseille where large numbers of escapees could bed down for the night before moving on to their next destination. The structure of this network, as Nancy soon learnt, was essentially like a series of communist cells. Everyone along the line knew and trusted totally the people on either side of them—those from whom they took the refugees and those to whom the refugees were subsequently taken—but for the sake of absolutely security one must never inquire beyond those people.

'That way,' Nancy points out, 'if ever you were captured and tortured and you were broken, the damage would be limited. Only a very few knew who was who along the entire network, while the rest of us were kept in the dark as much as possible. It was the only way to do it.'

Not surprisingly, some of the first people to move along this network were the same British officers who had been interned at Fort Saint-Jean. Gentlemen to the end, they had formally renounced their vow not to try to escape to the French authorities—*they gave them fair warning, what?*—and shortly afterwards disappeared along the 'Garrow Line' as it had become known. In early 1941, Garrow himself disappeared from the fort, but instead of passing along his own line, he stayed in Marseille to oversee operations. He remained in constant touch with Nancy and they kept moving people along the line.

'Every soldier we got home was another thorn in Hitler's side, of course, and we were happy for that, but I think the main thing remained to get them *home*.'

Some of these refugees, of course, were not Allied men getting back to homes they'd left long before, so much as continental Europeans leaving homes that had just been shattered. There was no better example of these than the growing numbers of Jewish people who were passing along the network. The stream of Jewish refugees that Nancy had first seen straggling through Paris in the mid–thirties had now become a full-blown flood—now that Hitler's infamous 'Final Solution' of murdering all Jewish people was fully under way—with the key difference that France was now no longer an automatic refuge for them as it had been then.

In October of 1940, the Vichy government had decreed that all foreign-born Jews in their part of France were illegals, and were to be rounded up and put into concentration camps forthwith. Just under eight thousand of them promptly were.

To the north, in the German-occupied zone, things were every bit as bad, with the Germans demanding that all foreign-born Jews attend a Parisian sports stadium at a given time. Once there, they were arrested and put in a concentration camp. In a horrifyingly short space of time, no fewer than thirty thousand Jews were in French concentration camps.[18] The Nazi hunt for foreign Jews in France was soon widened to include French-born Jews as well, meaning that while some of the Jews to pass through Nancy's safe hands were from places as far afield as Poland and Czechoslovakia, the majority were French. Typically, Nancy would gather them in from some safe house, perhaps at Nice or Cannes, and take them with her on the train to Marseille. There, she would either secrete them at a nearby apartment which she rented for the purpose or, if that was full, into a discreet corner of Henri's factory.

'Mostly, I didn't talk too much to any of the refugees,' Nancy says, 'because that was the best security policy. The less I knew about them, and the less they knew about me, the better it was for all of us, should any of us be caught by the Gestapo, but sometimes ... you couldn't help but be drawn in.'

Sticking particularly in her memory are these Jewish families, fleeing a stable and often affluent existence, and never knowing whether they would ever see sunset, but sticking together through it all.

'It was the children who made the biggest impression on you,' says Nancy, 'and I would always try to get biscuits on the black market just for them. Their parents would often have this haunted look about them, as if they were constantly replaying what had happened in previous months, and recalling all those around them who hadn't made it, but had instead been rounded up. But sometimes the children's eyes would shine like this was all one big adventure. When that happened, the contrast was always extraordinary. Many of the parents just kept holding their children tightly, as if they were always afraid someone was going to tear them away ... which at that time wasn't so crazy.'

Sometimes too, among the many Allied servicemen passing through, Australians and New Zealanders would turn up, and if the occasion presented itself they could talk of common things in their past. The servicemen spoke of how much they missed things such as the surfing at Bondi or the shearing at Cootamundra, and Nancy would add her own reminiscences of surfing and promenading at Balmoral. She didn't miss such things herself, *per se*, but it helped ease the tension to talk about it.

When Nancy received word that the coast was clear—either through a carefully coded phone call or from a trusted member of the network, or finally from a stranger with the right password—it would be time to move again. She would gather her small knot of refugees to her, (sometimes as many as seven) and they would all board the train separately but would stay close enough to keep each other roughly in view. At their destination they would then travel to the foot of the Pyrenees, most often to the town of Perpignan.

This charming town—lined with palm trees along many of its boulevards and situated just thirty kilometres north of the Spanish frontier and ten kilometres west of the Mediterranean—was always a good launching point, but not only because of its geographical location. More to the point, it was full of Resistance people who, true to the town's proud Catalan history, refused to bow to invaders whatever their superior strength might be. As a journalist visiting Perpignan, Nancy had once wandered around *Place des Esplanades* atop the the hill which dominates the historic part of the town, and looked over the mighty *Palais des Rois de Majorque*. This thirteenth-century castle, she had reflected, had famously rebuffed many, *many* invasions through the ages, and it was as good a reminder as any that resistance was simply in the blood of the locals. Once Nancy had guided her escapees into Perpignan, they would often rest for a night in a safe house, before she walked with them into the foothills to the south until, at a designated dark spot, she handed them over to what they called 'passers', the guides who would take them over the other side of the mountains into Spain.

Not surprisingly, it was only a fairly short time before Fort Saint-Jean was effectively shut down and all those who had not already scarpered were transferred to the far more secure Saint-Hippolyte-du-Fort, well to the north-west of Marseille. This in no way diminished the use of the 'safe-houses' network, because it served far more escapees than simply British servicemen escaping from the local prison. As the use of the line increased, Garrow inevitably brought more help in to organise it and this is when, early in 1941, Nancy met a Belgian doctor with the unlikely name of Patrick O'Leary. (In fact his real name was Dr Albert-Marie Guerisse, but throughout the war he stuck to his *nom de guerre* of O'Leary.)

When Belgium had fallen to the Germans, O'Leary had refused to stop fighting and soon made his way onto a ship in the British navy, HMS *Fidelity*, which in turn came to a bad end when intercepted by a French navy cutter who handed the crew over to the German authorities. After a circuitous route he had been interned at Saint-Hippolyte-du-Fort, but Garrow had organised his escape and then recruited him to stay in France to help with his network. Nancy kind of liked O'Leary but never quite hit it off with him the way she had with Garrow.

'He was not a bad looking bloke,' she says, 'but very conceited and self opinionated, not at all like Garrow, though they both always had an air of authority about them. He was tall, with thinning blonde hair and about thirty years old, I suppose.'

Whatever else he was, O'Leary proved to be an extremely good organiser, and he had not been long on the scene when Garrow ceded much of the organisation to him. O'Leary had, after all, quickly proved himself by masterminding the tunnelling escape of thirty-seven Allied airmen from another military prison near Nice, in an action that also involved Nancy.

'I didn't have anything to do with the tunnelling,' Nancy says, 'as that was all organised by O'Leary with the prisoners, who scattered the dirt around their exercise yard through holes in the bottom of their pockets, but I was there when they came out, so that I could ferry them to their next destination.'

One of the particularities of this O'Leary-designed escape was that it would be one of the first times that escapees would be spirited away in a British submarine launched from Gibraltar. The sub would surface just off the tiny Mediterranean beach of Canet-Plage, thus meaning the escapees would not have to face the risky trek over the Pyrenees. All well and good, but because of the sub's very severe space limitations there were meant to be only thirty-seven escapees coming through the tunnel. Come the time, however, as so often happened in wartime, things didn't go according to plan.

'There came the big day,' Nancy once recounted to the Australian magazine *Woman's Day*, 'when the airmen began emerging from the tunnel in a small but dense wood five hundred yards from the fort. Whisking each one away with a guide, we heaved a sigh of relief as the thirty-seventh man appeared and was fading away from the spot when I almost passed out. Another man was appearing from the tunnel, and another, and yet another. There was commotion inside the fort and we scattered .... Now to get the charges to the submarine.

'Oh, Patrick O'Leary, the nonchalance again with which you told me the beach selected for the submarine was a flat open one covered with anti-invasion fortifications and heavily guarded by the Germans.'[19]

It worked nevertheless, after a fashion, and they did indeed get thirty-seven of them away on the sub—not that the method was used for long, as it was finally judged too risky to send submarines in that close to occupied land. The excess escapees on this occasion were secreted in safe houses, and later made their way over the mountains successfully into Spain.

Henri—who by this time, despite the war, had managed to get his business back on its feet—continued to be a great bank-roller for many of O'Leary's and Nancy's activities, but other methods of financing also had to be organised. One method was to send one of their operatives over the border to the British embassy in Switzerland, where he would be provided with toothpaste tubes within which were secreted tightly packed wads of banknotes. Never *near* bloody enough, it seemed to Nancy and O'Leary, when they opened them back in Marseille, but it was a help. Another way was to tap on sympathetic French business people for a loan, with the assurance that the British government would repay them once the war was over. To prove their bona-fides, Nancy and

O'Leary would ask the potential donor to come up with a phrase, any phrase—say, 'the rain in Spain is going down the drain'—and then tell them to listen to the BBC news service the following night, where at the end of the news bulletin that message would be repeated in the 'Personal Messages' section. In the meantime, Nancy and O'Leary would pass the message to London and, sure enough, the following evening the often amazingly impressed businessman would hear the phrase and suddenly have confidence that what he was handing over really would be only a loan.

This local French charity consolidated increasing British funds. Newly financed by this largesse, Nancy's activities progressed apace. An endless stream of refugees continued to come along her line; she still acted as a courier all along the Riviera and inland whenever important packages had to be delivered, thus helping to set up 'Xavier's' network which, as he explained, would leap into action once General de Gaulle gave the command; and she funnelled refugees along their way for Garrow and O'Leary. Sometimes Nancy could link the two roles, by dropping a package to a pharmacist in Antibes and then going on to a safe house in Cannes and bringing some refugees back with her to Marseille. It was all extremely dangerous work, but it wasn't necessarily the danger that bothered her.

'It was the boredom of it all,' she says frankly and startlingly. 'For all the supposed glamour of resistance work, the reality was a lot of it was deadly dull.'

In short, just as the job of medical anaesthetists was once described as ninety-nine per cent sheer boredom mixed with one per cent overpowering terror, so too with a lot of Nancy's tasks. It was work that had to be done, and she was proud to play her part in the war effort, but it didn't necessarily thrill her soul. One morning after returning from shopping, Nancy's maid Claire informed her that she had visitors, and that one of them had already made himself at home more than somewhat. She entered her living room to find Captain Garrow, as punctiliously proper as ever, but with him was another Britisher who made her skin crawl as soon as she laid eyes on him. It was not merely that he had settled down on the very chair where her beloved Picon always slept when she was out, nor even that he had helped himself to her whiskey without asking, nor *even* that he did not immediately leap to his feet as soon as she entered the room, as had Garrow ...

'There was just something about him,' she recalls, 'something sinister and shifty, that I did not want in my house.'

And no-one, read *no-one*, was allowed to remain in her house when she didn't want them to be there. She'd house six hundred of them if they were escapees on their way to Britain, and be polite about it along the way, but of all the things she simply *would not stand for*, impoliteness was near the top of the list.

'*Out!*' she said to the stranger, even before Garrow had properly finished introducing him, 'Get out of my house!'

Nonplussed, and overwhelmed by her outrage, the stranger—who she subsequently learnt was Paul Cole—left, with a distinctly underwhelmed Garrow trailing behind. As he would tell Nancy shortly afterwards, he was prepared to accept that Cole had not necessarily behaved like an officer and a gentlemen, but Nancy's treatment of him was way over the top in return.

It took all types to make up the network they were a part of, and everyone had to learn how to get along with everyone else, even if they didn't hit it off right away. Tragically, however, Nancy's instincts about Cole soon proved to be totally correct. Cole was not what he appeared to be, and the consequences were dire. He had told everyone he was an army captain who'd been left behind at Dunkirk. In fact he'd scarpered from the British army before Dunkirk even happened, and even then he was only a sergeant and not a captain—and his correct name was Harold Cole, not Paul. The reason he had undergone that name change was particularly acute; for when he had deserted he had taken with him money intended to run the sergeants' mess and when the army enquired into his background they found that he had a 'long record of civilian convictions for housebreaking and fraud'.[20]

And *still* it got worse! For while all such transgressions belonged to his past life, his crimes in the present were more to the point. At a quick glance it seemed that Cole was a hard-working member of the Resistance movement, constantly helping to ferry people and money along the line. But then things started to go wrong. In September of 1941, Cole was spotted with his mistress at entirely the opposite end of the country to where he was meant to be organising an escape. Then, a large sum of money that was meant to be delivered to an agent in Lille never arrived, and Cole was the last man handling it.

When O'Leary called him and accused him point-blank of stealing it, Cole swore he had faithfully delivered it as asked. At this point the said Lille agent was called into the room, whereupon Cole dropped the façade and admitted it. He was locked in a back bathroom while they discussed whether or not his punishment should be as simple as a bullet behind the ear, but the debate proved futile, for even while they were discussing it, they were interrupted by the sound of shattering glass and they quickly discovered that Cole had made good his escape, *out* the bathroom window.

This was a catastrophe without disguise ... Cole had quickly made his way to Gestapo headquarters and in return for their protection—and possibly more money—he had given the Gestapo the names of every Resistance worker he knew on the network. A wave of arrests followed, resulting in fifty of those workers being executed. These executions stand as tragic testimony to the danger of doing escape-line work—it later being estimated that 'one escape-line worker lost his life for every fighting man who was led to safety'. Nancy, for some time, was quite nervous that she would also get a knock on the door in the middle of the night, but it didn't happen. Rightly or wrongly, she believes it was because she had given Cole such short shrift that she'd never had a chance to be compromised by him.

'I always think that's how I never got arrested,' she says, 'because I didn't like the way he came into my place, because he kicked the dog out of the chair and he drank my bloody whiskey.'

As to Garrow, alas, he was arrested—although this may or may not have been because of Cole's betrayal, it was never clear—and promptly put in prison at Fort Saint Nicholas for three months' solitary confinement, before the sentence called for him to do ten years at Meauzac concentration camp.

In the wake of this disaster, O'Leary had to move more deeply underground than ever before for fear of being taken away himself by the Gestapo. Certainly Cole would have betrayed him, but so carefully did O'Leary move that the Gestapo did not have the first clue where to begin looking for him. Nancy continued to work with O'Leary—meeting him in clandestine hideouts, but never more at her home—and yet became angered when she formed the impression they were not doing enough to get Garrow out of gaol.

'It was almost like they were so busy doing everything else that the task of getting Garrow out was no more than a distraction to them,' Nancy says, 'even though he'd set up the network in the first place—and I just wasn't prepared to accept that.' To her already full list, Nancy thus added, 'organise Garrow's release'.

She began to send Garrow food parcels, write him letters, and even managed to see him once. She also paid for the lawyers to look into his case in the vain hope that the last shreds of integrity in the Vichy justice system would provide enough moral force to release him. Alas, her hopes in this regard were in vain. When Garrow's three months of solitary confinement were over and word was passed to Nancy that Garrow was going to be transferred to Meauzac concentration camp—well to the north, near the town of Bergerac on the Dordogne River—Nancy and Henri went down to the Marseille Railway Station to see him being transferred from the prison truck to the train that would take him to the camp. They could barely believe that the chained, emaciated man with cadaverous eyes, making his way along the platform was Garrow.

'It was one of the most devastating things I've seen,' recalls Nancy, 'to see this proud man manacled like a dog, dragging his chains behind him with all the other prisoners, absolutely emaciated like they just hadn't been feeding him. I couldn't believe it had come to this and clearly he was not going to last long under those conditions.'

Equally clearly, the only way they would be able to get Garrow out of gaol was to *break* him out! Through careful enquiry, and using the contact of a former prisoner who was also one of Garrow's friends, Nancy ascertained that one of the guards at the Meauzac camp might be open to bribery, and this now seemed the best course to pursue. She set to work, having arranged with O'Leary that if she could get to the prison guard and get Garrow out, then the O'Leary Line—as it *now* had become known—would move heaven and earth to quickly spirit him out of the country and back to England. The prison that the Scot was interned in was actually more a Vichyiste 'concentration camp'—built since the beginning of the war—and it was situated in the tiny picturesque town of Meauzac in the beautiful country of La Dordogne. In mid-November 1942, Nancy travelled there by train, armed with nothing more than a desire to get Garrow out and the tip that one of the guards could be bought.

At least getting to the camp was no problem. Nor was meeting with Garrow very difficult—as Nancy had written him a series of letters which she knew would be read by the authorities, in which she had pretended to be Garrow's first cousin. A simple stroll from her lodgings in the town centre and there was the camp, and there on the other side of the barbed wire was the Scot himself. Even more emaciated than before, but delighted to see her, his heart at last filled with hope that something might be done to save him. She promised she would do everything in her power, but was professing a greater confidence than she actually felt. For what could Nancy do but make herself conspicuous in her visits to Garrow and hope that the guard would somehow make himself known to her, in whatever fashion he chose? With that in mind she continued to visit Garrow every week, and always made a point of being particularly expensively dressed herself, in the manner of a woman who could afford to pay well for the release of a prisoner if she chose to. It worked, after a fashion ...

One afternoon, she was just walking back from the prison to her hotel when a man on a bike rode past her and dropped a note wrapped in a stone at her feet, all without a word. The note made reference to her 'cousin' and said if she wanted to talk about him further she should be on La Linde bridge at midnight, where they could talk. How did she know that this wasn't a rapist inviting her to an isolated location at a time of his choosing in the dead of night? She didn't ... but she carefully made her way to the location at the appointed time anyway. As the waters rushed beneath and the clouds flitted overhead in the moonlight, she was alone, all alone ... and remained that way.

'The man never came,' Nancy says incredulously. 'He never came! I waited till two-thirty in the morning, but he was a no-show.'

Nothing if not persistent, Nancy returned to Meauzac the following week anyway—at least feeling as if something was starting to break—and was just having a drink in a local bistro when she sensed a presence beside her. She looked up, and there was a man she vaguely recognised, one of the guards from the prison.

'May I join you?' he enquired.

'Of course, please sit down ...' Nancy returned.

'I have seen you visiting Monsieur Garrow ...' he began carefully.

'Yes, it breaks my heart to see him in prison,' she replied, 'and I'm here to do everything possible to relieve his situation.'

'That might be possible ...'

Now they were getting somewhere and once on the same wavelength, they concluded the 'deal' quickly. If Nancy could provide 500,000 francs, of which 50,000 francs—the rough equivalent of 250 British pounds—would be available immediately, *and* procure a guard's uniform that would fit the prisoner, then this guard would guarantee that Garrow could walk out of there under his own steam. Done. Nancy didn't have that sort of money actually on her, but the wife of Henri Fiocca would never have to wait long for such things. She simply went to the local post office, telegraphed her husband with the request and was walking out an hour later with the cash in her hand, which she then gave to the guard.

Not all of this went unnoticed. The next day, as she went to see Garrow as usual to tell him the fabulous news, she was obliged to take a tour to the commandant's office. This gentleman proceeded to give Nancy the figurative third degree, as to just why it was that she had received such a large sum of money the previous day?

'I have *not* received a large sum of money,' Nancy replied point blank.

The Commandant insisted that she had, and he knew for a certainty that she had received fifty thousand francs. Using her own father-in-law for inspiration, Nancy curled her top lip into a superbly superior sneer and said 'That might be a lot of money for *you*, Monsieur, but I assure you it is not a lot of money for me.'

Chastened, if not humiliated, the warden—perhaps feeling more like a petty official than ever—backed off more than somewhat. Nancy made a formal and bitter complaint to the post office for betraying her business, just as she imagined a completely innocent woman would have done, and shortly afterwards returned to Marseille ... until the next weekend when she would visit again.

In the face of such activities, Henri, bless him, never complained. Long an admirer of his wife's energy and bull-headedness he simply continued to nod benignly at the series of seemingly crazy schemes she put before him, and wrote the cheques required to finance them. The main thing was that the escape plan was well underway and with the guard's uniform indeed now procured—and the O'Leary organisation was fully engaged after Nancy had convinced its principal that they had to help—the plan was at last about to be put into operation when subsequent events forced a delay ...

At the first light of dawn on 8 November, 1942, 110,000 Allied troops under the command of General Dwight D. Eisenhower disembarked from almost five hundred ships and hit the beaches of French North Africa, under the banner of Operation Torch. They had established a beach-head and were pushing eastwards, ever eastwards, against the German forces of Field Marshall Erwin Rommel. The operation was a stunning success from the first and, following reports on the BBC, Nancy thrilled to every new breakthrough.

'From that point on,' she says, 'France knew that it was not alone, that it had not been abandoned after all. Morale soared and there was a real sense that the remnants of what had been the French army were forming up together again, and were going to be a force.'

She was less thrilled though when just three days later in response a clearly shocked German high command sent Wehrmacht troops across the demarcation line that separated Vichy France from Occupied France, and essentially put *all* of the German jackboot—heel, heart and soul—over the entire country. That this was done at the behest of the traitorous Vichy Premier Pierre Laval in order to 'defend France' from a possible Allied attack on the Mediterranean coast, changed nothing.

'The occupation came with bewildering swiftness,' Nancy recalls. 'One day they weren't there and the next day, they were there in force.'

She happened to be on a Marseille tram, just stopped on the Boulevard de Gambetta when the first of the Nazi soldiers arrived, and an enduring image of that time has stayed with her ever since.

'A whole troop of them passed in front of the tram as we were stopped,' she remembers, 'and the tram-driver took one look at them and his bottom lip started trembling. Still without making a sound, he began to cry, the tears rolling down his cheeks as we drove on. Then suddenly the tears stopped rolling as he pulled himself together, and got this really hard look on his face—like whatever it takes, *whatever it takes*, I will see the end of you. I have never forgotten that.'

More than ever, the Vichy government was a mere puppet of the Nazis, and the environment in which the O'Leary group was operating changed quickly. Firstly, it meant that for a large section of the populace it was no longer possible to imagine simply that the war was something for the north of France and not their problem. ('As incredible as it sounds,' says Nancy, 'that is the approach a lot of them took.') Now that it was barely possible to spit out the window without hitting a Nazi of one form or another in the eye, it became a matter of clear necessity for people to decide if they were with the Germans or against them.

To a certain extent, it was the women of Marseille who led the way. As Russell Braddon detailed in his own biography of Nancy Wake, soon after the Germans arrived in the towns of the south, many were joined by their wives and girlfriends for the duration.

These women, Braddon says, rushed to duplicate the French female *chic*, in much the same way as Nancy had once done.

'So, noticing that all the Frenchwomen went hatless, the officers' women also stopped wearing hats. Immediately the Frenchwomen started wearing hats again. But they made it impossible for the officers' women to copy their example because the hats they wore all sported a green feather. The green feather symbolized a green bean and the 'green beans'—*les haricots verts*—were what the French had nicknamed the Germans! For any woman in Marseille to wear any hat at all after that was to fling a subtle insult at the Reich: the officers' women had to remain hatless.

'But the Frenchwomen did not stop there. When the officers' women obtained the best French stockings, the local women went stockingless. When their rivals also went stockingless, the Frenchwomen took to wearing revolting knitted stockings in which they still contrived to look *chic*. At this the opposition gave up the unequal struggle and victory went to the conquered.'[21]

Generally, while the fact that Vichy France was also now occupied meant that the Resistance could expect a lot more help from citizens wanting to become active against the Germans, it also made it infinitely more dangerous as the Hun was not only at the gate, he was *everywhere*.

Even more dangerous than the Germans themselves though, in many cases, was the wretched 'Milice' a kind of informal and home-grown occupying army commanded by the Gestapo and made up of those French who were not only *collaborationists* but proud to be so. At the behest of Premier Laval, the Milice had been formed in early 1943, with the specific role of quelling internal dissent, rounding up Jews, hunting down *partisans* involved with the Resistance and generally furthering Nazi aims on a dozen different fronts ... using whatever means were necessary.

Placed at the head of the organisation was Frenchman Joseph Darnand, a World War I veteran of extreme right wing political background who was so pro-Nazi he even took a personal oath of allegiance to Hitler as he was sworn in as an SS *Obersturmfuhrer*. Such a man as this knew what kind of people he wanted, and he got them—not just the scum of the earth, but the scum *of* that scum. Starting in 1943, Darnand and his lieutenants went about recruiting for the Milice thirty thousand members prepared to embrace daily brutality as a madman murderer embraces his axe.

When the numbers prepared to answer that job description didn't quite add up to the required thirty thousand, Darnand arranged for the Vichy judicial system, even such as it was, to offer hardened criminals who'd just been convicted of serious felonies a term serving the Milice instead of getting a zebra suntan in prison. Nearly all so offered, chose the Milice. Nancy's views about such men were best expressed by an editorial that appeared in one of the underground's leading newspapers. 'Kill the Miliciens', the editorial exhorted, 'exterminate them, because they have deliberately chosen the road of treason. Strike them down like mad dogs. Destroy them as you would vermin. Kill without passion and without hate. Kill without pity or remorse, because it is our duty.'[22] (And certainly, while Nancy wasn't in a position yet to do that herself, she was getting there...)

Working often in tandem with the Milice was the German Gestapo, also arrived in Vichy France now that it had more formally come under German control. The name Gestapo was composed from *Geheime Staatspolizei*, as in German Secret State Police, and the organisation was singularly devoted to exterminating all opposition to Nazi rule within Germany and all of its subjugated territories, as well as rounding up Jews to be sent to the genocidal gulags known as concentration camps.

In all such matters, the Gestapo was effectively unanswerable to any greater authority—having been given the power of 'preventative arrest', essentially to imprison someone on mere suspicion that they were enemies of the Nazi cause. There was no right of judicial appeal to any action taken by the Gestapo. If, on one of the many security checks they now conducted on trains, checking papers and the like, they did not like the look of you, you were theirs to do with whatever they liked.

The arrival on the scene of the Gestapo and the Milice and the German occupying troops themselves now brought to five the organisations who could bring Nancy to serious grief—when added to her existing problems of the black market police, and the standard-brand French Gendarmes.

'It certainly kept me on my toes,' recalls Nancy, 'though the fact that there were so many repressive organisations also meant that there was more potential for someone to "fall between the cracks" because there was a lot of administrative overlap, where one body assumed that another body was responsible for something, and vice versa.'

The Germans, of course, were not merely an administrative problem however, a point graphically illustrated on many occasions. Beyond the mere added danger of more eyes looking around, there was also the absolute physical fact that German troops were thick on the ground and determined to wipe out organised resistance.

In Marseille the most virulent hotbed of resistance was smack-bang in the middle of the twisted, turning and tangled streets of the Vieux Port where, for perpetuity, a variety of petty criminals, Mr Bigs, pimps and prostitutes had gravitated. The Germans decided that too many of their officers had disappeared into that wretched warren never to return again; too many times had the trail of a hunted 'criminal' been tracked right to its edge before completely going cold. They were tired of having to watch constantly for buckets of raw sewage suddenly descending from the skies when they were on patrol there, and appalled at the number of times fatal accidents seemed to befall Miliciens who ever became isolated while on patrol there. If it wasn't a wardrobe that mysteriously came cartwheeling down a set of stairs at the wrong moment, it was something as unsubtle as a silent knife between the ribs. So one terrible afternoon the entire area—on the personal order of Hitler—was suddenly surrounded while whole squadrons of Germans and local police scoured it street by street, house by house. Occupants were either arrested and detained—soon to be sent to camps—or if they were very lucky, simply told to clear out. Then the Vieux Port was put to the torch.

No fewer than twenty thousand Marseillais were suddenly

without a home as just under two thousand buildings were razed. Nancy first became aware of it when Picon started barking for seemingly no good reason and shortly afterwards the air was filled with the overpowering smell of smoke. This was not the sometimes delicious smell of eucalyptus leaves burning as in an Australian bushfire, but rather the acrid thick smoke of burning houses, of people's whole lives going up in flames. Nancy looked out from her balcony upon the inferno going up just a few kilometres from where she stood. The streets soon filled with refugees, people pushing barrows and the like, with whatever they had been able to save from the German torch.

'I thought, those bastards,' Nancy remembers, 'those absolute *bastards*!'

Nancy's rage at the Germans sometimes boiled over in spite of herself, even when she was engaged in undercover work. On one occasion she was travelling in a first-class train compartment bound for Nice opposite a German officer and a diminutive French soldier. When the ticket collector came to check tickets, he peremptorily ordered the Frenchman to leave as he held only a second-class ticket. The soldier, with Nancy hanging on every word while the German officer disdainfully looked out the window, quite reasonably protested that he couldn't sit in the second-class compartment because it was full, while there was plenty of room here.

The ticket collector insisted regardless, saying the *loi* was the *loi* was the law, and that the soldier would have to move back to the carriage behind to the standing-room only positions. It was at this point that Nancy exploded in fury.

'*You*, a Frenchman,' she roared, 'want to send one of your own countrymen who *fought* for this country, back to a second-class carriage, while you're quite happy for a *Boche* officer to sit here in comfort!'

She followed up with some choice French epithets as to his likely parentage—'not distinguished' is a fair summation—and finished by flinging from her purse the necessary French francs for the soldier to keep his seat. The soldier remained in his seat, while the ticket collector, abashed and humiliated, withdrew ... as did the German officer shortly afterwards when the subsequent stony silence likely proved a little too much for him.[23]

'It was probably a crazy and dangerous thing to do,' Nancy acknowledges, 'but I simply couldn't stand it. That kind of thing always made me furious.'

Often after such episodes, Henri would come home to find Nancy sitting with a drink in her favourite chair, distractedly patting Picon a little too fast and hard, as she tried to calm down. Henri would then do his bit, leading her to a couch where they could sit together, holding hands, and he would try to get her to settle down. A good man, he admired Nancy's outrage at injustice—for he shared it too—but was constantly trying to get her to temper its expression as he worried greatly for her safety.

With Henri's blessing though, Nancy continued her weekly visits to Garrow in the Meauzac concentration camp. Yet it soon transpired that the move of the Germans into Vichy territory had immediately thwarted the plans for the Scot's escape. This was for the simple reason that with the new German authority over the prison, the guards had been replaced by gendarmes, meaning that the uniform Garrow had intended to walk out in, was now worse than useless.

Fortunately it only meant a delay in the plans, and not cancellation. O'Leary himself took charge of fabricating a new uniform, while the guard with whom Nancy had initially made contact kept his word and managed to secrete it in the prison at a spot where Garrow could get to it. The upshot was that on the evening of 8 December, 1942, the newly adorned Garrow managed to attach himself to the end of a guard detail that was marching out of the prison after changing shift, and in short order—after blowing his nose with a large handkerchief at the exact moment that he passed the key checkpoint—he was breathing free air for the first time in a year. A little further away one of O'Leary's men was waiting with a car, and over the next few days Garrow had the supreme pleasure of being passed from hand to hand over the same escape line that he had personally set up, until he reached a safe house on the outskirts of Toulouse, where he stayed for over a month.

'We had to fatten him up a bit,' recalls Nancy, 'so he'd have the strength to get over the Pyrenees.'

Three weeks after he'd arrived, when a lot of the mad searching for him had died down, Nancy visited him in the safe house and the two were able to spend a wonderful afternoon together.

'It was marvellous to see him, and he was extremely grateful for everything we'd been able to do to get him out,' Nancy says. 'I must say I felt very proud of our accomplishment, and I was delighted when a week later he safely made his way across the Pyrenees.'

The early months of 1943 were simply a blur of activity for Nancy, just as it was for the O'Leary line she was working with on one hand, and the French Resistance she was with on the other, as she continued to be a courier *par excellence*. As the Allied Command had intensified bombing raids across Germany and selected targets in occupied territories, so too had the Wehrmacht intensified its own 'ack-ack' (anti-aircraft) defences to shoot the planes down, meaning there were more downed airmen than ever in continental Europe trying to keep out of the clutches of the Nazis and find a safe way home.

'Of course I can't remember all the Allies who came through,' she says, 'but what I do remember is the extreme happiness they had to be heading home again, frequently after they had felt that everything was lost.'

While it was deeply satisfying to be able to do one's part to help more and more good men home, still it came with more and more risks, for as the flow of escapees and refugees increased so did the numbers of people required along the O'Leary line to help cope with the increased traffic. What had begun as an extremely intimate collection of thirty people had now grown into an enormous organisation with two hundred and fifty helpers throughout France.

'And that meant,' Nancy points out, 'that even O'Leary was suddenly obliged to rely on people that he didn't actually know well, making it all the more easy for a traitor or a Nazi operative to penetrate the network and betray us, just as Cole had on one occasion. But what could he and we do? We couldn't turn away the airmen who needed our help, so we just had to keep expanding the best we could and hoping that everything would be all right.'

The problem for Nancy specifically was that with her own increased activities it became progressively more difficult to maintain the façade that she was nought but Madame Fiocca, dedicated to nothing else but frippery. In fact, by this time she had heard that the Germans were—if not aware of specifically *her* activities—at least aware of *a* woman's activities, whose description she fitted! They had code-named her 'the White Mouse', she heard, because of her amazing ability to disappear just when they thought they had her cornered.

'I must admit I got a swelled head,' she later told a journalist. 'I thought "God, I have got a code name in Berlin".'[24]

For all Nancy's feeling of being flattered, more to the point at the time was that it was clear that the brutes were closing in.

'I started to come to the conclusion,' she says, 'that it could only be a matter of time before I was exposed and I would have to be very, very careful indeed.'

One day returning from yet another sortie on behalf of King, Country and the Allies against the wretched Germans, Nancy stopped as usual at the corner bistro to get some supplies for lunch as well as cigarettes and ice. The owner there was a dear friend whom Nancy would trust with her life—an Italian-looking Frenchman who had fought bravely against the Germans in World War I and had positively *cultivated* a deep and abiding hatred for them ever since—and he had news.

'Nancy,' he said carefully, '*je ne veux pas* to scare you but when you left this morning I am almost sure you were followed . . .'

Somehow, Nancy was not surprised. Though she had not noticed someone following her that particular morning she had had a sense of things 'closing in' in recent times, and this possible scenario fitted in perfectly. The telephone had been making strange 'clicking' sounds, which were meant to be the classic signs of it being tapped, and just three days previously Claire had surprised a man going through their mailbox. If they really were onto her, it was quite possible that she was under surveillance to see just who else she was going to see, who else was implicated in her nefariousness. Clearly things had come to an impasse, and she had to move. And quickly. Thanking the man, she hurried back to her house to await the return of Henri for lunch ...

Henri was adamant. There was simply nothing else that could be done. She had to get out, go, go, *go* before the dreaded knock came on the door. He would follow her, he faithfully promised, once he could sort out arrangements to keep the business running without him. It was simply out of the question, he insisted, that he leave now with her. If he did, they would surely lose everything, and among many other things he felt a powerful sense of duty to both his father and his employees to keep it going strongly.

So, conscious that every *minute* could be the difference between making a clean escape and spending that night—and perhaps the foreseeable future—in a Gestapo cell, the two quickly made their plans. She would leave right away, spend that night at a safe house in Toulouse, and try to follow the same escape route that she had helped so many Allies along—across the Pyrenees to Spain and thence to England. Her own part in the Pat O'Leary line was about to come to a close. It was later estimated that during Nancy's time with them, she had played her part in helping 1,037 people escape the clutches of the Germans in wartime France.

In thirty minutes flat, Nancy packed a huge trunk with the best of her things which could make its own more leisurely way along that same route—via the postal services—while she also filled a small bag with the essentials she would need that very night. Secreted in the folds of her purse was her finest jewellery, including her engagement ring with its three-carat flawless diamond and her gold bracelets and diamond brooches.

Then goodbye. It was about 2 p.m., an unusually cold day outside. Holding each other tightly just inside the door, there really wasn't an enormous amount to say. She promised that she would get word to him as soon as she had safely completed her journey across the mountains. He promised, once again, that he would follow her trail soon. Still aware that every minute counted, they held each other, whispered their love and the fact that they would soon be re-united, and then Henri, desperate that she get to safety as quickly as possible, slowly loosened his hold. Not so fast. Nancy was conscious that there was one more thing to say. A simple now or never thing that came out of her instinctively.

'Henri,' she said delicately, as she looked straight into his eyes. 'I know that while I'm away, you won't be faithful to me ... and that nothing I can say will make you be faithful. So that is okay, but I want you to remember one thing. When we meet again, you must not ask me whether I have been faithful to you because I don't know what I'm going to do in England with all those bombs falling. That must be the agreement between us, yes?'

Henri looked back at her, seeming to be slightly stunned at the direction in which the conversation had suddenly turned— everything was happening so incredibly fast—but then nodded his head rather meekly, and replied.

'*Oui*, Nanny.'

And one more thing.

'If anything happens to me Nanny,' he said, 'you must always remember that in your safe deposit box at the bank, you have been well provided for, yes?'

Yes, she would remember. Henri had always told her that in that box there was the equivalent of sixty thousand pounds in gold, notes and bonds. Money was the least of her concerns now though. A few more whispered words and it was time. Finally, much as they used to on the Marseille train platform, they embraced and parted, her only words being a very loud '*À toute à l'heure!*' (See you shortly) for the benefit of the Vichy Commissaire next door. Whether or not it actually fooled him is a moot point, but this faux farewell certainly did not fool Picon, for even as she was moving down the stairs, the little dog let out a long series of wailing yelps, communicating to his mistress the extreme distress with which he viewed this departure. Even down in the street it continued and it was all Nancy could do not to burst out howling herself and return to take the dog up in her arms. She kept walking, a little self-conscious that her left breast must have looked a little larger than normal, courtesy of the large wad of notes given to her by Henri which she'd stuffed in there just before leaving.

Nancy cried all the way to the station, fearful among other things of the situation in which she was leaving Henri. Still, within half an hour she was on a train bound for Toulouse and, though she found she was constantly looking over her shoulder and wondering if every new passenger in the carriage might be the Gestapo, only a few hours later she was safely ensconced in that city's best hotel for those involved with the Resistance, the rather down-trodden Hôtel de Paris.

She had chosen to go to Toulouse because that was where O'Leary happened to be at the time, and she wanted him to devote his full resources to getting her out safely. They dined together that night in a black market restaurant he had especially picked—they abounded in France during these times, with the going rate being about ten times pre-war prices—and looked at her options. Actually there was only one option. She had to get out of France and get back to England, and as they well knew crossing the Pyrenees was the best way to do it ...

CHAPTER EIGHT

·⁀·

Escape Across the Pyrenees

I believe in an extra consciousness that looks after you.
It only comes into play in extreme circumstances . . .

ROGER MARSHALL
Mountain climber

Of course it was one thing to decide to cross the Pyrenees, and quite another to actually do it, for as Nancy well knew, it was always an extremely precarious business. And so it proved for her. During the next week she made the attempt twice, with the very same guides who had ferried her previous escapees, and twice they had to turn back because of the weather. After a week, she tried once again, and again it began to look ugly. When, from the outskirts of Perpignan, she gazed south at the tops of the Pyrenees and saw that they were lost in angry storm clouds she knew it would be nothing short of suicide—and a particularly cold suicide at that—to head out into such weather, so there was nothing for it but to once again get on the train and turn back to Toulouse.

But while this was disappointing for Nancy, things were about to get a whole lot worse. Just outside Toulouse station and the journey's end, the train suddenly stopped and was boarded by armed policemen with guns demanding that all get onto waiting trucks where they would be taken down to the station to have their papers examined. Nancy jumped for it. Over the tailboard of the truck and away.

'And I really might have made it, too,' she says, 'but as soon as I got around the corner, I ran into a whole bunch of students who were demonstrating against something and I couldn't get through them, so the police caught me.'

Quickly, Nancy slipped out the one piece of incriminating evidence she foolishly had on her—a British five pound note given and signed as a memento by five fliers she'd recently helped escape—and ate it.

'Henri used to say that I could eat money like no-one he ever knew,' she says, 'but this time I really did!'

Back at the station, a particularly big ugly brute of a policeman demanded to know exactly why it was that Madame was on a train bound from Perpignan to Toulouse, when her *carte d'identité* clearly stated that she was a resident of Marseille. It was no crime to be on that train certainly, but in these times every trip had to have a purpose, and a legal purpose at that. So just *why was Madame on that train?* Telling them the truth was as out of the question as even mentioning her previous residence at the Hôtel de Paris, so Nancy simply lied through her teeth, coming up with as plausible a reason as she could at short notice. She had been on a business trip to Perpignan with her well-known industrialist husband, Henri Fiocca, she said. They had a bitter falling-out and she knew not where he had got to, but she demanded, nay *demanded,* that they release her immediately. It didn't seem to make much impact. At least not as much impact as the cell door did, when it clanged shut behind her. They said they would check out her story, and in the meantime she could think about whether or not she wanted to tell the truth.

After these first few hours of interrogation, Nancy had at least learnt what specifically they were looking for. A cinema in Toulouse, which had been showing a film of the well known Corsican and Fascist Tino Rossi, had been blown up—obviously by the Resistance—and the police were under great pressure to come up with a guilty party, *any* guilty party. That at least was the impression Nancy garnered when, late that evening, the police dragged her out of her cell, and told her no-one had ever heard of anyone called Fiocca in Marseille and everything she said was lies.

'What that meant,' Nancy says, 'was that they didn't even care enough to make the call to Marseille to check out that part of the story. They wanted someone to be guilty, and I was close enough.'

Madame was given one more chance to confess that she had indeed blown up the cinema, *non?*

'*Non.*'

'*T'es une pute!!!*' the policeman roared as he slapped her hard across the face. You're a prostitute! Some more pushing and shoving followed, together with slapping, and at last she was taken, not back to her cell, but to a stinking hole-in-the-floor toilet where she was told she would stay for the night. Possibly, she thought, tomorrow she would be tortured. The thought of this was extremely disturbing, but for some reason she never understood, she always had confidence that if it came to it she could withstand their worst. Maybe, on the morrow, she would see.

If the situation was grim, not to mention smelly, there at least remained some kindness in the world, some decency. That evening at about nine o'clock a key rattled in the toilet door, it opened, and through it came one of the quieter gendarmes she had seen through the day. Lifting his finger to his lips, indicating the need for her to remain quiet, he signalled for her to follow him, and he took her to an internal office where he had prepared food and freshly brewed coffee for her.

'They've all gone home now,' he whispered, 'and won't be back until *six heures* tomorrow morning. You can sleep here on the desk with my greatcoat over you, and I'll come and wake you in the morning just before dawn to take you back to *la chiotte*.'

With which, he left. If the night was not comfortable on the desk beneath the coat, it was still luxury compared to passing the night on a cold concrete toilet floor with no cover whatsoever. And she was also warmed, of course, by his simple human kindness.

The following day, it was on again. By now, for some reason, the police were convinced that she really *was* a prostitute, and from Lourdes yet! *And* she'd been involved in the bombing. The irony of the situation of course was that while Nancy was telling an out and out lie about why she had been on the train in the first place, so too were the police trying to frame her up for something she absolutely hadn't done. The questioning continued throughout the day, without food or even a toilet break, but then again that night she was offered a whole night's toilet break beside the same hole in the floor as before. Again the kind gendarme came, insisting she spend the night on the office desk instead. So it went for four days, until she looked up and thought she really must be hallucinating. For there was O'Leary smiling down upon her with a beatific grin!

Fool! She studiously ignored him, confused about why he was there. She at least knew that having steadfastly denied that she had any involvement with the Resistance movement, it would not be a good idea to show any recognition of the most active Resistance man in the region. Then she realised. O'Leary was not there, as she had immediately assumed, because he was under arrest. He was there as a free citizen, come to visit her. The two policemen beside him did not have arms placed upon him in the manner of someone who might bolt at any second; they even seemed to be behaving quite deferentially around him! After saying something to the two *flics*, which made them laugh, he came up to her, made to kiss her on both cheeks, and with a touch of his lips whispered into her ears that would she *please* start looking like she was fond of him, because the police had been told that she was O'Leary's mistress.

Within thirty minutes she was on his arm and walking out of gaol, still incredulous about her sudden change of fortune. The more she thought about it, the more she came to the same conclusion: the *one* thing her mother had ever been right about was that she must have been born lucky, for as they walked away—Nancy still half-expecting a piercing whistle to blow behind her, calling her back—O'Leary told her what had happened. The Resistance's contacts had been wily enough to discover exactly where Nancy was, and also to learn that after four days and nights she had not betrayed any of them. O'Leary knew that in good conscience, there was only one thing he could do. Try to rescue her. He and his lieutenants briefly considered going in with all guns blazing before arriving at a far less noisy though only marginally less dramatic plan. O'Leary, an expert on the French psyche, decided that he would personally go and see the commissioner and pretend that Nancy was his mistress and that they had been travelling on the train together—which was the real reason she had been so vague about where she was going. The reason he had not been hauled onto the trucks like all the rest was because he had been able to show them that just like they he was a member of the Milice (with which, he handed to the commissioner his fake papers).

So come, come, come, *Monsieur le Commissaire,* we're all men here, we all have problems with our mistresses, and this is more a matter between men of the world than police and citizens. The killer was that O'Leary also made out that he was an extremely close friend of the notoriously cruel Premier of the Vichy government, Pierre Laval, and that O'Leary knew he would take it as a personal favour if the commissioner would release his mistress Nancy into his care. The commissioner hesitated, then demurred, saying that he would have to make a call to Laval's people to see if the story stacked up, whereupon with infinite cool O'Leary set himself to play his last card. Having checked before coming in exactly where Laval was, he now laid that card on the table.

'Commissaire,' he said gravely, with just enough steel to indicate he wasn't so much asking a favour as demanding his right as a personal friend of Laval, 'Pierre is in Berlin at this moment, and cannot be contacted. Even *I* could not get through to him, otherwise I would not be wasting my time here with you. But I will not answer for what he will say, and *do*, if Madame Fiocca is detained a moment longer.'

The boldness of the escapade as recounted by O'Leary, nearly took Nancy's breath away. Here was O'Leary, one of the most important Resistance figures in the region, marching into the police headquarters like Lord Muck, and *demanding* the release of Nancy on the grounds that he was good friends with the Premier of the Vichy government! The result had been superb, of course, but the consequences of failure simply did not bear thinking about. The Commissioner wearing O'Leary's balls for earrings and his guts for garters would have been merely a beginning …

That night, and every night for several weeks thereafter, it was arranged that Nancy would stay in the home of a Françoise Dissard, a two-plaited sixty-year-old French spinster close to the Resistance movement whose three great passions in life were her nephew, smoking cigarettes and hating Germans. The fact that her beloved nephew was even then in a German concentration camp not only meant she smoked more cigarettes than ever, but that she also put all her passions in a kind of cyclical overdrive with each one feeding off the next. This meant she was a blur of smoke, love and hate throughout the time Nancy was with her. (Sometimes it seemed the smoke was coming out of her *ears*, but whether that was cigarettes or pure fury, Nancy was never sure.) Françoise was a good stick, and a generous host as the Australian recuperated from her ordeal and pondered her next move.

During this contemplating, Nancy often stared at Françoise's telephone sitting in the corner beside a lamp. It was black and grotty, with the silver of the dialling mechanism cruelly dulled by the cigarette tar that coated her hostess's fingers. It was painful to Nancy that if she simply picked up the phone and dialled, then she could be talking to Henri! Nancy wanted so much to make sure that he was okay and to assure him that she was still safe. Her body simply *ached* for it. Or perhaps it was a physical and spiritual ache whereby, after loving a man as passionately as she had for the last six years, she simply felt out of kilter without his body beside her every night. She wanted to call and tell him that too, but always reluctantly reached the same conclusion. Contact was craziness. Contact risked compromising Henri completely. For now, she must just cut him off completely.

Clearly, she must keep her mind focused on the next step as her need to get across the Pyrenees was as compelling as ever. With that in mind, in the next three weeks she made no fewer than three sorties to Perpignan to try to organise a passage through. On each occasion, though, she was obliged to return, disappointed, as one mishap after another meant that the escape line she was on was suddenly broken up by the Gestapo and, more particularly, by the extremely active Miliciens, who forced them all underground. After all, the consequences of being caught aiding and abetting fugitives to escape rightful Vichy justice were severe, so it was not actually surprising that she'd turn up to a rendezvous to find herself all alone, or to knock on the door of a 'safe house' and simply receive no answer.

'It was simply extraordinary,' she remembers, 'and extremely frustrating, that after sending so many people over the Pyrenees myself, when it came time for *me* to go over, I just seemed incapable of doing it! It was like fate was conspiring against me.'

Nothing if not persistent though, Nancy was just on the point of heading off for the sixth time when Françoise told her she needed Nancy's help. This amazing woman, half spear, half battle-axe, had single-handedly engineered the breakout of ten Allied prisoners from a nearby gaol. They would shortly, she informed Nancy matter of factly, be arriving at the apartment and lying low with her for a few days until, she hoped, Nancy would help them make their way over the Pyrenees. The efficacy of her audacious action never failed to amaze Nancy. It was indeed extraordinary that this sixty-year-old woman—so manic that she could smoke with one corner of her mouth while sipping black coffee from the other—could contrive a prison break-out scheme that actually worked, but that is what she had done.

Françoise's contact at the prison which held American, Canadian, New Zealand and French men, was a guard who had promised to help as long as he could escape across the Pyrenees too. Agreed. Through her contacts with a friendly pharmacist, Françoise managed to procure a very potent sleeping draught, which she mixed in a bottle of wine—then she put the cork back on and gave it to the guard. He in turn gave the wine to his co-warden on the night in question, who promptly drank it and disappeared so far into the land of Nod that he did not stir even when the cell keys were removed from his belt, nor even when he was dragged into the said cells where the door clanged shut behind him ... nor finally with the heavy, echoing *click* of the lock seconds later. The first that Françoise and Nancy knew that the plan had worked was when there was an insistent knock on the apartment door at two o'clock in the morning. When they opened it, nine men in filthy, stinking prison garb, and the guard himself, quickly entered. With adrenalin in higher supply than whiskey, they all talked till dawn and beyond, at which time they finally conked out and substantially slept through the daylight hours.

For the next three days Toulouse was virtually torn apart as the police tried to find the escapees, but simple mathematics—there were some 100,000 homes in the town at that time, and only so many police on the ground—meant that Françoise's flat always had a fair chance of not being searched, and this is exactly what happened. The men spoke *sotto voce* to avoid making any noise to attract the neighbours; at Nancy's behest avoided flushing the toilet; and played cards till their noses bled. Nancy spent the days cooking and cleaning, particularly the latter as it was a matter of urgency to send the men back out into the world in clean clothes.

While in peacetime cleanliness was next to Godliness, when people were moving undercover in occupied territory it was higher still—for dirtiness and dishevelment were right next to suspiciousness and just one step again removed from arrest and an ugly death. The Gestapo and the Milice were always on the lookout for people who appeared as if they'd slept out overnight and, extremely conscious of that, Nancy scrubbed—*out, out, damned spot*—and ironed the clothes of her companions until her otherwise rather delicate hands were *ruined*! Her manicurist back at Marseille would have howled at the desecration of such fine hands, but Nancy did not. She was frankly too busy laughing and listening as all of them in the tiny flat—hidden on the fourth floor of an old building lost in a rabbit-warren of cobblestone alleys— traded their life stories. A special closeness came upon them as they remained in their tiny hideaway while the sirens continued to wail in the world outside.

At last though, the clothes were cleaned and dried, the latter was particularly difficult because they simply couldn't put their garb in direct sunlight. It was now possible to make another assault on the Pyrenees, still brooding all this time in the south, waiting for them. The other firm rule of travelling in these circumstances was to keep to small groups—large clusters always attracted attention—and so, departing in the early evening, Nancy was soon in a carriage heading south on the Perpignan line in the company of a New Zealand airman, two Frenchmen and O'Leary. The Belgian had come along to see if he personally could help guide them through this time, while the rest of the group were together in a forward part of the train.

They were just settling down for the long journey ahead—with Nancy drawing deeply on a Gitane, and watching the reflection of the smoke in the window as she pondered what likely lay ahead—when a conductor burst into their compartment. *'Vite, vite! Les allemands vont chercher!!!'* Quick, quick, the Germans are about to search the train! Even as he spoke they all lurched slightly forward as the train suddenly slowed down in the middle of nowhere, confirming his panicked words. Nancy and O'Leary and the other three all looked at each other and instinctively knew that they only had one option. O'Leary pulled the window open and Nancy was the first to climb through it, with the others pressing close behind. The train continued to slow, but the landscape blurred past her in the moonlight regardless as they were still travelling at a fair clip. Still, all things considered, it was a pretty simple choice ... because there was no other—to stay would mean certain arrest, followed by imprisonment at the very best.

'Now, Nancy, *now,*' O'Leary yelled at her through the window, 'and we'll meet at the top of that big hill you can see to the sou ...'

She leapt, instinctively putting her hands out before and making ready to roll with the impact. She did exactly that, as the train continuing to roar by her as she rolled.

Winded, she was still instantly on her feet and heading for cover, in this case the thickly grown vineyard that the railway line smoothly bisected. She had just gained the first semblance of such cover when she heard them, and almost felt them. Bullets, hurtling past her, and torching through the vines as she went. The Germans on the train had quickly realised that several passengers were making their escape and were now firing in their general direction. A bullet flying past your ear sounds exactly like a kitten miaowing softly, and she continued to run as the air was filled with kittens.

She kept running, zigzagging a little through the barely perceptible vines as she went hoping to throw off their aim, until at last the bullets stopped and she was momentarily able to crash to earth.

From there she listened intently for any sound that might indicate that the Germans were out after her and her fellow Allies. Certainly there were sounds of people crashing through vines from the direction of the now halted train—she could see its twinkling lights about two kilometres to the south, and just hear some kind of commotion coming from it—but there was no telling if they were friends or enemies. Quite possibly ... both. There was nothing for it. In the distance she could see the dim silhouette of the large hill in the distance that O'Leary had pointed out, and she now stoically made her way towards it, as heartbroken as she was.

'I was absolutely devastated,' Nancy recalls, 'because I realised that somewhere in that jump and roll, and then that frantic run through the vineyards, I had lost my bag with all my precious jewellery and *carte d'identité* in it. My most treasured possessions, gone, just like that. I couldn't go back and look for the bag of course but I really just wanted to cry my eyes out.'

Perhaps some three hours later, totally exhausted, she arrived at the designated rendezvous at the top of the said hill to find she was the first. She had decided that pace was the key to safety, while the others had quite probably plumped for stealth, not making a move until they were absolutely sure that any noise near them was not a German patrol who would shoot them on sight. Shortly thereafter one of the Frenchmen arrived, a nice sort of bloke by the name of Guy who she'd got on well with back at Françoise's. He'd been a policeman before the war, with a young family, and yet despite his concern for their security had simply been incapable of collaborating with the Germans as so many of his colleagues had done. So he'd joined the Resistance. Now, he was just happy to still be alive, and kept patting himself, almost as if he was counting all limbs and organs to make sure they were present and accounted for. At one point he brought out a carefully secreted photo of his wife and young child which he very proudly showed Nancy in the moonlight. Then O'Leary stole in, a little the worse for wear, battered and bruised in equal measure but, like them, simply glad to be intact.

When after another two hours still there was no sign of the rest of the group, Guy offered to go on a quick reconnoitre to see if he could scout them out, an offer that was accepted. He headed off back down the mountain, and shortly disappeared into a darkness containing he knew not what. (They never saw him again, hearing only that he had been arrested and died some time later in a concentration camp.)

The rest of the group, five in all, bedraggled its way together just before dawn and made its way to a barn where it lay up for the rest of the day and the following night. In spite of herself, Nancy was reminded of the time she'd run away from home and hidden under her sister-in-law's house, when the police had come looking. Throughout their time in the barn, one of them always stood guard in the loft to look out for any approaching trouble, while in the night particularly all the rest huddled tightly together for warmth, with Nancy right in the thick of four male bodies. (Wartime situations frequently did not lend themselves to prurience, as innocent as she was, and she felt sure Henri would understand.)

Finally, after two bitter nights, their need for food, drink and a more refined kind of warmth overcame their desire to continue hiding from the German patrols, and they began to carefully walk their way out of their predicament. Their destination, traipsing through the night, was a safe-house O'Leary knew of in the same tiny town of Canet-Plage where the British submarine had once come to pick up the thirty-seven escapees. There they hoped to get fresh clothes, money, food, and a chance to either continue over the Pyrenees or to beat a retreat to a point from which they could launch themselves again.

Five hungry days and four wicked nights later they arrived, wobbly on their pins through all the freezing famine of it all, but desperately glad to have made it. Not that all their problems had disappeared. Nancy, in particular, required urgent attention for a terrible case of scabies she had picked up— literally from having to sleep in pig pens—and had to be scrubbed from head to toe in disinfectant by one of the Canadians.

'Standing there naked being scrubbed by a man I barely knew was not nice,' she says, 'but it was no time for modesty.'

Nor was it time to be fashion concious. All of their clothes were filthy and rotted through and they had to use local Resistance contacts to get different outfits. Nancy's, when it came, looked like a potato sack with slits cut into it, but at least it was clean and roughly presentable. It was strange, she reflected, how she had started in life wearing hand-me-downs, graduated to wearing some of Coco Chanel's finest garments, and now here she was wearing hand-me-downs once again!

Whatever, at least they were now ready to move again, and clearly there was nothing for them but to head back to their safe base, Françoise's place in Toulouse. Toulouse, always Toulouse!

'It was amazing,' recalls Nancy, 'that by this time it was about three months since I'd left Henri to cross the Pyrenees, and I was now further away from getting there than I'd ever been! There is only one way I can describe it, and that is to say I had shit on the liver. Something didn't add up . . .'

Unless of course, all the bad weather apart, there was a leak somewhere in their organisation—which would explain the Germans and Milice blocking their way every other time she and others tried to move. Unless, somehow, somewhere in the labyrinthine relationships that constituted 'the underground', someone was coming by the information that was compromising them every time they headed south . . . and was passing that on to the Germans. Nancy, with Françoise's full support, put her fears to O'Leary, only to see them airily dismissed. Couldn't be right, he said. Security too tight, he said. Everyone is checked before they become party to sensitive information, he said. Nancy remained convinced that there was something rotten a lot nearer than the state of Denmark, but began to prepare for her next assault on those blessed mountains one more time anyway. Truth be told, there was nothing else she could do. She couldn't possibly head back to Henri and neither could she remain precariously with Françoise in Toulouse. She had to get back to England.

O'Leary meanwhile, kept up his activities organising his underground network and the day after Nancy had voiced her concerns to him—on the morning of 2 March, 1943—he went off to a meeting at a Toulouse café with a new recruit to the O'Leary line by the name of Roger le Neveu.

'I had never met this Roger,' Nancy recalls, 'and only knew of him that he had particularly asked to meet the "woman from Marseille" that he'd heard so much about. I didn't want to go because I was washing my clothes getting ready to leave again, and O'Leary probably wouldn't have taken me anyway for security reasons.'

One authoritative account describes what happened subsequently like this:

'When O'Leary arrived at the café, le Neveu was waiting for him. O'Leary sat down and said, "Tell me quickly, do you know who has been giving us away in Paris?"

"Yes," le Neveu replied with a grin, "I know him very well." O'Leary felt the muzzle of a revolver press into his neck, and a voice behind him said, "Don't move."[25]

'Roger' it turned out, was better known to the Gestapo as Agent 47, their *own* agent 47. In the German language, he was a *Vertrauensmann*, a trusted man or informer who had been able to worm his way into the Resistance.[26] Nancy and Françoise were waiting back at the flat when shortly afterwards a message was passed to them by one of their own who'd witnessed the whole thing. They were shocked, appalled and trepidatious in equal measure.

Still, just as O'Leary had once had every confidence that Nancy would not break quickly under interrogation, so too was Nancy now fairly confident that O'Leary would not compromise them. That did not change, however, their urgent need to abandon the apartment. Françoise who was in France for keeps, come hell or high water, went one way—to another nearby apartment—while Nancy went the other.

She, as always, headed south in the general direction of the Pyrenees. This time, in the absence of O'Leary—he was even then, alas, on his way to Dachau where he would remain until war's end—she headed towards Toulouse station with one Bernard Gohan, a former pilot for Air France, who had just joined the organisation.[27]

It was as well that he was a particularly good-looking chap, because as it happened Nancy would soon be raining kisses on his lips ... all in the name of survival. Just as they made their way onto the railway platform, her constantly searching eyes—always on the lookout for danger—looked straight into the eyes of the very policeman who had been most brutal to her several weeks before, slapping her and calling her a prostitute. This man looked back, perhaps trying to place just where he had seen this woman previously, at which point Nancy decided there was only one way out. After a tiny whisper to Gohan, the two suddenly became an ambulant embrace, necking like teenagers as they walked along. If the policeman had wanted to get a closer look at Nancy's face it would have involved him doing the extremely un-French thing— not to mention dangerous thing—of disturbing another man while he was on the job, and in this fashion the two made their way past the policeman, onto the departing carriage and out of Toulouse.

Their first port of call was Marseille, where Nancy had to warn some of the people who were most at risk after O'Leary's arrest. It was one of the most difficult things Nancy ever did, to be in the same city as Henri and yet make no effort to contact him, yet she knew she had no choice.

'I simply couldn't risk it,' she says. 'I would have liked nothing better than to meet with him for even a few seconds, but such was the situation at that time, I felt I just could not risk compromising him. With the arrest of O'Leary by the betrayal of Roger it was clear that there were double agents everywhere, and the best thing I could do to protect Henri was simply to pretend that that part of my life never existed.'

So it was, that on the particular night she was in Marseille, Nancy walked on by, not even a hundred metres from their old apartment, on her way to the second apartment she had long maintained for escaping refugees—such as she was now! She passed by so closely that she could see the lights shining brightly in their apartment, indicating he was at home. She could just imagine him there, inside, no doubt nursing a whiskey and hopefully wondering just where she was at this moment. But there was nothing she could do.

After arriving at her flat to find it filled with Allied refugees and members of her network she spread the word in Marseille that O'Leary had been taken by the Gestapo and that all bets were off until they could establish whether or not he had broken under torture—though as it turned out most of them already knew O'Leary was gone. They decided that she and two escaping Allied airmen, who also needed to get away from O'Leary's previous haunts, would go to the apartment of an old friend in Nice with whom Nancy had done a lot of Resistance work, Madame Sainson. As the train pulled out of Marseille station, Nancy, for one of the very few times during the entire war, wept.

'I suppose,' she says, 'it was just the sense that all of my life there had so totally come apart, and now I was really, *definitively* leaving it.'

The train rolled on to the east. On to Madame Sainson—she of the warm honey-brown eyes, with the amazing big black eyebrows always standing solemn guard above, no matter what the rest of her face might be doing. In sum, her visage was just like her— warm and loving but armed with a great deal of strength as well.

This woman, whose code name was Delilah, was something of a legend in the Resistance mostly for her capabilities but also, in part, because of her eccentricities—she delighted, for example, in taking tourist-type photos of some of her escaped airmen in front of some of Mussolini's finest along the Nice promenade. Somehow or other, it seemed not to matter how many refugees passed through her hands, nor how little her resources, she would always find a way to get them fed and to move them on safely without attracting heat from the authorities. Nancy knew her well because in the route of 'safe houses' across France that led to the Pyrenees,

Madame Sainson had oft-times been the contact just before hers in Marseille. This meant that Nancy had frequently visited her tiny and rather rundown apartment to collect a group of escapees and take them on to her own home, and during that time the two had become extremely close. Now, though, Nancy was not here to pick up a 'package', she *was* the package!

Careful though—before Nancy knocked on the door she looked at the doormat.

'This was one of Madame Sainson's only three gestures towards security. If there was any danger, she kicked the mat crooked, then she chained the door firmly (which was her second precaution) and laid a hand grenade ready inside the door (which was the third). Anyone mad enough to knock when the mat was crooked merely invited Madame Sainson to open her door the few inches allowed by the chain and to deposit an exploding bomb at their feet.'[28]

Fortunately the mat lay square against the door. All quiet on this front at least! She knocked, and no sooner had the door opened than Madame Sainson stood before her, uttered a brief squeal of delight, and then crushed Nancy in her fleshy embrace, raining kisses upon her cheeks. *Nonc-eee, Nonce-eee, Nonc-eeeeeee!*

'She was lovely, Madame Sainson,' Nancy remembers, 'one of the warmest people that I have ever met. She was so brave, so very, very brave. I would have died for her and I know she would have died for me. She had such a wonderful sense of humour, everybody loved her. We laughed our way through the war.'

For Nancy, after the rigours of the last few weeks, it was delightful to be back in a comparatively safe and comfortable home ...

What they needed most at that time was information, specifically information about whether or not O'Leary had broken—and whether they were all now entirely compromised. The easiest way to find out was for one of them to return to Toulouse briefly to check with their people, to see if their homes had been searched or if enquiries had been made about them. Bernard agreed to do just that, as Nancy was still without an identity card since losing her bag in the vineyard. A few days later he was back, with good news. O'Leary had obviously remained strong because all was as it should be.

In the meantime, Nancy and Madame Sainson had been preparing for Nancy to have a go at crossing the Pyrenees one more time—on this occasion hopefully without a 'Roger' anywhere in the network to forewarn the Germans that a group of escapees was on its way. Making the trip with Nancy and Bernard this time would be a New Zealander and two Americans, together with a couple of French girls they were to pick up along the way.

There was a short delay while Madame Sainson arranged for their local friendly forger to provide false identity papers for the lot of them, but once that most crucial detail had been taken care of, they were away. There was, true, the minor problem that their network had been so split asunder thanks to Roger that they were essentially flying blind, with no idea just who to approach once they got to Perpignan, nor what the correct password was, but Nancy had what she was pleased to call, 'an idea'. Nancy's idea was that she would go to a partisan's house which she had once seen O'Leary visit when he was looking for a guide, and simply front the bloke. No password, no nuttin'. Just tell him who they were, what they needed, and how they wanted him to help them get across the Pyrenees.

Of course if Nancy's plan failed, the act of fronting a Resistance man without the proper password could likely get her shot on the spot as a spy. But still Nancy had confidence enough to go ahead, so that was that. When they arrived in the town, she knocked on the door of the said residence, as proud as you please, and when the bloke opened it, she let him have it: 'I am Nancy Fiocca, and you are in charge of our guides. I work for O'Leary, so do you, I want to go to Spain. I've had enough trouble here, so don't give me any crap.' An initial look of stupefaction quickly gave way to a smile, and then he laughed outright at the very audacity of it all, before inviting her inside for a drink. From there, it was quickly organised.

Perpignan was thirty kilometres north of the Spanish border. Twenty kilometres either side of that border was a military zone in which the only people allowed to move were those with residential permits. Nancy's rag-tag group would walk the first few kilometres in darkness to a point where they would be met by a coal truck. There, they would climb into the back of the truck, be buried beneath many coal bags to get them through the various checkpoints, and then emerge dirty but defiant to be dropped off at a point where all they had to do was get over the Pyrenees, go another twenty kilometres or so, and they would safely be in neutral Spain! Simple really.

At least the first part of the plan went without mishap, as they set off in the early days of May 1943. The walk was easy; the coalbags were heavy; the dust they produced filthy and choking. But it all worked and after several hours' walk the Pyrenees soon enough lay right before them, theirs to conquer if they dared. Huge and forebearing, cold and treacherous. At sunset, in a deep part of the border-land forest, the group met their two guides—a swarthy man by the name of Jean who looked like he would as soon snap the lot of them over his knee as guide them, and a singularly beautiful young woman by the name of Pilar who was as taciturn as a rock.

And so they walked. And walked. And walked some more. And all the while they kept climbing. Sometimes through falling snow and howling wind, always through bitter cold. Every two hours there was a ten minute break, and then on again. No talking, no coughing, no smoking. Walk. Climb. Walk. Climb. The air getting thinner, the snow getting thicker. Lots of slipping and sliding and slapping the buildup of snow from their bodies.

Jean himself said very little, Pilar nothing at all, but they knew their business. That business was to get small groups of people over the Pyrenees in both darkness and light, in safety from the Germans. That essentially meant going over, and not around, the largest obstacles, scurrying from near-summit to near-summit rather than sticking to the passes and valleys where the German patrols were thickest and, more importantly, where their wretched dogs could operate. Fortunately, up this high, their sniffer dogs simply refused to sniff, so the Germans generally stayed lower.

That at least was the theory. When on one occasion Pilar happened to stumble on a German army ration can, the inescapable conclusion was that danger was abroad at any level.

There was little enough to find humorous in their situation, though afterwards they would always recall with a wry smile Jean's response whenever he was asked—which was often—just how far they had to go. '*Una montana mas*,' he would growl in his thick Catalan accent. One mountain more. Usually he was the one who led the way, while Pilar kept the stragglers moving at the rear, though sometimes they reversed positions. For a good forty-eight hours in succession they walked, with their only unscheduled breaks coming when one or other was caught short by Mother Nature taking revenge for them having consumed some rotten black market lamb that had given them all a terrible bout of food poisoning. It seemed there was always just one mountain more until the thick fog of exhaustion so engulfed them that almost no-one even bothered saying anything at all. They simply kept moving, stuttering their way through the whiteness, perpetually wondering if they were going the right way, but ultimately trusting to Jean and Pilar. Jean was a seventh-generation smuggler across these mountains and though they couldn't see a discernible track through the crags, that didn't mean he couldn't. With no choice, they simply had to trust him.

The one exception to this was one of the Americans who simply never shut up, despite Jean's growled admonitions to keep silent. 'His feet hurt,' he said. 'They were going too fast,' he whinged. 'They needed more time to rest,' he implored. 'Why hadn't they brought more toilet paper,' he wondered out loud. 'He couldn't imagine what had possessed him to go with such a group,' he said. 'Can we *please* slow down,' he cried. While most of the rest simply suffered in silence—except the other, deeply embarrassed, American who exhorted his compatriot to shut up—Nancy at least tried her luck in getting him to shut the hell up by sidling up alongside him and telling him that she would shortly push him into a gorge if he didn't put a zip in it. Nothing worked. He kept complaining. Finally, the recalcitrant American sat where he plopped.

'I'm not taking another step,' he said surprisingly vehemently for such a clearly exhausted man, 'not *one.*'

This time, something inside Nancy *really* snapped. In the last few months she had had to leave her home, her husband and her dog; she had been thrown in prison and slapped around; she had jumped out of a moving train; had been fired upon; lost her jewellery; had to sleep in pig-pens; had starved for five days and frozen for longer; had scabies; and had tried to cross the Pyrenees fruitlessly on six occasions. She was not a happy little Vegemite. And now they were fighting for their lives in the high reaches of the Pyrenees, with German patrols all around, and this petulant prick of a person was having a tantrum because he was tired and cold and ... and, in the process, was putting *all* their lives at risk.

Personally, Nancy couldn't have cared less if they left him where he lay—knowing he would soon turn into a human popsicle—but for the deep security risk that would raise. A dead body lying atop receding tracks in the snow would lead directly to them. That meant this bloke had to be 'encouraged' to keep moving, come what may. Nancy took it upon herself, deciding that a variety of methods would be better than just one. First she kicked him, then she swore at him, then finally she dragged him for a few yards along the snow by his hair.

'I will report you to the American Consul as soon as we get there!' the American cried shrilly, now shaking with rage, but moving again all the same. 'You just see if I don't!'

Thinking he must have confused her with somebody who could give a shit, Nancy merely gave a death's-head grin and kept moving forwards.

She also came up with a plan a little later on to keep one of the French girls moving. After she complained of total exhaustion, Nancy saw to it that at just the right moment the Mademoiselle tripped and landed in a pool of extremely cold water. This gave her an extremely stark choice, wet through as she was—keep moving and live, or stop where she was and freeze to death quickly. Upon consideration, the Frenchwoman decided that she actually could keep moving after all.

At long last, after they crossed a high point of some 12,000 feet where they could see a stormy Spain stretched out before them for a hundred horizons in one direction, and France stretched equally in the other, their way began to definitively descend. Yes, there was a fearful blizzard still blowing—with the driving snow and wind nearly blinding them at times—but it was ultimately bearable because they knew that after well over two days of all but solid trudging through some sixty kilometres of wretchedly difficult country, their journey was near an end.

Finally, Jean led them into a hut deep in a forest where they were able to light a fire, warm themselves and dry their clothes. After a few hours' rest, they crossed the shallow bed of a river and landed on the ochre-red earth of *España* proper, and were shortly afterwards led by Pilar to a nominally 'safe house', a farmhouse where they could get a couple of nights' rest before a car would arrive to take them to the British Consul in Barcelona. Jean had already gone on ahead to alert the consulate of their presence, and there was nothing to do but wait for the blessed car to arrive.

On their second night there, they were all sleeping in the barn under cover of hay, and just drifting off to sleep, when the air was suddenly rent by guttural male commands in Spanish and female screams in response, coming from the direction of the farmhouse. Pilar, their female guide, would shortly be doing her own fair share of screaming, for no sooner had the barn filled with a bunch of gun-wielding *Carabineros*—Spanish police—than one of them put a speculative pitchfork in the middle of the haystack, and connected right with Pilar's bottom. She unleashed a cry to wake the dead, sprang out of the haystack and through the window before the *Carabineros* quite knew what hit them. For the rest of them in the haystack, there was clearly no point in remaining there to get better acquainted with the pitchfork, so one by one they all emerged, blinking, into the light and the two groups faced each other. On the one side, a bunch of Spanish macho men who had actually been looking for contraband bound for the Spanish black market; on the other, five males of soldierly age and three females, one of whom was hellishly attractive. What to do? Why, of course, do what every self-respecting police force all over the world has done on such occasions through the ages: they took them down to the station for some further questioning!

On this occasion the forlorn and dilapidated little station was situated in the nearby village of Besalut and the lot of them were marched down there and put in a tiny cell with nine other prisoners, at least until the morrow.

'Not that we made it easy for them,' Nancy recalls. 'All the way there we kept singing loudly and badly, as well as doing a series of leap-frogs over each other and just generally carrying on.'

There was actually good reason for showing such bravado, for despite now being in the hands of the authorities, things weren't actually that grim. To begin with, the British Consul in Barcelona by this time must have known they were there, and when a car from that consulate turned up the following morning to find them gone, it wouldn't be too long before they were tracked down. Secondly, whatever else, at least these authorities were Spanish and Spain was not at war with England at all. They should be fine ... that, at least, was the theory. After three days of waiting with no sign of the British consul, Nancy was taken into a room for some *serious* questioning—serious enough that they chained her up before beginning—she had cause to wonder whether they were in fact in very big trouble indeed. And so the questions began, with the help of a translater. Why were you hiding in the barn?

'My name is Nancy Farmer, and I am an American, and this is all I have to say to you.'

Where have you come from?

'My name is Nancy Farmer, and I am an American ...'

Where did you meet your companions, who were with you in the barn?

'I think I told you, my name is Nancy Farmer, and I am an American ...'

And so on. To each response, Nancy kept doggedly repeating that she was an American—from the very same America, as a matter of fact, did she mention that was even then emerging as the world's most powerful nation, since it had joined the Allies' cause after the Japanese bombing of Pearl Harbor. A nation which would be *very* pissed off if one of its citizens was treated badly. A nation which just might reconsider its well publicised plan at that time to send shiploads of wheat to a seriously hungry Spain ... Having also mentioned to her interpreter that she would complain to her friend the American Ambassador about the treatment that she had received, Nancy had some vague hope that things might go better for her shortly, but even she could not have imagined how much better.

Within twelve hours the Spanish authorities had suddenly altered their approach to her radically and she was installed in a warm hotel, and shortly thereafter was able to make contact with the British Consul at last. Although she would soon be formally charged with entering Spain illegally and fined the equivalent of one thousand pounds—which the British Vice-Consul, who was attending the brief trial, handed over on the spot—the upshot was the same. After seven attempts, she was now actually in Spain and was free to head on to England. She quickly sent a coded postcard to a friend of Henri's to indicate that she had safely made it over the Pyrenees, and began to make her arrangements. After the usual amount of stuffing around to get the proper papers which would allow her to travel in Spain, she set off first by train to Madrid, and thence Gibraltar, the British protectorate that sits at the southern tip of Spain.

It was one thing of course to be back on British territory at last, and quite another to get back from there to Britain itself. Before the war it would simply have been a matter of popping on the next ship bound for London or Liverpool, but now it was necessary for those ships to travel in convoy. With so many Allied refugees trying to accomplish exactly the same thing as Nancy, there was enormous competition to get on one. She spent the time waiting doing two things: 'I went up to a hotel on top of the Rock and got pissed every day, and I also read lots of newspapers catching up on what had been going on in the war.'

If the grog was great, the news was also pretty good. The Germans had had terrible reverses on the Russian front and despite a slight resurgence, continued to be bled in the north. In Germany itself, on 16 May, 1943, the Royal Air Force had launched an extraordinary operation whereby nineteen Lancaster bombers had launched 'bouncing bombs' on dams in the Ruhr Valley and had taken out two of them, thus flooding the German industrial heartland and severely disrupting production for the Nazi war machine. Out of Africa, the news was even better as Field Marshall Erwin Rommel's famed Afrika Korps had suffered severe reverses against the combined forces of the Allies, led by such notable figures as General George Patton from the USA and Field Marshall Montgomery from Britain. In early May, German resistance had all but collapsed and no fewer than 125,000 crack German troops had been taken prisoner! This heightened the possibility that an Allied invasion could be successfully launched from North Africa into the heart of Europe. Good. Good. Good! There clearly remained a lot of venom left within the German war machine, however—not least in France where the situation remained essentially unchanged, and in the oceans where Nazi naval power was still extremely strong— but the upshot of the news was indeed up, and it was a rare pleasure to be able to read it uncensored.

At last, after an agonising wait of two weeks, the word came through. Nancy would be on a convoy of seventy ships leaving for England the following day. It was wonderful news that, after such a long wait, she would finally be on her way, but even then it was a long way from guaranteed that she would actually arrive. When she boarded the good ship *Lutstia* her fellow passengers were a vast group mixture of Gibraltar residents, fellow refugees, British military, and many, many Maltese wives of British officers travelling to London to be with their husbands ... plus one other delightful passenger besides.

Nancy was just settling in on the boat, being chatted up by a singularly good-looking officer whose jib she very much liked the cut of, when she heard a joyous shout behind her: '*Nonc-eeeeee!*' She turned and there was none other than Micheline, the girl she'd taken with her from the English convent all the way back to France when the war had first broken out. At least she used to be that girl.

Now she was not only a young woman, but also a young mother, delightedly showing off six-month-old Patrick, the son that she had with that same Canadian, Thomas Kenny, whom she had met at Nancy's and Henri's dinner table and had subsequently married. Kenny, like Nancy, had been busy in setting up escape routes and had also had to escape to England at a certain point when the Gestapo was after him—briefly leaving his heavily pregnant wife behind, as she couldn't travel. Micheline and her baby were now on their way to meet him in England. All up, it meant that, just like Nancy, Micheline had seen her previously happy life vanish with the winds of war. She too had fled with Patrick across the Pyrenees and, well, here she was!

'It was a joy to see her again, together with her young son,' Nancy remembers, 'and it just seemed extraordinary that after nearly four years, with all the amazing things that had happened to us since, we would be both returning to Britain with the same person we'd left it.'

Micheline, felt the same.

'It was wonderful to see Nancy,' she says, 'but I couldn't help but notice the changes in her. She used to be so ... light ... and sort of frivolous ... but now there was a real toughness in her, I suppose because of all the things she had been through. It was still the Nancy I loved, but there was now a hardness there that I had not seen before.'

The convoy sailed at dusk and Nancy and Micheline, with baby Patrick sleeping in his mother's arms, spent the rest of the evening chatting in a darkness imposed by the need to extinguish all lights. As they caught up with each other's news, the lights of Spain twinkled in the distance off to starboard. All up, they were like young kids on Christmas Eve, happily laughing and gaily gossiping, all the while with the consciousness that wonderful things lay ahead for them in the very near future. After everything they had separately been through in their recent past, it was a rare delight to be heading back to England with the prospect of a life in which they were not perpetually looking over their shoulders for the Gestapo. Not that they were still home free, for all that.

While they needed no reminding of the precarious nature of their trip, that came soon enough. On the first day out of Gilbraltar, they were subjected to lifeboat drills in case a German torpedo should come their way. On the second day, sure enough, there were sightings of German submarines; at least the accompanying destroyers could greet the U-boats by dropping depth-charges to give them something to think about. From the deck, Nancy and her fellow passengers could see massive plumes of spray burst into the air as the depth charges went off. They then watched to see whether it might possibly be followed by a stricken submarine floating to the surface, but ... no such luck.

The main thing was that *they* were still afloat, and still heading towards Britain. Many before them had not been so lucky. In the early part of the war, British merchant ships had been easy prey for the ravenous packs of the infamous German U-boats that hunted them, and between 1939 and 1942 no fewer than 1,950 Allied and neutral ships had been sent to the bottom. Throughout 1942, the U-boats had torpedoed over six million tons of shipping, while their own numbers had increased from 91 to 212. As recently as March of that year—just a couple of months before Nancy's convoy set out—the U-boats had achieved their greatest kill-rate ever, sinking 627,377 tons of shipping.

It was at that point that Britain's Ministry of Shipping had insisted that things be done differently and the organisation around convoys, such as the one Nancy was now on, had been the result. Allied shipping travelling together in large numbers meant that help was always near at hand if disaster struck, and it also justified allocating scarce destroyers and warships to protect them in the water, even as patrolling planes—especially armed Liberator planes from America—swooped the skies looking for all possible predators.

In a way those destroyers and planes were like protective hens, constantly fussing around the baby chick passenger ships, trying to ensure that any feral foxes in the neighbourhood didn't get close enough to do any damage. One particular episode on the ship was recounted by Nancy in her autobiography and bears repeating:

'The officers who had been stationed in Malta disappeared every morning between breakfast and lunch time. One morning I was wandering over the ship trying to pass time. The bar would soon be open and I was trying to retrace my steps, but I got lost. I walked along several corridors but all the doors were locked. Eventually I found one that was not locked and in I walked to find that around the corner all the officers were being lectured on security by their senior officer. I was surprised, but they were spellbound. I excused myself and made for the door opposite, which was locked. The senior officer let me out and enquired as to how I had entered that conference room. I pointed in the direction from where I had come. They had locked every door but the back one. They used to call me Olga Palouski [sic],[29] the beautiful spy, after that.'

The roving packs of German U-boats notwithstanding, the convoy proceeded without damage and ten days later they were delighted to arrive off the craggy coast of sunny Scotland, and shortly thereafter in the port of Greenock. True, there was a minor hassle for Nancy when the customs official refused to allow her entry because she had neither a passport nor identification papers, but after she sent a single rather crisp telegram to Captain Ian Garrow of the War Office—the same man she had helped spring from the Meauzac concentration camp!—things quickly sorted themselves out.

Nancy bid Micheline and Patrick a fond farewell, making earnest plans to meet up in a couple of weeks' time, and headed south, south towards London. Good ol' Garrow had been busy meantime. By way of small recognition for all the sterling work Nancy had done to get Allied refugees safely out of France over the past three years, she was plucked from the train on the outskirts of London by the Assistant Chief of the British Intelligence Service, Captain James Langley, and driven the rest of the way to the suite they had booked for her at the St James Hotel. For Nancy, who had not so long ago slept in pig-pens and climbed across icy mountains, it was heaven on a stick.

Six months after kissing Henri goodbye, she'd finally completed her journey and was back safely in England.

'My overwhelming feeling,' she remembers clearly, 'was "I made it!, I made it!"'

She had at that, as had Micheline. The well meaning customs officer of three years previously who had warned them that if they left Britain for war-torn France they would never return, had got it wrong. Granted, it had taken her a while—it was now 17 June, 1943, and she had left in September 1939—but here she was.

CHAPTER NINE

I Spy, With My Little Eye ...

'Freedom is the only thing worth living for. While I
was doing that work I used to think that it didn't
matter if I died, because without freedom there was
no point in living.'

NANCY WAKE,
Sydney Morning Herald, 25 October 1968

Both Nancy and London itself had changed dramatically since
the last time the two had been together. The once majestic city
had since endured tons of bombs dropped on it, and Nancy was
staggered as she walked around and saw just how much ruin had
been visited upon it. Whole streets and buildings were reduced to
rubble, while others remained standing but were boarded up and
abandoned. A blackout still applied at night, and at the first shrill
call of an air-raid siren everyone scurried to bomb shelters, though
this was thankfully a much rarer occurrence than it had been
during the Battle of Britain.

As for Nancy herself, when she was last living in London her
frivolous lifestyle saw her spending her time at bars and clubs,
picnics and pub-crawls. Now she had only minimal interest in
such things, though she did at least go and see all the theatrical
shows that were on, of which there were many, thriving as they
were on the people's need for entertainment during such hard
times. The first film she sought out was *Gone with the Wind*, as
she had caught a glimpse of Vivien Leigh in a smoky nightclub in

Gibraltar and been struck by her extraordinary beauty. Nancy also socialised with the many Allied servicemen and French whom she'd previously known in France. And after the word had spread that 'Nancy's back' there were a lot of them, starting with Garrow who on the night of her arrival took her to dinner at Qaglino's, one of London's best restaurants of the time.

'After that, at least fifty of them invited me to their homes and I met their wives, or mothers or fathers or friends,' she says. 'The ones with money took me out to nightclubs, restaurants and generally entertained me, which was very nice indeed.'

Nancy also busied herself with renting and decorating the apartment in Piccadilly she'd decided to rent—one of three she'd looked at seriously, and the only one that wasn't subsequently bombed into ruins. (Once again, her luck held.) She was decorating the apartment and making it as stylishly comfortable as her Marseille home against the day when Henri might soon be arriving. It was for the same reason that she spent a lot of time buying such things as clothes, linen and the like—for she felt sure that he would arrive with only what he had been able to carry over the Pyrenees. He had, after all, faithfully promised that he would try to reach her soon. Finally, she bought French champagne and Henri's favourite liqueur brandy in Soho with which she intended they would celebrate his arrival.

'I had had no contact with him of course,' Nancy says, 'but just assumed that he would be keeping to our original plan, for him to follow me to England.'

All up though, even while she was making her arrangements to settle in, she couldn't help but notice that the capital was full to overflowing with service men and women going to, or coming from, *action*—there was a crazy kind of buzz in the air—and Nancy was not unaffected by it. Soon enough, though, it was becoming apparent that Henri simply wasn't coming, and she knew more clearly than ever what she wanted. She wanted at least to be in the same country as Henri, if not the same city, which she knew would still be too dangerous for both of them. And she wanted to get back into it, to get to grips with the Germans as she'd vowed she would all those years ago in Vienna when she'd seen the storm troopers whipping the Jews. Clearly, that meant visiting the headquarters of Charles de Gaulle's Free French, to see what they might have for her.

'Some of my friends advised me to go to the British services first,' Nancy recalls, 'but I was still angry with the British at that time, because I never thought they looked after our network in France the way they should have. There we were, constantly risking our lives to keep the network going, and we always had to try and scrounge the money necessary; forever finding too little money in the toothpaste tubes they sent. We were always short of money ... and I hadn't forgiven it.'

So it was that one bright morning she arrived amid the hurly-burly hustle-bustle of General de Gaulle's Free French Movement headquarters in central London to see just what role she might play in one of the many underground programs they were now running back in France. And why wouldn't she be confident? After all, due to her undercover work in Marseille and the Riviera she already enjoyed a certain reputation among the intelligence cognoscenti— as evidenced by the British Intelligence Service sending a car for her—and she had already demonstrated that her courage and resourcefulness were valuable assets on the ground behind German lines. Surely the Free French would snap her up.

Alas, Colonel Passy, a recruitment officer for the Free French did not agree. After listening to her account of her activities over the previous few years, he said that while he admired the work she had done—and was already well aware of it, by the by—the simple fact was that they did not have an opening for her right now.

Puzzled, and not a little miffed, Nancy left. The next day, the most extraordinary thing happened. *How* extraordinary!

Nancy was in her flat and about to go out when the phone rang. It was an acquaintance from the British Intelligence Service wanting to know just exactly 'What were you doing in the General's headquarters yesterday?'.

Sang-froid, be thy name. 'What general was that?' Nancy enquired pleasantly.

'General de Gaulle.'

(Oh *that* General.) Still, Nancy hadn't survived and flourished for two years right under the heel of the German jackboot for nothing. Though she knew she had absolutely nothing to be ashamed of in having made the visit, instinct guided her to admit nothing. No, she blithely assured her interrogator, you must be mistaken. It wasn't me there yesterday, it must have been somebody who looked exactly like me. Unfortunately, the man proceeded to tell her exactly what she had been wearing, what time she had arrived, what time she had left, and where she had gone from there. Suddenly it all fell into place.

Though nominally the Free French and the British were on the same side, in fact there was a lot of suspicion between them. From the French side of things, General de Gaulle maintained the fiction that he and his represented the only true government of France, even if they were in exile, and thus, all British activity breached their sovereignty and could only be done with their permission. The British on the other hand, while happy for de Gaulle to maintain that fiction in radio broadcasts to France, believed that there was a war to win here. And the way they saw it, as the French had already been proved manifestly incapable of defending their own territory, the job had fallen to the Brits and they intended to get on with it! Much argy-bargy had subsequently resulted ...

A possible reason, therefore, that her services had not been required on the previous day was because the French thought she was there on behalf of the British—spying on what they were up to—and so had given her short shrift. Well, she *never*! The obvious question then beckoned—where to, from here? She couldn't go back to Marseille to resume her life and she had absolutely no interest in returning to Australia. Why not, a friend asked her over lunch, look up 'Buckmaster's Group' and see if they had anything for her? Why not indeed ...

Colonel Maurice Buckmaster was the head of the French Section of the Special Operations Executive (SOE), which was essentially the British counterpart to the Free French, set up in the wake of the

Dunkirk evacuation to 'foster and encourage the growth of the partisans'. Therein lay a tale ... '*How wonderful it would be,*' Churchill had written in a memo to his personal representative to the Chiefs of Staff, '*if the Germans could be made to wonder where they were going to be struck next, instead of forcing us to try to wall in the island and roof it over!*'[30] Essentially the role of the SOE—sanctified by a British War Cabinet decision on 22 July, 1940—was three-fold. The initial stage was to get information out of the infernal blackness of France. Where were the Germans garrisoned? In what numbers? What were their points of vulnerability? Who were the French who could be counted on to actively engage in the task of helping to liberate their own country?

The next thing was to facilitate partisans in Occupied Territory to both hamper and hammer the German Army in whatever way they could to debilitate them. And the final aim was to prepare those same partisans to aid the Allies should the great day arrive when they would launch their armies to re-take France. In Churchill's words, the SOE was there 'to co-ordinate all action, by way of subversion and sabotage, against the enemy overseas'.[31]

And if the role of the SOE was to facilitate activities against the Germans generally, there was no doubt which country had top priority. France, as all agreed, was going to be the key battleground of the war. Closest geographically to Britain, it was also far and away the most industrialised of the six nations under German subjugation and, as the Nazis well knew, unless the Axis powers harnessed France's resources they would quickly fall behind.

In June of 1942, the Germans had launched *la relève*—the relief—whereby for every three French who volunteered to go and work in German industries to make armaments and the like, one French prisoner of war would be set free. This had raised two hundred thousand Frenchmen for the workforce, which was judged to be still not nearly enough, and the net was widened. In September of that same year, the Vichy government passed a law that said that all men between the ages of eighteen and fifty and all women between twenty-one and thirty-five had to make themselves available to go to Germany if the government adjudged their call-up to be 'beneficial to the overall interests of the nation'. Still not enough, and in February of 1943, all pretence of volunteerism was off. With the passage of *Service du Travail Obligatoire*, every French person of reasonable health and workable age had to make themselves available to go and work in Germany.

The results were immediate. In their tens of thousands many French men, particularly, headed for the bush where they joined up in bands which became known as *Le Maquis*, a uniquely French word meaning 'scrubby underbrush'. Now, as it was explained to Nancy, a lot of SOE's activities were centred on getting those Maquis properly organised with guns in their hands and ammunition along their belts.

Nancy considered the above for about a minute before deciding to apply for a position with the SOE. She cannot remember where her initial interview took place, though it is likely that it was held in a flat in Orchard Court that the SOE kept for such interviews and pre-mission briefings. While the SOE's real London headquarters were in famed Baker Street (just down the road from where Sherlock Holmes used to fictionally live), that and many other details about the workings of the operation were closely guarded secrets.

This time the interview was more to her liking. It was conducted by an SOE officer and it quickly became apparent that they were not only aware of her activities back in Marseille, but were also in deep admiration of her. After several more discussions, she was offered a position with the organisation. They explained they wanted to train her up, then drop her back behind German lines in France so she could start preparing for the day which they felt would be soon at hand when the Allies could launch the invasion to re-take France from the Hun.

She was in! If that was her top secret mission—and it seriously was top secret, for because of the Official Secrets Act she had to formally commit herself to never discussing it—as far as the rest of the world was concerned, Nancy had merely joined a fairly benign organisation known as FANY, short for First Aid Nursing Yeomanry. Created in 1907, this unit provided opportunity for wealthy upper-class women to serve their country's war effort, but had more recently also served as a cover for operatives such as Nancy. She was actually issued with their uniform, and signed up on FANY papers using her maiden name of Wake—it somehow seemed right, being back in Britain and putting on hold her old French life, at least for a time. After the initial paperwork she saw nothing more of FANY, for no sooner had the SOE taken her in and given her the rank of ensign, than she began an extraordinarily intense sixteen-week training period which would take all her energies.

The SOE was very big on making sure its agents were multi-skilled in various facets of espionage and counter-espionage, from making bombs to defusing them, from killing a man with your bare hands to learning how to disarm one coming at you with a knife. The first stint of Nancy's training was in an establishment just outside London known colloquially to its inhabitants as 'The Mad House'. The reasons for this are lost, but Nancy certainly found it mad enough.

In the company of many other potential agents—all of whom, like her, could speak the language of the country they were to be dropped into—she was put through a battery of tests and obstacle courses to see how she coped. Among other things she was given the classic psychological Rorschach test of being asked to look at pages stained with ink blots and then to describe what she saw.

'I see ink blots,' she said quite reasonably.

When the psychologist, a New Zealander, expressed his extreme disappointment that she should say such a thing, Nancy in turn expressed her own extreme disappointment that an able-bodied man such as he should be wasting his time on this sort of malarkey when he would clearly be a whole lot more effective if he simply picked up a rifle and went off to do his duty to God, King and country.

'I said,' she remembers, 'why the hell aren't you back in New Zealand looking after that country instead of doing all this shit?!?!' And I walked out and I refused to do anything more.'

In short, the unfortunate Kiwi probably got more of a

psychological insight into Nancy Wake than he'd bargained for. What's more, he'd had his own personality assessment done for free! Apparently though, her one-time countryman wasn't too put out by it, for she subsequently heard that the psychological report he had given on her mental strengths had been glowing.

It was while at the Mad House that Nancy met the man in charge of the whole shebang, Colonel Maurice Buckmaster. Buckmaster was an urbane yet energetic Englishman like they used to make 'em, and he and Nancy hit it off immediately. Like Nancy, he was a devoted Francophile who had lived in France as a young man while working as a tutor and, similarly, he had an extensive background as a journalist— having worked for the famous French newspaper *Le Matin* in Paris—before becoming the manager of the car-manufacturer Ford in the same city.

'He was a lovely man, an Englishman of the old school,' Nancy recollects, 'and I loved him. He was a gentleman, and he really cared for each and every one of us.'

It should be noted that this adoring view of Buckmaster was not universal. So successful were the operations the good colonel had helped set up, that the story had circulated that Hitler himself became aware of his name and is reputed to have said: 'When I get to London I do not know who I shall hang first—Churchill or this man Buckmaster!'[32]

Another person Nancy met in those first days and who made a big impression on her, was the conducting officer for the Mad House course, a radio expert by the name of Denis Rake, known to everyone as 'Denden' ...He was unlike any man she'd ever met before. Openly and proudly homosexual at a time when it was usually social 'death-at-the-box-office' to so proclaim oneself, he was charming, funny and, most importantly, an absolutely first-class radio operator who not only knew how to maximise the chances of any given radio sending a clear, clean signal back to London, but also understood so well the spaghetti of wires and transistors found inside most radio sets that he could give his students rudimentary instruction in how to fix any possible problem. Most of all, he was a man of extraordinarily varied experience and pedigree. He had joined the circus with his parents when he was only four years old, before his father had gone away to fight in the Great War and had finished up being executed by the Germans side by side with Edith Cavell. (Cavell was a British nurse working in a Belgium hospital during the First World War. She faced a German firing squad when they discovered her role in helping hundred of Allied forces to escape from behind German lines.) Denden continued to work under the big top over the next eighteen years all over the Continent, during which time he became fluent in the German and French languages. He was a man with a particularly rich and resonant voice and later in England he had appeared on the stage in such high-profile productions as *No, No, Nanette*. At World War II's outbreak Denden had gone immediately to France with the British Expeditionary Force before being evacuated at Dunkirk. He'd then joined the SOE, gone back to France, been captured, and then escaped. And still all of this was not the most remarkable thing about him!

Most extraordinary of all, in this context at least, was that he had succeeded as an SOE agent and was highly regarded *despite* the fact that he hated revolvers and refused to use or practice with one; despised parachutes and insisted he be sent into France by boat; and detested explosives and refused to have anything personally to do with blowing anything up. In any other organisation just one such refusal of basic practices might have been enough to see him expelled, but in many ways the SOE was designed specifically for eccentrics and Denden was a good enough radio operator that everything else about him was tolerated. For her part, Nancy got on well with him, though remained in wonder at his open and determined pursuit of a homosexual life.

'Denden thought,' Nancy recalls, not to put too fine a point on it, 'that every man *should* be homosexual, and if they weren't, it was just because they hadn't had a chance to try it with him yet.'

Not to worry, it didn't bother Nancy unduly, and all she knew was that she liked him.

Which was as well, for at one point right at the end of the course, she happened to enter a room where one of her fellow female trainees, a Frenchwoman, was having a furious argument with Denden. Nancy simply ignored it, going about her business as if nothing was happening at all. She didn't even look up when Denden shortly afterwards stormed out, slamming the door behind him. Nor was she particularly interested when the aggrieved woman began a tirade about what a disgrace he was, and how he would be better off completely out of SOE, and she was just the person to see that he was drummed out.

'Of course,' she continued, 'I'll need you to be a witness to how rude he was to me.'

Suddenly Nancy was all ears.

'I will do no such thing,' she announced grandly. 'It is absolutely nothing to do with me, and I happen to think that Denis Rake is a great asset. I would advise you to calm down and leave the whole thing alone.'

From there, things quickly turned nasty. The woman, sensing that Nancy might have been slightly tipsy after the lunch she had just returned from, accused her of being drunk, and quickly reported this 'fact' to one of SOE's more punctiliously proper officers, Selwyn Jepson, together with the fact that Ensign Wake was refusing to acknowledge what she had heard Rake saying to her. Jepson called for Nancy and upbraided her. She promptly told him, in highly specific terms, where he could stick his upbraiding. He, white-faced with fury, ordered her to leave the premises and return to her flat in London. She'd no sooner shut the door to her apartment and put her bags down, than a telegram arrived, informing her that she was required to send her FANY uniform back to SOE headquarters. It really looked as if her whole SOE experience would be over before it had truly begun. *C'est la vie.*

Thinking back, she says 'I was upset, but probably more upset at Jepson for throwing me out and the Frenchwoman who'd caused it all, than I was at losing my commission.' Well bugger 'em. She'd have another go at joining the Free French. But first, she rang the said SOE HQ and told them they could have their bloomin' uniform back, but only if that Jepson came to pick it up himself and apologised to her first![33]

Fortunately, even in these extremes, Nancy had many powerful friends in Britain's armed services—a lot of whom, like Garrow, probably owed their lives to her—and once apprised of her situation, they moved quickly. They explained to people in high places: yes, Nancy was volatile, passionate, fearless. Nancy was simply like that. It might be a problem in a training course, but it was *exactly* what was required of an agent living with the Maquis in France. Colonel Buckmaster, who'd been appalled at Jepson's action in the first place, had himself been manoeuvring to retrieve Nancy, and one way or another she was asked to come back in for another chat ... Everything was quickly smoothed over, and she was invited to rejoin the course.

'I was relieved,' Nancy says, 'but still not apologetic to Jepson or the Frenchwoman. I never wanted to see either of them again.'

From the Mad House, Nancy's next mission was to head up to Scotland where she had to do a lot more physical training. It was while on the train to Edinburgh that Nancy had cause to admire, as ever, the extraordinary resilience and cheerful stoicism of the British people. Never mind that the entire nation was at that time under the threat of daily German bombings and all out German invasion; never mind that a system of food rationing had been placed on them all. The Brits, clearly, were making the best of it, pip-pip, chin up and best foot forward, what?

'You see,' Nancy explains, 'when I looked out from the carriage window on the way up to Scotland, I was looking into the backyards and tiny gardens of all these houses that backed on to the railway line, and what do you think? They were all growing vegetables. All of them had these great vegetable patches going wherever there was a spare patch of dirt. They were magnificent! England, and the people in England, were growing everything themselves, never mind what the war had to say about it. And they could feed everybody. I've never forgotten it. I don't give a bugger what anybody says—we owe a lot to Britain. I loved Great Britain—and I will die loving it ... '

And so to the training ground proper. She arrived at a wonderfully picturesque part of the Scottish coastline called Inverie

Bay, and over the next two months the sun rose and fell on the lone female, Nancy, in a class of thirty-seven. Often their trainers were Dunkirk evacuees who had seen action in the thick of battle and who were now passing on the skills they had learned in the field, so this rising generation could go back and smack the enemy once and for all. It was a singularly intense period in Nancy's life and at its base was a simple rule, expounded by Colonel Buckmaster: 'Everything that the [trainees] did they had to do in the French manner,' he has written, 'whether it was combing their hair or leaving their knives and forks on their plates (or removing them from them), answering the telephone or calling for a waiter'.[34] This obsession with totally French-ifying all their agents extended to having a dentist on call who removed all English fillings in their teeth and replaced them with the far more Gallic-looking gold ones.

More to the point than just *looking* like natural born French though, was that they had to be highly trained operatives working behind enemy lines, capable of coping with all contingencies. One of the things the course taught them was that, with training, their hands could become lethal weapons. Certainly, when taking on the enemy it was preferable to be armed to the teeth with every modern weapon they could get their hands on, but there could well come a time when the only weapon to hand would be the hand itself and they had to be ready. With that in mind, all students were encouraged to do a series of tiny karate chops with their hands against the sides of tables and chairs constantly to turn the soft fleshy part into a more lethal hardness. They were also trained to strike an opponent's neck around two inches below the ear at a point where the spinal column was at its most vulnerable. Compared with the generally big brutes around her, Nancy was only eleven stone and five foot seven inches (about 170 cm), so she was never going to be able to generate a lot of physical power; but her instructors assured her that if she hit exactly the right spot she could still be effective enough to kill someone.

'It was odd in a way,' Nancy thinks back, 'learning how to kill someone in such a cold-blooded fashion using only your bare hands, because you could never actually believe that you would ever have to put it into operation, but I concentrated as hard as anyone on those lessons, against the day I *might* have to use it ...'

If the Mad House had got on her goat more than somewhat for the pure inanity of it, then the training in Scotland was right at the other end of the scale, for not only were the lessons there practical, but she was clearly learning things that she would need to know if she was going to be effective back in France. The students weren't just taught how to blow up a train, for example, they were taught how to do so to cause maximum damage to the enemy. The best thing, they were told, was to derail a goods train in a cutting—meaning that it would then be blocking the line for a long time, as it couldn't be easily moved aside. If it was a German troop train though, better do it on high ground as more Germans would be killed as it tumbled down the slopes. If there were possibly French on board though, they were to be more careful. Steer by the star of causing as much damage to the Germans as possible, and as little to the natives. Victory lay partly in having the local population fully behind them, not in killing them.

'It was mostly very good stuff,' Nancy remembers. 'If I could see the point of learning something, then I think I was a lot easier to get on with, and I certainly saw the point of a lot of what they were teaching us.'

There were further lessons in weapons training, in shooting with the latest weapons and in stripping, cleaning and reassembling Bren and Sten guns; in surveillance; Morse-code; radio work; how to disable a car with a handful of sugar, sand or even with a few spoonfuls of honey in the petrol tank; where best to place explosives to blow up a bridge; the *absolute* importance of punctuality when rendezvousing with another agent, and so on. All that said ...

'I was *not* going to let them rule me,' she affirms. 'I knew more about resistance work than they did, and I might sometimes have reminded them of that, but I also knew that I didn't know anything about explosives and that sort of thing, so I mostly behaved myself.'

Mostly anyway. As one account of her time there has it, 'for much of the course she cheated unashamedly, taking short cuts on cross-country runs, skipping physical training practice on the pretence of having a cold, and circumventing obstacle courses with an ingenuity that earned her full marks for initiative.'[35]

Ingenious always and that was just the way she was made, and it was fortunate for her that her instructors decided to put her approach down under the heading of *Initiative* and not *Cheating*. Even with such short cuts though, the course was nothing if not gruelling for the 31-year-old Nancy. After all, given her previous soft life living out of a champagne glass on the Riviera—her Pyrenees trek notwithstanding—it was no surprise that she finished most days extremely tired indeed.

At least there was some respite from all the endless drilling in deadliness and ceaseless instruction in insurrection.

'We also had a lot of fun, and a lot of laughter,' says Nancy. 'As a relief from the seriousness of everything else, there was a lot of skylarking and pranks and that sort of thing, and being a bit of a skylarker myself I absolutely loved it.'

Whatever the hardships of such a course, at least they were hardships shared with others, and she soon bonded closely with many of her fellow trainees as well as some of her instructors. In the evenings, they would all dine together in full uniform in the Officers' Mess and afterwards, if there were no night exercises arranged, Nancy and the others in their group would often drink until midnight. Far from being frowned upon by their superiors, such sessions were even encouraged, and for a very good reason.

As Maurice Buckmaster subsequently wrote in his book *They Fought Alone*, 'they were also primed with spirits to see how they behaved under the influence and whether their tongues were loosened in agreeable company'.[36] Recruits were similarly encouraged to participate in some light gambling with cards to determine if anyone had a problem in that field. This aversion to having someone with a gambling problem was for a very good reason. In the spring of 1942, SOE had trained up a professional gambler by the name of Nigel Low through much the same course as Nancy went through, and dropped him into France with a large sum of money in French francs to finance his designated Resistance group. 'Low reached the Riviera,' Colonel Buckmaster would write in 1958, 'and from that day to this we have never heard of him again!'[37]

At night, they would often be observed while they slept— sometimes when they were drunk, sometimes sober—to determine if they had a propensity for talking in their sleep, and if they did, in what language. If their drinking sessions then had a serious purpose from the point of view of the authorities, as far as the trainees went it was simply something to look forward to at the end of the day—and it was through such sessions that Nancy really came to know most intimately the people she was with. Once again, Nancy was the only woman on this part of the course, and there were many men who wanted to take this intimacy further still, but she was, for the most part, not interested. For the most part . . .

'There was one man,' she says carefully, 'an American, who was married and had three children. But whatever we had was momentary passion and brief companionship, it was not love.'

She still had not heard from Henri at this point, though it wasn't as if he actually had an address to write to her if he'd wanted to, nor a phone number to call. She often thought about him, and very much still loved him, but she had given him fair warning, had she not, that she would not necessarily be faithful to him while they were apart, and he was not to ask about it.

And so back to training. There were always more things to learn, such as how to live off the land should they ever have to survive deep in the forest without any provisions—this mostly involved wild turnips, hence its sometime sobriquet of 'the turnip course'. All of this was against the day when she would hopefully be dropped in France to actually start using all her new-found skills. But when would that day be? Nancy could do nothing but wait and hope that she would be assigned a mission soon after her training was over. Some ten weeks in, just as her time in Scotland was coming to an end, they heard that some of the big brass were coming up from London to check them out. Nancy suddenly conceived a great curiosity to know just what the report that was being assembled on her—as it was for every student—contained. Certainly it was going to be difficult to get her hands on that report, because it was locked in a filing cabinet in one of the administrative offices, but, after all, hadn't they just been taught how to pick locks and break into safes with no-one the wiser? By golly, they *had*! By comparison with working behind enemy lines, this would surely be a piece of cake . . .

So it was that Nancy together with Raymond—an extremely reluctant French fellow trainee whom she had roped in for the occasion—soon embarked on her own 'top secret' project. They wandered into the office during a particularly busy part of the day and, waiting until Nancy's query diverted the clerk's attention elsewhere, Nancy herself snatched the dangling key from its hook and pressed it into a lump of plasticine she had brought with her for the occasion. Done! A visit to the workshop the following day, some handy work with molten brass poured into the mould in the plasticine, and Bob was their *oncle*.

'That evening Raymond stood guard while I slipped into the office to try it out, and it worked!' Nancy exults.

She quickly scanned both their reports by the soft light of her torch. Nancy's report was very good, and she particularly remembers a phrase saying that 'Her morale and sense of humour encouraged everyone', and Raymond was also happy with his. Job done, to everyone's satisfaction!

After the long stint in Scotland was over, there remained a few more three-day training sessions to do at various sites around Britain. Perhaps most crucially of all—for without it working, all else would be wasted—they went to an establishment called Ringway near Manchester where they were given serious parachute training, a key skill which didn't necessarily come naturally to Nancy.

'Remember what your mother told you!' the instructor kept bellowing at her in a simulated exercise. 'Keep your knees together! Now roll, *roll* as you land!' Twice in her training program she was taken up in a plane at night and told to jump out—which she did—but she never liked it one little bit, and didn't mind saying so.

At another establishment, Beaulieu near Bournemouth, Nancy was taught the structure of the German armed forces and how to recognise rank from the insignia on the uniform, which regiments were responsible for which role in France, and how to determine what kind of German plane it was simply by looking at its silhouette. It was at the same place that she and her fellow trainees were instructed on how to maximise their chances of surviving a Gestapo interrogation. The bottom line in such interrogation, they were told, was to do everything possible to hold out for at least twenty-four hours to allow all those who would be compromised by your breaking time to get away. Nancy, as all the others, was dragged from her bed in the middle of the night and put through simulated questioning together with some rough treatment.

In yet another course, she was taught how to make amazingly powerful explosives from simple chemicals that you could buy over the counter at any pharmacy in France—on the chance that when they were on site in France that there might be a breakdown in supplies of explosives from London. Now, *now* they were talking!

'For me,' Nancy says, 'this was the best part of all the training because I didn't know anything at all about explosives and knew I needed to learn as much as I could. The key thing, as it turned out, was to make sure that all the ingredients were weighed absolutely precisely. So you would be down there in the morning for about four hours, weighing everything out, and then you'd blow it all up in about five seconds!' It was at this particular establishment that she met and became very friendly with one of the most famous of all of SOE's female operatives, Violette Szabo, the first female on a course with her in the last eleven weeks. Sadly, Szabo came to a very tragic, though heroic, end. While fighting with the Maquis in France several months later, she and a local partisan leader were ambushed by the Germans in the area of Salon-la-Tour and, in their rush to escape, Szabo fell with a grievously twisted ankle and could not continue. Insisting her comrade leave her, she used her last bullets to keep the Germans pinned down, allowing him to escape. When captured herself she was sent away to the infamous Ravensbruck concentration camp where she was executed. The story has a postscript ...

'Nearly two years afterwards, at Buckingham Palace, the King handed [Violette's] little daughter, Tania, the George Cross. "It is for your mother. Take great care of it," he said. As the little girl and Violette's parents came out of the palace, the photographers asked Tania to show them the medal. The little girl lifted it up. "It's for Mummy," she said. "I'll keep it for her till she comes home."'[38]

'We got up to a lot of mischief together,' Nancy remembers of the singularly beautiful Frenchwoman. 'I adored her. As women we always had an advantage over the men because of our common background in cooking. We were a lot more used to weighing out ingredients than they were. We slept in the same room, worked together, and loved it.'

As the only two women on this particular course the two came in for their share of good-natured 'ragging' from the men, all of which they took in good humour. When one particular instructor went a little far for their liking though, they decided to exact revenge.

'In front of everyone,' Nancy recounts, 'Violette and I jumped onto him. I held him down, and she took his pants off.'

In just a few minutes the instructor's pants were flying from the compound flagpole ... as the whole barracks rocked with laughter. When the conducting officer of the camp got their goat by not inviting them to a party, exclusively for staff and instructors, they decided to communicate their displeasure in an equally novel fashion.

'When he was out,' Nancy remembers, 'Violette and I took all the furniture out of his room and left it absolutely bare, with just his helmet left on the floor. And then we locked ourselves in our own room with all the furniture up against the door so he couldn't get in, and when he came back that night as drunk as anything he couldn't believe it, just couldn't believe it. He just stood there, and screamed and tried to break our door down, but it wouldn't give.'

Again, there was ultimately much laughter all round. Such were the times—all good friends and jolly good company, *Suh!*

At last, after sixteen weeks of intensive training, Colonel Buckmaster asked to see Nancy in the SOE flat at Orchard Court, which was mostly used to brief agents who were about to depart on their missions. She had seen a lot of the Colonel over the previous months when he would regularly drop into their training, and had always enjoyed their encounters.

'Nancy,' he began, 'I've looked at your report and it's very good indeed.'

'Yes, I know ...' she responded unthinkingly before suddenly stopping, appalled at what she had just said.

'What were you going to say?' the good Colonel rushed in. 'What? How? How could you possibly know what is in your report?'

Something in the way he said it, confirmed to Nancy that she could trust him.

'Do you promise you won't tell the General?' Buckmaster made no reply, so she charged on regardless. 'I broke into his office in the middle of the night, opened the safe and read it!' she said happily.

'You *what?*'

'I broke into his office in the middle of the night, opened the safe and read my report!'

'You WHAT!?!?!'

'Well you needn't shout at me, you taught me how to do it, you should be proud of me.'

Suddenly Buckmaster laughed, and shook his head ruefully.

'Nancy,' he said, 'we've got to get you out of this country straight away. You're a menace!'

While in any other branch of the services such an action might have seen an immediate court-martial being instituted against the perpetrator, in the case of the SOE this was exactly the sort of thing they were looking for in their recruits. Even allowing for his exclusive use of the male generic, Buckmaster's writings on this seem to fit Nancy well.

'All of our agents,' he penned in his reminiscences, 'possessed a quality which I can only describe as that most likely to make an officer—initiative. We had no use for those who could not think for themselves and we placed a premium on those whose common sense could be relied upon. Inflexibility was the most dangerous drawback to a man's selection; a man had to make his own appraisal of a situation, obeying where obedience was necessary, acting on his own good authority where he found a good cause to vary the judgement of superior officers.

'It was no use trying to do things by the book. There was no book.'[39]

One of Buckmaster's key offsiders at the SOE, Vera Atkins, later reminisced about Nancy thus:

'Ah Nancy. She was a real Australian bombshell. Tremendous vitality, flashing eyes. Everything she did, she did well. With all her gay laughter, she had a serious and sensitive streak.'[40]

Despite this assessment, at the time Atkins expressed doubts to the Colonel about the Australian, wondering if she would be up to making an impact in France when she did not have a rich husband and all his resources to back her up. Buckmaster overruled her.

Now, where was he ...? Ah, yes, telling Nancy about her forthcoming mission. She was ready, he said, to be dropped back into France and that this would happen possibly as soon as the following Friday, 28 April, 1944. She would, indeed, be the first of her whole group to be sent. Nancy listened, spellbound, as he explained her mission. She would be dropping, she was told, just a hundred kilometres from Vichy itself, into l'Auvergne—in an area near the town of Montluçon with which she already had a passing acquaintance from her many journalistic sorties through the French provinces.

It was extremely rugged country, she knew, with most of it belonging to the famously unforgiving Massif Central, and in the kind of business she was to be engaged in, l'Auvergne was clearly among the best of all possible worlds to be operating in. For if the Atlantic Ocean was God's gift to fishes, and the Sahara desert came as the particularly generous gesture He made towards dust mites, then l'Auvergne was equally among His greatest of gifts to guerrilla fighters. Mostly mountainous and inaccessible, with peaks as high as two thousand metres, it was covered in thick forests and was criss-crossed by many tiny back roads. Scattered around and about were various farmhouses, the hardy occupants of which would be almost exclusively anti-German. It was known as *la fortresse de la France* for the very good reason that it was just that. What it meant was that huge bodies of Maquis could live in comparative safety deep in the woodlands, and yet still be able to get out quickly and hit the Germans hard, before just as quickly melting away again. There were several thousand Maquis there, she was told, and her job was to make contact with them, assess their needs—both financially and for arms—then organise by radio for parachute drops from Britain to fulfil those needs. Then came the hard part, to train the Maquis up from there. Nancy couldn't wait to get started.

This operation was vintage stuff for the SOE, as M.R.D. Foot explains:

'The Special Operations Executive's task was to co-ordinate subversive and sabotage activity against the enemy; even if necessary to initiate it. In every German-occupied country there were spontaneous outbursts of national fury at Nazi rule. SOE's objects included discovering where these outbursts were, encouraging them when they were feeble, arming their members as they grew, and coaxing them when they were strong into the channels of common advantage to the Allies.'[41]

Although Nancy would be only one of many SOE operatives lighting such fires, it was a crucial role and one that she was raring to fulfil.

She would be accompanied on her mission by Major John Farmer, code-named 'Hubert', who had joined Nancy's training program near the end and whom she knew slightly. Her radio operator, she was delighted to find out, would be none other than the man she'd been nearly kicked out of the SOE for trying to protect, Denis Rake! The two had always got on well, the more so since the episode with the accusing Frenchwoman, and she looked forward to working with him. A minor complication was that because Rake point blank refused to jump out of any bleedin' aeroplane, he was to be flown in and landed by a tiny Lysander plane at a safe spot several hundred kilometres away, to make his own way to join them just a couple of days later.

As for Nancy, her own code-name would be 'Madame Andrée' to the French Resistance, and 'Hélène' to London. In this business, where double agents abounded and you could be betrayed at any time, pseudonyms and code-names were everything. Everyone in the Resistance movement was assiduously trained never to refer to other partisans by their real name, even if they knew it. That way, when one of theirs 'turned'—perhaps under torture—the damage could at least be limited. The reason, therefore, that Nancy had two code-names was so that even if she were compromised in France, she would not necessarily be compromised in England and vice-versa. As to the code she would use when communicating with London, like every agent she was required to choose a memorised verse or poem on which the code for subsequent messages about armament drops and the like could be based. Most others chose biblical passages or benign poems that they were familiar with, but Nancy wouldn't cop a boring verse. Her personal code line for the SOE during the war was this:

> She stood right there,
> In the moonlight fair,
> And the moon shone,
> Through her nightie,
> It lit right on,
> The nipple of her tit,
> Oh Jesus Christ Almighty!

Such a bawdy verse was typical of the temper of her times. Yes, they were engaged in a life and death struggle against a deadly foe, and, yes, the stakes were huge, but there was still time for a laugh, and Nancy certainly did her fair share.

On the last night before heading off on her mission, the Thursday before the scheduled Friday jump, Nancy and her closest companions from the training course went to the famed Astor nightclub in Piccadilly and not only danced up a storm to the sound of the big band playing such songs as *In The Mood* and *As Time Goes By*, but drank as if there were no tomorrow.

'Well,' Nancy allows, 'we were *fairly* sure that there would be a tomorrow, but there was absolutely no guarantee that there would be a day after that.'

So they drank, and laughed, and danced, and drank and laughed and danced some more. One of her male friends from the training course with whom she danced that night was René Dusacq, a former Hollywood stunt man—in one movie he stood in for the swashbuckling Errol Flynn—and now a first class weapons instructor. At one point, in a quiet dark corner of the club with Nancy he had become briefly emotional at the thought that they would all soon be separated to go their different ways, and there was no telling how many of them would survive to meet again ... but the moment quickly passed. In fact no-one wanted to dwell too long on the possibilities of disaster befalling them, and it was never a subject that they considered for long. And, well, if they all held each other a little more tightly when they danced to the sound of the band singing a cover version of Vera Lynn's famous lyrics, '*We'll meet again*', then it was quite understandable.

And so it was that at four o'clock in the morning, they were outside the Astor Club on the street and as drunk as lords weaving their way down along Piccadilly towards Nancy's flat. Every fifty metres they would do parachute rolls just as they had been taught—arm forward and curved to break the fall, legs tightly together—even as all of them sang an entirely different song at the top of their voices: '*Gory, gory what a helluva way to die, gory, gory what a helluva way to die, and we ain't gonna jump no more ...*'

CHAPTER TEN

.⸺

Back to France

'Set Europe ablaze.'

WINSTON CHURCHILL

His original instructions to the Special Operations Executive in 1940,
their guiding charter, as it were.

'Tu sais, quand tout cela sera fini, nous dirons—
c'etait le bon temps, quand meme.'

'You know, when all this is over, we will say—these were still good times.'

FINAL LINES OF *Les Croix de Bois* [42]

And this *would* be a helluva way to die, Nancy thought grimly two nights later. She was sitting on the cold floor in the back of the Liberator B–24 on the way to her drop-off point and desperately trying not to vomit into her oxygen mask. When her original mission had been delayed by a day to give her and Hubert more time to memorise all the key details, she had headed off to the Astor Club again that night, where much the same revelry occurred as the night before. She woke that morning with the worst double hangover of her life, felt wretched throughout the day, and then made the singular mistake of eating Spam sandwiches and drinking coffee before taking off just after 10 p.m. Greenwich Mean Time from a military airfield in southern England. She'd eaten them just before Colonel Buckmaster had turned up at the airfield to wish Nancy and Hubert all the best and to present them with small gifts, Nancy receiving a small silver compact makeup case. (War or no war, he knew well enough by now that Nancy always liked to look her best.) The good colonel kissed her goodbye—in the French fashion of course—with a gentle peck on the fleshy parts of both cheeks.

'I tried as often as my work at the office allowed,' he has written, 'to accompany the [agents] to the aerodrome, for this moment before take-off was the most upsetting to the nerves; it was then that melancholy or morbid presentiments could most easily assert themselves.'[43]

Well, he wasn't going to let that happen here ... the very last words he said to Nancy as she disappeared into the bowels of the plane were, '*Alors Andrée, je te souhaite une bonne merde*'. While the literal translation of this is more than a little vulgar—'Well, Andrée, I wish you a good shit'—what he meant by it was, 'I wish you luck'.

(This curious cultural quirk of language dates back to the Battle of Waterloo in 1815 when the French suffered one of their most infamous defeats at the hands of the English, beaten almost across the board—except in one part. Enter General Pierre-Jacques-Etienne Cambronne. At a point when his men were badly outnumbered and were falling back at the hands of the overpowering Britons, the English General called out to Cambronne to surrender himself and his troops. Cambronne replied '*la garde meurt mais ne se rend pas!*', essentially 'my men will die sooner than surrender'. The English General repeated the demand, and Cambronne gave the same reply. For a third time came the demand, and this time Cambronne exploded with a one word response 'MERDE!' So the legend goes, his men took up the cry and, suddenly motivated as never before, charged the British and won the day. A sterling tradition was born. For Nancy, it was a charming thing for Buckmaster to say, and infinitely better than the encouragement he might have delivered had he kept to the English tradition of 'Break a leg!')

As the flight of the Liberator continued, Nancy felt worse, with her temples pounding and a general queasiness rising which simply would not quit. Those Spam sandwiches were right there. She wasn't quite sure what would happen if she vomited inside her oxygen mask at an altitude of fifteen thousand feet but she felt sure it wouldn't be healthy. There was nothing to do but keep swallowing, and hope for the best.

The Liberator B–24—powered by four 1,200-horsepower engines sucking in a combined total of 2,750 gallons of fuel— droned through the night. Though nowhere nearly as famous as the legendary B–17 'Flying Fortress', for a mission such as this the B–24 was perfect as it could not only fly higher than the B–17, and further and faster, but most crucially it could take more punishment from the 'ack-ack' guns below than any plane in service. This was just as well, because as this one came in over the coast of France, the German guns below sent up their traditional welcome to all planes coming from England, and many of the explosions were uncomfortably close, with each near miss sending the plane bucking like a wild bronco jumping up and over every cloud. Nancy, still with a severe hangover and freezing to boot— the B–24s were neither pressurised nor heated—simply rode it out.

'There was nothing else you could do in situations like that,' she says simply. 'If you were religious I suppose you might have prayed, but I wasn't so I just had to hope that none of their flak would hit and bring us down.'

Less on a wing and prayer than a wing and a wish, Nancy Wake continued on her appointed course through the night. However precarious their situation, at least she knew that the pilot and crew were experienced in these matters. In the first three months of 1944, Churchill's Wartime Cabinet had moved operations arming the Maquis right up to number two on their priority list, just behind sending bombs right down German Jerry's throat. So it was that the RAF, with the aid of two squadrons of Liberators from the US Army Air Forces, had successfully flown 759 missions in which they dropped either operatives such as Nancy and Major Farmer or matériel to the Maquis below. This was a seven hundred per cent increase on the number of missions completed in the final quarter of the previous year.

As the Liberator bomber at last left the worst of the ack-ack fire behind it, Nancy's thoughts turned to what might lay before her.

The short answer was that once they had landed, they would be met by one of their own agents already on the ground in the region, Maurice Southgate, and he would facilitate their meeting shortly afterwards with the Big Boss of the Resistance in that area, a man by the name of Gaspard. After that, they were on their own. London's information was that Gaspard commanded somewhere between three and four thousand Maquis in separate groups concentrated around l'Auvergne. Nancy's and Hubert's mission was to assess the fighting capabilities of these groups, their needs for weaponry and finance, and subsequently advise London via Denden, their radio operator, who would shortly be joining them. From that point on, they were to do all in their power to turn the Resistance of the Auvergne into Germany's worst nightmare and ...

And suddenly, it was time. Just after 1 a.m. local time on the morning of 31 March, 1994—a little over two hours since they had taken off—the aperture in the floor of the plane opened, the wind whipped inside and they saw the darkened French countryside appear in the silky soft moonlight some six hundred feet beneath them. 'Dropping zone up ahead,' came the rather strained Texan drawl of pilot Harold Van Zyl through the intercom. Nancy—trying desperately to recover from yet another very strong urge to vomit—made ready, checking for the umpteenth time that the straps on her parachute were just so, that she had done everything possible to ensure that when the parachute flew free and hopefully caught the air, she would stay fully attached to it.

She was dressed, oddly enough, as simply a very lumpy version of her normal self. For the jump she had on her favourite camel-hair coat atop regulation army overalls, but beneath this army issue she wore silk stockings and stylish shoes beneath heavily bandaged ankles to protect her bones and tendons against the impact of landing. In the pockets of these clothes were two revolvers. On her head, a tin hat. In her small backpack, she had several changes of clothes and, among other things, a red satin cushion that she simply adored and two hand-embroidered nightdresses she'd insisted on bringing. On her arm, topping the whole thing off, her handbag stuffed full of just over one million

French francs with which she hoped to help finance the Maquis, plus her favourite red Chanel lipstick and tightly packed articles of feminine hygiene, while securely memorised in her head she had a list of targets for demolition—railway junctions, bridges, underground cables and factories that had to be attacked and destroyed the moment D-Day arrived. In the same spot, securely stored away, she also had the addresses of various safe houses in the area, together with the names of their residents and the passwords by which she would be recognised. Finally, secreted in the second button on the cuff of her left sleeve was a cyanide pill which guaranteed an all-but-instant death should she ever find herself in a situation where that was clearly preferable to what lay before her.

In short, if she had landed just next to the claret jug at a top-of-the-line French dinner party, she could have been ready for action and passing the camembert in all of thirty seconds—*or* she could have landed in the middle of a fire-fight between Germans and partisans, and equally have acquitted herself well.

It was as well to have all contingencies covered, because truth be told none of them, not the SOE back in London, not the pilot nor the navigator, neither she nor Hubert, had the first idea just what kind of reception they were about to receive. Standing beside the open bomb-bay—what the Americans called a 'Joe-hole' by reason of the 'Joe' who jumped through it—with the wind pulling at the pant-legs of her overalls and making that urgent flapping sound, Nancy gazed into the howling abyss to see just what it was that she would be jumping into. And there she saw it.

Down in the darkness, she could now clearly see huge bonfires burning, and off to the side a discreet light flashing on and off. For all she knew, she was about to descend into the rim-fires of Hell her mother had long promised her—complete with a control tower to guide her in—but, more likely, this was indeed the promised reception from the Maquisards of the Auvergne. The Liberator made several circles of the airfield, ascertaining just which would be the best line to make the drop, and then pulled away in a long and lazy loop before coming in for the pay-dirt run. Hubert went first, stepping forward into the hungry and gaping maw, causing the static line connected to his parachute to suddenly snap taut and so automatically release it. Then it was Nancy's turn. Her turn ...

The dispatcher signalled it was her time to jump. There is usually a moment's hesitation among parachutists new to the art when the time comes to actually leap—a moment in which they consider whether or not to forgo all this madness and possibly say 'I'm *not* going to do it', before firmly sitting back down—but Nancy maintains that in this case she was an exception.

'I have never been so pleased to get out of a plane in my life,' she says. 'The Spam sandwich and coffee were still going round and around. I will always remember the dispatcher, seeing me white in the face and wanting to puke, saying "If you're afraid, Witch, we'll take you back" and I said, "All I want to do is get out of this bloody plane"!' (Such a last-second refusal had in fact happened before, most inauspiciously on the occasion when the first SOE agent was due to be dropped into France on the night of 14 November, 1940. Arriving over the designated target area in Brittany, the agent had an overwhelming panic attack and point-blank refused to jump. They all went home.)

Nancy did however ask the dispatcher for one little bit of help. The dispatcher was a nice kind of bloke from Colorado by the name of Hank Hettinger, to whom she'd chatted briefly before the flight had taken off. As Hettinger, now living in Lakewood, Colorado, remembers, 'She asked me to give her a push. She wasn't going to back off, and she was very brave—the only woman we ever dropped—but she wanted me to get behind her and push her into the 'Joe-hole' at the right moment. I waited until exactly the right moment, and gave her a big shove.'

Before Nancy knew it she was out there and falling. Immediately, her own ripcord was pulled open by the line connected to the plane. From the sudden rush of cold air all around her, she felt the blessed braking and then the sudden surge upwards as the parachute flared out, and she began slowly wafting downwards. By the time she was within perhaps three hundred feet of the ground, she felt her tension rise again and for obvious reason. She knew that by now she would be clearly visible to those on the ground and if this were an ambush, or if there were any Germans on the field, the bullets would be coming her way shortly. A parachutist is never so vulnerable as when suspended in the sky—at which point a single bullet through the large target of the open canopy could send the flyer tumbling to a certain death—and there was absolutely nothing Nancy could do but wait suspended in the blackness. But, happily, no bullets. She simply continued her descent unmolested, though despite her frantic tuggings on the right side of her parachute, nothing could prevent her from drifting away from the field with the bonfires. Instead, she was carried to an adjacent field where she landed in a bloody great tree, with the parachute itself caught in the upper branches. The insufferable *indignity* of it!

In the middle of the night, it was as silent as it was dark. 'Black as the pitch from pole to pole', she couldn't see even the tiniest glimmer of the bonfires that she knew were nearby. Downwind she could even smell the smoke from them, momentarily evoking memories for her of when the Germans had torched the Vieux Port of Marseille. Then she heard voices. Coming closer. '*Ahhh, voilà un parachute là-bas!*' a voice cried out. There was no instant relief to hear that the language used was French. Nancy knew only too well from her own bitter experience that a French voice was no guarantee that its owner was not in cahoots with the Germans and as the voices came closer she drew her revolver. Suddenly, from right beneath her, came a clear resonant French voice, too beautiful and laced with humour to possibly belong to someone about to shoot her.

'Ahhh, that England should send us such a beautiful flower,' came the rich, laughing voice of a man.

Just as she had planned, though in an entirely different fashion, Nancy returned fire.

'Cut out that French bullshit and get me out of this tree,' she growled, as she finally located the release mechanism of her parachute and pulled it.

No sooner said than done, she was shortly standing beside a singularly good-looking Frenchman by the name of Henri Tardivat, a thirty-something one-time maths teacher and rugby player from the nearby town of Montluçon, who was the leader of the local Resistance movement. As it turned out, he was the one who had been assigned to meet her and Hubert and he had never even heard of this Southgate that was meant to be meeting them. Of him, there was certainly no sign, but looking at Tardivat Nancy didn't actually mind that much. Something about this bloke was very reassuring, and it was a charming beginning to what would be a good and enduring relationship between her and 'Tardi', as she soon came to call him.

There would still be problems to overcome initially, and the first of them came right then and there. SOE training had impressed upon them the necessity of burying their parachutes as soon as they landed—so as to rid themselves of the worst of the incriminating evidence—but when she set out to do just that, Tardivat intervened. Fabric as sheer as this, he said, while stroking it rather sensuously, was far too rare in wartime France and there were a dozen different uses to which it could be put, none of which included putting it beneath the soil to rot.

'I argued and argued,' Nancy recalled, 'but he simply would not be moved.'

She finally relented and they got going, the parachute carefully secreted in the boot of Tardivat's car.

Back in London at that time, Colonel Buckmaster would likely have been woken from his slumber to receive a cryptic phone call.

'Two umbrellas have been seen around Central,' a voice would have told him. (Two parachute drops have been successfully made in l'Auvergne.)

'Well, I hope they've rolled them up and taken a nice stroll down the mall,' he would have replied. (I hope they've got rid of their chutes and moved off to their rendezvous.)[44]

Well, at least the last part of that was true.

With the headlights of his car extinguished for stealth, Tardivat whisked Hubert and Nancy away to the nearby village of Cosne-d'Allier, where they were put up in the home of one of the local sympathisers, a man by the name of 'Jean', and his wife. And nice people they were too, but very, very French. Soooo French were they that when, very late that night, after having many nightcaps with their hosts, Nancy and Hubert were shown to their sleeping quarters, they were staggered to see *one* double bed awaiting them! Nancy looked at Hubert. Hubert looked at her. They both looked at their hosts. The hosts looked back at them. What was *zeee* problem? After some discussion, Jean and his wife could vaguely understand why Nancy didn't want to sleep in the same bed as Hubert, but just why Hubert would have a problem sleeping in the same bed with Nancy was simply beyond them! In any case that bed was the only soft horizontal surface they had available so there really was no choice. Nancy finally slept beneath the bedclothes, while Hubert slept upon them, covered in coats.

It was a rather awkward beginning to what would always be a rather awkward relationship between them. Some partnerships, of course, have a natural chemistry, where everything just clicks from the first to the last moment. Others don't. Nancy's and Hubert's was of the latter variety. Both were dedicated, professional and courageous SOE agents. Neither though, it is fair to say, soared to the highest summits of their spirit while with the other.

'Once he got his uniform on later, he was okay,' Nancy concedes grudgingly, 'but before that he was a pain ...'

'Hubert', for his part, actually John Farmer of course, now eighty-four years old and living in France just across the border from Geneva, also acknowledges that theirs was not a match made in heaven.

'She was a woman of very high energy,' he says. 'Incredibly high energy, but she also had very clear ideas of how she wanted everything to be done, and how she wanted everything done was *her* way. She was a great agent, there was no doubt about that, but not always the easiest to get on with ...'[45]

But fortunately, one way or another, the two would work out their differences and operate together professionally.

The plan from here called for them to lie low and out of sight until the SOE man on the ground, Maurice Southgate, came for them. But 'lying low and out of sight' was never something that came easily to the oft excessively exuberant Nancy, so when after two days of inaction her hostess invited her to come for *une petite promenade autour de la ville*, she thought '*Pourquoi pas?*'. Why not, indeed? A few minutes later the two were out in the village square, while Hubert stayed back in the house. Amazingly, for an operation that was meant to be top secret, most of the villagers seemed to know exactly what Nancy was doing there and why she had come ... and were most happy about it. Nancy should have been worried, she supposed, that their arrival in France had not been entirely secret but, in spite of her concerns, she was happy to chat. Clearly, this was a part of France that had never rolled over to either the Germans or Pétain, and she actually felt that she was on reasonably safe territory. And, in a way, she was reliant on the instincts of her hostess, who was risking every bit as much as Nancy if the Germans ever caught up with them. If *she* felt that it was safe, Nancy reasoned, then it probably was. Hubert expressed a different opinion when she got back to the house and explained what she had been doing. He was all for abandoning the house then and there, and starting again at one of the other safe houses, but after discussion they decided to give it one more night. The way Nancy saw it, if the village knew they were there, so too would Southgate, their starting point for getting to Gaspard.

The following morning one of Southgate's men, Hector, did indeed arrive. He walked into Nancy's bedroom unannounced just as she was soaking her feet in a large basin of hot water, and was lucky not to receive a bullet from the revolver she had by her side.

'After all,' she reasoned, 'this was a man whom I'd never met, coming into my room without knocking, and for all I knew he could have been Gestapo ... '

But that calamity averted, she and Hubert were all soon hail-fellow-well-met with Hector, who informed them that Southgate sent his regards, but he was having a spot of bother with the local Gestapo and had his hands full at that time. Hector promised that, in his stead, within at least two days either he or one of his men would be back to take them to see Gaspard. Good. But after two days, and then three, there had still been no contact and, as it turned out, they were destined never to see Hector again, just as they would never make the promised contact with Southgate. Something, somewhere, had gone very wrong. (They heard shortly afterwards that both men had been arrested by the Gestapo.)

A week after landing in France, they were still no closer to making contact with Gaspard and decided that they would have to start rowing their own boat. After long discussion she and Hubert decided to tell Jean exactly who it was that they were trying to reach and see if he had any ideas about how they might get to him. If in one way this move contravened the way they had been trained—tell nothing to anyone, not anything, not ever—then in another way it was classic SOE strategy. That is, effective agents had to adapt to the environment in which they found themselves, *sniff* out a way to go forward whatever the obstructions. Jean had no idea where Gaspard might be found, but he at least had a fair clue where one of the lesser leaders, Laurent, could be contacted, and was happy to take them there. The following morning, they set out in Jean's ancient car—a *gazogène*, meaning it was fuelled by charcoal!—and by going from contact to contact throughout the day, each one getting them closer to Laurent, by nightfall they had actually made their way into the latter's camp high in the hills in an abandoned chateau perhaps twenty kilometres outside Montluçon.

Nancy looked around the gathered group of Laurent's fighters, her eyes taking in the myriad details of what these famed Maquis actually looked like in the flesh. The first thing that came to mind was 'haggard'. For all their mightly legend, they looked to a man unwashed, underfed, bedraggled, bellicose and slightly hunted … but committed to their cause regardless. Laurent himself was a classic compact Frenchman in his middle age, who was at least delighted to see them and promised to contact Gaspard. He apologised for the difficulty they had experienced in reaching him, but given that the Gestapo was also looking for him at the time—courtesy of the fact that a fortnight before he had shot dead several Germans in Clermont-Ferrand—he and his men had decided that a certain 'uncontactibility' had its usefulness.

Doubtless, Gaspard felt much the same way and for much the same reasons. Still, Laurent felt he could find him all right and shortly thereafter he disappeared on the promise that he would make it happen. Three days later, he was as good as his word.

After a twisted and turning trip through many back roads, Nancy and Hubert were ushered into the great man's presence at his citadel in the deep forest near Saint Flour. In person, Gaspard proved to be a tall and extremely self-satisfied sort of man of great presence and a bully-like kind of bearing. He, in strict contrast to the way Laurent had received the SOE duo, informed them that he had no idea who they were or what they were doing here, and neither was he particularly interested in their promise that they could provide munitions for him. So ... pretty much ... *adieu*. Right. They would find out later that Gaspard passionately believed that his group would be receiving help from de Gaulle's Free French forces in North Africa, and so viewed it as disloyal even to think about taking aid from *les Britanniques*.

At the time, Gaspard made it clear that his dismissive views were simply not to be argued with. He was, after all, the leader of thousands of desperadoes and he would not argue the toss with a couple of blow-ins from Britain who'd sailed in out of a clear night sky—and who, if they were successful, were obviously going to challenge his absolute authority. Furthermore, the fact that Nancy and Hubert still didn't have a radio operator meant that they had very little ammunition to use against him even if they had wanted to. Well, that was that then.

Hubert and Nancy took themselves off a little to discuss what their next move should be, while Gaspard and his men held their own pow-wow in the kitchen. Fortunately for the SOE agents, they did so in front of an open window and Nancy overheard a particularly crucial part of their grand plan. Having heard rumours of just what SOE agents carried with them, Gaspard's men were convinced that she must have a lot of money on her at the very least, and one of them volunteered to seduce her, take the money, and then kill her that very evening! Oddly enough for a lone woman in the middle of four thousand male Maquis, Nancy maintains that news of this plan did not panic her. 'I'd have broken his *fucking neck*!' she says flatly, confident at least that all of her rigorous silent-killing training would at least serve for something. It had, after all, now become second nature to her to keep tapping the lower side of her hands on tables to harden them and turn them, as promised, into lethal weapons. And indeed she might have broken his neck, but it proved unnecessary. That evening after dinner, when the man in question made his first moves by enquiring whether she would like to go for a little walk, she let him have it point blank.

'Je suppose que tu veux coucher avec moi?' she asked him flatly.

'I ... I ... would be most honoured,' the man stammered in reply, not quite sure where this was leading or whether he loved or hated it.

'And then kill me and take my money ... is that the plan?'

'*Non, non, non!*'

The man flat-out denied it, his hands out wide in defensive supplication. Clearly this woman was a lot more than they had bargained for.

This impression was confirmed that night. It so happened that Nancy and Hubert had arrived at a time when Gaspard's Maquis were preparing a raid for that very evening to the nearby town of Saint Flour, where the owner of the sportstore was a known *collaborateur*—and, the way they saw it, he needed to be encouraged to do his bit for the cause. That is, they wanted to drive into town beneath the noses of the German garrison, smash the store windows, quickly help themselves to whatever they fancied, particularly boots, tents and every bit of camping equipment they could get their hands on, then head for the hills.

It sounded like an extremely good idea to Nancy, she wanted to go, and said so ...

'*Quoi?*' said Judex, the strapping Maquisard organising the raid, stupefied. What?

'*Je ... veux ... y ... aller,*' replied Nancy, for all the world as if she were talking to a notably stupid person who needed careful enunciation so he could understand. The Maquisard thought it not right, and much too dangerous for a woman to make such a trip. Nancy replied, in suitably graphic language, using the very best of the French swear words she'd picked up over the years, that she actually couldn't give a shit what he thought about it, because she had come here to help them fight and that was exactly what she was going to do.

So she went. And then a funny thing happened. Somewhere around the time of the glass breaking and her tearing through the store filling her arms with everything she could carry and then squealing away in the truck—with rubber burning and alarms ringing behind them—she remembers having a sudden surge of optimism, confidence and pleasure, for the first time since parachuting into France.

'I decided I *liked* this kind of thing,' she recalls.

This was a lot more like it! Yes, she had been happy and honoured to do her part to help stranded Allied forces and other refugees move along the Pat O'Leary Line and to do all that courier work for the Resistance movement; but the truth of it was that that kind of work also entailed endless hours of waiting, of standing in trains, of always taking the long way around instead of pursuing her natural instinct which was 'damn the torpedoes, full speed ahead!'. But if she really could establish herself as a member of her own band of Maquis—and essentially become a fully fledged Maquisard herself—she would be in the thick of the action, not dodging the enemy all the time, but every now and then just storming the ramparts just like this.

But however impressed the other Maquisards had been with her actions on this occasion, and Gaspard did hear of it, the problem remained. Without Denden, the radio man, Nancy and Hubert were as near as useless. With this in mind, they were amenable to Gaspard's 'Plan B', which would see them 'parked' with one of the lesser leaders of the Resistance, Henri Fournier, who could be found in the picturesque village of Chaudes-Aigues, high in the *département* of the Cantal, named for its abundant hot springs.

Fournier had his own band of Maquis, and he might very well be interested in what they had to offer, Gaspard told them dubiously, in the manner of a man who was fairly certain that they had nothing to offer *him* whatsoever. Still, it was a shrewd move on Gaspard's part, because if it turned out that these two pests could produce their promised weaponry then he could always claim them back. But in the meantime they were Fournier's problem.

By sharp contrast to Gaspard, this Henri Fournier was their sort of man. Not only did this former hotel executive not promote any plans whereby Nancy would be ravished, robbed and killed, but he also came across as a plainly decent man. The fact that he had used a lot of his own money to finance his group of Maquisards also impressed them, as did the fact that he privately acknowledged that Gaspard could be as difficult as Chinese calculus. He soon had them installed in a hotel in a remote village even higher in the hills, called Lieutadès, and promised he would be in regular contact to see that they had all they needed until their radio operator arrived. Speaking of whom ... *where the hell was Denden!?!?*

'It was the most incredibly frustrating thing,' she says, 'to be actually in France, fully trained and ready to go, and yet without a radio operator it was worse than hopeless. The radio was the pipeline to the power of London, and if you didn't have it you were more a hindrance than help to the group you'd come there to aid.'

At last though, *at last*, one bright morning in the middle of May, while Nancy was sitting on the wall of the Lieutadès cemetery, a car pulled up and out hopped Denis Rake wanting to know if she had already picked a suitable plot for herself.

'Denden, you darling,' Nancy exploded. 'Where have you *been*?!?!'

Don't ask. Essentially, they soon found out, he had been pursuing an amorous affair with a man he had met in London several weeks before. Denden mouthed some inanities about how sorry he was to have kept them waiting, but his heart didn't really seem to be in it. To Nancy's mind, it was clear he had been having the most *ravishing* time with the new love of his life while they had been simply wasting their time without him.

But it was good to see him anyway. And while Denden wasn't necessarily thrilled to see Hubert, he was very pleased to see her.

He would tell Nancy later that when they had first told him that he would be returning to France to work as a radio operator for a female, he'd had a right *turn*, didn't he, point blank refusing 'to work for any skirt'.

'But you know her,' they replied, 'you've already met Nancy in your courses.'

'Oh, *Nancy*,' he had sagged with relief. 'Well, why didn't you say so? That's different. Of course I'll go.'[46]

It was time to get to work. In their specific line of business that meant judging each Maquis group's needs and then radioing London to parachute the supplies in to them. At least Nancy had spent her time waiting for Denden in assessing Fournier's group and her conclusion there was overwhelmingly positive. Not only did his group of Maquis need arms, she thought, but clearly they *deserved* them.

'In my experience there,' she thinks back, 'the most important thing in judging the quality of a group of Maquis, was the quality of their leader. If he was up to it, and could not only impose discipline but organise them into a cohesive fighting unit, then they were worth backing. But if he was just an outlaw by another name, with no real idea how to form his men into an effective force, then I was not so inclined.'

Clearly, Fournier and his men fitted into the former category. Fournier was a fine man who was strong enough to impose his will on the band around him. If they had leadership, they certainly needed weaponry. Mere courage would never get them far in this game, and their assorted hotch-potch of rifles, hand guns, knives and wire garrottes would be no match against an enemy with a machine-gun.

Fournier was delighted with their plans and to know that shortly planes from London would be dropping whatever he needed. They proceeded to organise just that. Fournier and Hubert made lists of required weaponry and ammunition, while Nancy helped Denis Rake to code it, and the latter warmed up the radio set he had brought with him to beam it all back to England. This proved to be a model of the way their little SOE unit worked for the rest of their time in France. Essentially Hubert would deal with the Maquis on plans of military tactics and strategies, while Nancy was the one to assess their needs and organise the drops, and Denden was the one who sent the message. If this meant that Nancy was left in the supremely powerful position of holding the purse strings for thousands of men—she wasn't complaining!

As it turned out, their first night of transmission proved to be a fizzer as Denis had got his dates mixed up and no-one was listening at the other end. The system—contrived to thwart the efforts of German detector vans searching for the likes of them—was that every date had a different transmission time when London would be listening specifically for them. They were expected at 6.53 p.m. on 17 May, for example, 5.32 p.m. on 18 May, and so on. But if they missed their 'skeddy' (short for schedule), then they were unlikely to get through.

It was a mild annoyance and the following night the Morse-message went up the wobbling antenna, waving in the slight breeze, and out from there. It was received loud and clear at exactly the right time far away in a beautiful country manor in rural England, in Kent, where no fewer than five hundred men and women on rotating shifts were exclusively devoted to receiving the agents' signals and then translating the codes. From their first transmission, Colonel Buckmaster would have been informed 'A frog is croaking in the mountains' (A radio transmission has been received from l'Auvergne.) Back in France, Nancy and the said 'frog', Denis, shortly afterwards received confirmation from London that the drop was on, and then some short time later the whole lot of them waited by a bonfire on a plateau on a mountain right beside Chaudes-Aigues. Around them, perhaps forty Maquisards, gazed expectantly towards the west from where the planes would come—if indeed this pretty *demoiselle* could deliver what she had promised, and the looks in their eyes said they were far from convinced. And they waited ...

Finally though, just after midnight, the low drone of aircraft engines coming from the north-west, from England, was followed by cases of armaments dropping from the skies beneath parachutes. Fournier and his men raced around after them, for all the world like children searching for Easter eggs on Easter Sunday morning, and had soon gathered them all in. They tore open the crates and emerged with a variety of explosives and an assortment of automatic weapons. Certainly, they would have to be cleaned and assembled before being ready for action, but they were guns all the same! As a kind of bonus present, with each drop came a manual translated into French entitled *How to Use High Explosives*. Now, *now* they would have something with which they could have a serious argument with those infernal Germans! The same thing happened on the following five nights—silky mushrooms emerged from the heavens, and beneath every one a present from London.

Nancy and her Maquis of course were not alone in receiving such largesse from the heavens, as her fellow agents all over Europe were on the receiving end of similar packages. During the course of World War II, the Special Operation Executive would send into France over 650 tons of explosives, 723,000 hand-grenades and approximately half a million small arms including 198,000 rifles, 20,000 Bren guns and 58,000 pistols.

By the time the planes came no more, Fournier and his men were among the best-armed partisans in France, which is more than could be said for their original contact, the once-mighty-but-no-more, Gaspard. Even though he nominally remained the leader of the Maquis in the area, there was no disguising the fact that firepower dictated the pecking order, and it was the once lowly Fournier who had clearly moved up in the ranks thanks to his gleaming cache.

Now that they were more properly an active and valued part of the Maquis and no longer 'parked', Nancy, Hubert and Denden moved out into the forest to be with the Maquis at all times and, among other things, to help train them in the new weaponry they had received. They soon discovered that life in the forest above Chaudes-Aigues with Fournier and his men was as 'rough as guts'. Most of the Maquis simply slept where they dropped at the end of the day, usually near heavily sheltered fires or under the thickest of the pine trees in the vain hope that they would have at least some shelter from the spring-time rain if it fell.

Nancy's situation was essentially no better, though she did at least allow herself two luxuries. If it looked like no rain was going to fall she quietly slipped into one of the two nightdresses she had brought with her, tucked herself beneath a mangy blanket she had secured, and put her head on her red satin cushion. It wasn't much, but it was something! For security reasons every few days they would move to a new encampment in the woods, usually a spot where there was some sort of a clearing and very limited access by way of tracks. Sentries could then be posted day and night at about a kilometre's distance away along those tracks to give fair warning if anyone was approaching.

As Nancy and Hubert conducted their training with the new weaponry—trying to instil some rigour on the previously rag-tag mob—they also set about changing other things. Nancy absolutely insisted that they stop stealing food, clothing and provisions from their fellow French. Whatever they took from the Germans, she explained, was fine by her, but what they were engaged in here was not simply a fight against the *Krauts*, but a fight for the hearts and minds and souls of their countrymen— and every time they stole chickens and sheep from local farmers, the fight to secure them became harder. She could give them the money they needed because London sent wads of money with the weaponry for precisely such purposes. She distributed it according to need in an almost classically Marxian fashion, oddly enough—and then they could buy the stuff from the farmers at market rates.

Whatever the Maquis bought in this fashion served only as a supplement to their normal diet of forest mushrooms, called *ceppes*, whatever natural game and birds they could kill with their guns and nets, and horse meat. Not for nothing would these men without toothbrushes and running water have breaths that smelt, to Nancy's assaulted nostrils, like dead skunks on a hot day. Thank God, she had brought enough of her own toothbrushes and tubes of toothpaste to last for a year!

In terms of 'Madame Andrée's' personal relations with the Maquis, they would prove to be extremely good, although she found she had to establish some firm ground rules right from the beginning. First and foremost among these was that, as a woman, she needed to be able to go to the toilet in peace *and privacy*, do you hear?

'After waking up that first morning in a forest with Fournier's Maquis,' Nancy recalls, 'I went out in the bushes to have a pee and I noticed that all the bushes around me were shaking, and other bushes were providing only very scant cover for men who'd been hiding there, waiting for me to do this, watching me. You see, they were men living in the forest without women, so my presence among them caused quite a stir, so I could sort of understand them wanting to do that, *once* ... but I also had to put a stop to it. I wanted their respect, not their leering eyes, and I couldn't have both.'

As the only woman among a band of seven thousand men dotted around the forests of the Auvergne, this was not necessarily easy, but she managed.

In the meantime, the 22,000 Germans garrisoned in the area had not been idle themselves. It had become increasingly clear to them that there was a serious Maquis problem close by which had to be crushed. One morning in the last week of May, 1944, they set out to do just that, sending no fewer than five thousand of their crack troops marching on Gaspard's headquarters in the forests outside Mont Mouchet, a headquarters where he had foolishly gathered some three thousand Maquisards in the one spot at the one time. If this broke the cardinal rule of guerrilla warfare—never give your enemy a massed target to strike at—well, many lessons were learnt by both French and Germans on this day.

They fought a pitched battle with, on one side, regular troops trained in battle orthodoxy and, on the other, French men on French soil who had lived in these parts for months and knew the battlefield intimately. Both opponents fought bravely and without mercy. If the failing of the Germans was that they had little experience fighting in thick forest, the failing of Gaspard and his men was that they had also broken the second cardinal rule of their craft. They did not have a prepared escape route to fall back on when the simple weight of German firepower forced the French to swallow their pride and retreat, for compounding Gaspard's problems was the fact that his group simply didn't have the weaponry or ammunition it needed. Courage alone could only get them so far.

All that notwithstanding, Gaspard's Maquisards gave at least as good as they got, inflicting heavy damage on the invaders; but in the end it was all they could do to slip away into the darkness, leaving behind one hundred and fifty of their own dead. Many of those who remained made their way to Fournier's group in the forested valley at Chaudes-Aigues, where Nancy was now installed. With these additionals there were now some seven thousand Maquisards scattered within the one small area—many of them on the plateau above Chaudes-Aigues—and all now principally dependent on a former Sunday School teacher from Neutral Bay, one Nancy Wake, aka *Madame Andrée*, aka *Hélène*, aka *Witch*, aka *Lucienne Carlier*, aka *Shirley Anne Kennedy*, for their wartime supplies.

Well as their newly powerful *chef du parachutage*, Nancy had news for them.

From this point on, no-one would get a tuppenny bunger from her unless they had, as a bare beginning, established escape routes which could be defended in an organised fashion as they withdrew. Without a choice in the matter the Maquis leaders, including a now chastened Gaspard, agreed. For Nancy, only a little over three weeks since she'd arrived on site, it was a great moment. The last time she had wanted to speak with Gaspard she'd had to search for him for days on end only to be told 'Non!'. Now, *he* was visiting *her*, acknowledging that he needed her help, and agreeing with her demands. As Nancy and Hubert soon found out though, Gaspard was nothing if not a fine fighting man—and not a bad bloke besides—and now that he had accepted just what they could do for him, he was a whole lot easier to get on with.

In no time at all, Nancy was travelling around to the rest of the seventeen Maquis groups that were scattered in her area of operation, assessing their needs, and as always with the help of

Hubert and Denden, ordering drops. Nancy gave each field where the parachutes could land a code name, and sent these names with precise map references from the exquisitely detailed Michelin map guide by code to London. Thus, calls were soon going out for 'Strawberry Fields' to be on the receiving end that night, or perhaps 'Oranges' or 'Lemons'. At the end of a transmitted coded request for, say, weaponry and money to be dropped on 'Strawberry', she would add a seemingly nonsensical phrase or verse such as '*Ding-dong-dell, pussy's in the well*'.

Then they, along with other agents across France, would monitor the BBC news bulletin to see if their phrase was there; for at the end of each news bulletin, the announcer would say '*et maintenant, quelques messages personnels*' (And now for some personal messages). Then, for as long as thirty minutes, he would read out what might seem like gobbledy gook to a passive listener—'*Ding-dong-dell, pussy's in the well*'; '*It'll rain in Lyons when the crows fly south in the wind*'—but which were actually precisely what operatives such as Nancy dotted around the country were waiting for. When they heard their key phrase, they knew that the drop was on, and had to prepare that night for the planes to come. One of the advantages of this scheme is that it also helped thwart the many Gestapo detector-vans constantly roving around Resistance hot-beds looking for illegal radio activity. Also, by putting their messages in code on the general BBC French service, radio traffic between agents and London was cut in half.

As a further precaution, these messages often really *were* nonsense, as the SOE never wanted the Germans to have any clues as to how much activity they could expect in the night skies by how many personal messages there were. If, in an emergency, London wanted to make direct contact with Nancy, they would say 'Personal to Hélène', before sending her a coded message. On very rare occasions, a *real* personal message was sent concerning something that might have happened, concerning the agent's family at home. On 5 May, 1944, for example, agent Harry Ree, operating in France heard the message '*Clementine ressemble a sa grandmere*'. This informed him he had a daughter.[47]

For Nancy, Hubert and Denden the system worked well, with the only down-side that their day had to move to the circadian rhythms of the BBC news bulletins, because they simply couldn't afford to miss one. The SOE operatives found that their power and influence with the Maquis increased with every successful drop, as the fighters realised just how munificent the SOE trio could be. And if there remained, nevertheless, one or two problems with being the sole woman in a ruggedly male culture, Nancy found a remarkable way of getting the respect of the men. Simply put, she simply drank them under the table—or as near to a table as they had out in the forest. For some reason she'd never quite understood, her tolerance to alcohol had always been enormous, and when one night she'd joined in a hard-drinking game with some of the Maquis around the fire, she couldn't help but notice that after about three hours, she would have been the last man left standing ... if indeed she had been a man. The following morning, there was renewed respect in some of the bloodshot eyes around her, and she decided this was as good a method as any to get the initial attention of many of the Maquis she visited. And it also never hurt any that the Maquis found she could swear with the very best of them.

'From then on,' she says, 'whenever I visited a new Maquis group and was invited to drink with them, I always accepted and made a point of going drink for drink with the leader.'

Although he'd known her longer than most, Hubert was still hellishly impressed.

'It was absolutely incredible,' he says now. 'I had never seen anyone drink like that ever, and I don't think the Maquis had either. We just couldn't work out where it all *went*, and how she could stay conscious! In my long life, it remains one of the most extraordinary things I have seen.'

The upshot was that the legend of Madame Andrée grew among the Maquis, not simply because she made the sky rain guns and money, but because she could knock it back with the best of them.

'Ultimately,' she says, 'they accepted me as one of themselves. I never wet-blanketed them. If they were talking and telling vulgar stories as I walked by, they would go on talking. They were men and they behaved as men, and I never minded.'

All up, Nancy settled happily into the life of the Maquis encampments. She particularly loved the nights with the men around the campfire deep in the forest, shadows flickering across their faces as they talked of the lives they had all led before the war. While often feeling sorry for the fact that so many had to leave behind wives, children and whole lives to do this, she came to greatly admire the men she was dealing with as courageous, principled and remorseless in their desire to liberate France. She loved the camaraderie of the Maquis, their unified desire to trample the *Boches* despite any hardship, and if she wasn't herself enamoured of that hardship, still she coped.

'It wasn't easy living without even the most basic rudiments of comfort,' she recollects, 'but there was no choice. I had to be with the Maquis to properly organise and arm them, and the Maquis were in the forest so that is where I mostly had to be.'

If she wasn't with the Maquis around the fire or training them with the new weaponry in the clearings, she was with Denden sending messages to London, and then monitoring the BBC transmissions and listening for their coded words. Then, the drops. Often, amid all the weaponry, ammunition and money, she would get personal letters and packages from her friends at the SOE in London—always marked *Personal for Hélène*—and filled with such things as the tea she liked, the chocolates she adored and the toilet paper she treasured most highly of all. Occasionally they would even send her newspapers and to her enormous satisfaction she found that things were generally going well now for the Allies, with the weight of the Americans continuing to be felt on every front.

'It was always wonderful, to receive such things,' Nancy remembers, 'because it made you feel connected with the people at home, like they really appreciated what we were doing, and feeling for us. I loved those personal packages.'

As well as supplying the weapons and ammunition, she and Hubert also spent a lot of time with the Maquis in those early days training them in their use, and this would usually occupy as long as four hours every morning, and this on top of the physical fitness training that she and Hubert insisted that they do if everyone wanted to continue to enjoy London's largesse.

'We were trying to turn them into a really disciplined fighting force,' Nancy says, 'and not just a courageous rabble with guns.'

As to what the newly armed Maquis were doing with all their new-found firepower, they were harassing the Germans, picking them off in parts without yet going in for full frontal assaults. As Nancy and Hubert explained to them, the real issue of the moment was to keep most of their powder dry until the Allies launched the D-Day landing, at which point they would all come fully into play as they unleashed everything they had against the Germans. It was fine to conduct raids here and there, one or two ambushes on the Germans to keep them nervous and below maximum efficiency, but they must never forget that the real battle was to come.

Certainly a lot of great work had been done in the early part of the war with the sabotage of many key industrial targets to weaken the German war effort, but now the game had changed, she explained. They were building up to the Big Day, *le jour de la liberation*, and all their actions had to be judged against whether it was likely to help or hinder the success of the forthcoming Allied invasion into the European continent. In his book *They Fought Alone*, Colonel Maurice Buckmaster gives an insight into the approach taken by the SOE towards sabotage in France. 'We had to plan the actual operations with a view to doing the maximum harm to the Germans while occasioning a minimum of reprisals against the civilian population. One of our ways of doing this, when aircraft became more readily available to us, was to arrange that the RAF should pass over a given target area at a given time so that the detonations which took place on the ground could be attributed to the aircraft which were flying over it. Strangely enough, the Germans would always co-operate in ascribing the damage to the bombers for this helped to hide from the French the presence of so active and powerful a resistance force in their midst.'[48]

A beacon in this field was Nancy's old friend Henri Tardivat, with his band of merry men in the forest at Alliers. He was a constant source of harassment to the Germans, and he perfected a technique of letting most of a German convoy go through before hitting with force the very last two vehicles. By the time the main firepower at the front had turned around they were confronted by burning vehicles, their own soldiers dead or screaming wounded, and a band of Maquis that had simply disappeared. The actual damage done to such convoys was important, and so, too, was the lowering of German morale and their growing sense of vulnerability. The parachutes kept landing, and the Maquis kept arming themselves and building up their ammunition dumps.

Clearly such damaging activity could not proceed long without the Germans moving against them again, and it was soon clear that the Krauts were indeed preparing to do just that. Nor was it just the Germans who noticed that things had changed. Around and about Mont Mouchet word had also got out that the Maquis were now well armed and financed, and together with the fact that the tide of the war was now clearly turning against Germany—Allied bombs were now regularly falling on Berlin, and in early May the Germans had surrendered in the Crimea—it was further encouragement for more and more young men to join the Maquis.

Alas, just as had happened before when the O'Leary Line grew too big to be properly secure, so too now with the Maquis. Whereas previously a new member would not be admitted unless he had the total trust of the small group of men already there, now in the flood of men joining them in the forest, it was always going to be easier for an infiltrator to succeed. Or at least try to.

One morning, Nancy and Hubert noticed a car driving past with two men in it. There was nothing remarkable about them, and she thought nothing more about it, until a few hours later when she was summoned to nearby Mont Mouchet by one of Gaspard's lieutenants. Gaspard's band of Maquis had captured a double agent the lieutenant said—a German pretending to be a Frenchman wanting to join the Maquis, but actually there on

Above: Madame Sainson with Allied escapees on the promenade beside the beach at Nice. Italian soldiers stand behind, entirely unsuspecting that the men are fugitives.

Madame Sainson with Nancy just behind her, circa 1985.

Above: Captain John Alsop, the American weapons instructor who was parachuted in to help train Nancy's Maquis.

Below:Captain Reeve Schley with French children after Liberation.

Above: German soldiers photographed from behind a hedge by Schley, Alsop and Nancy.

Below: On the steps of their chateau, 'Fragne', just outside Montlucon, Nancy's Maquis present arms and salute her—on the occasion of her thirty-second birthday—just before they were part of the liberation of Vichy, in the latter part of 1944.

Above: To arm the Maquis, Nancy and her fellow Special Operations Executive (SOE) agents relied on retrieving packages of materiel dropped from the skies by the RAF. This photograph is believed to have been taken of an SOE training group in rural England, early 1944.

Below left: Germans retreat along the road which ran past 'Fragne', the chateau outside Montlucon where Nancy's Maquis were hiding.

Above: Nancy Wake and John Forward, in the early 1980s.

Below: Nancy with her second husband, John Forward, in the early 1990s.

Nancy and Denis Rake hamming it up in a friend's London apartment in the mid-1950s.

Below: Nancy's collected medals.

Right: Nancy joined the FANY (First Aid Nursing Yeomanry) in 1943.

In her later years, Nancy settled with her husband in Port Macquarie, on the north coast of New South Wales.

a mission to assassinate Gaspard. He'd even had the password to get past the first checkpoint, but he'd slipped up thereafter, and they'd got him. Would Nancy come? Nancy went and smelt the horror before she saw it.

It was the stench of burnt human flesh and it was coming, she soon discovered, from Agent 47, Roger le Neveu—the one and the same who had betrayed O'Leary in the Toulouse café! Whence the smell? Nancy remembers, only too well:

'They stuck a red hot poker up his arse as they tortured him for information and I think it was very terrible what they did,' she says bluntly. 'But in a way, it was the sort of thing that was a reaction to things the Germans themselves had done. If you lived, as these men had, with seeing German atrocities on a daily basis, you had to understand some of their own outraged actions in return. But I told them, I would not put up with torture any more ... and that was really the end of it.'

As they had already extracted the information from him, Nancy suggested they shoot le Neveu to put him out of his misery. This was done, a single shot ringing out, to her great satisfaction. Nancy herself would see many such atrocities in the course of the war, perpetrated by both sides, some of which were horrific almost beyond belief.

On one occasion she had left the Maquis encampments to visit a nearby town when the Germans suddenly blocked all major entrances and exits to the town in an effort to round up a particularly troublesome partisan leader who they had long been looking for. They failed to find him, but as they searched from house to house, they captured the man's seven-month pregnant wife and his two-year-old daughter. The Germans took extreme action. Taking the woman and child to the village square, she was chained to a lamp-post while a crowd gathered—impotent in their rage against the heavily-armed Nazis. The woman was asked where her husband was, on pain of her life. She refused to tell. Once. Twice. Thrice.

The German officer in command gave her one last chance. Now for the fourth time, she refused. At this point the officer screamed an incomprehensible order to a nearby soldier, and in all her days Nancy would never forget what happened next.

'The soldier,' she says, 'went up and slit her stomach with his bayonet and her unborn child was hanging out and the woman's little girl was screaming her head off. And they wouldn't let the people do anything for twenty-four hours, they made the whole bloody place watch this poor thing, tied to this post in the square for twenty-four hours. She was dead as a doornail.

'I was just *disgusted*, outraged, frustrated that I couldn't do anything to stop the atrocity or help, but I had to remain disciplined, and not sacrifice myself to a futile gesture. I knew, at least, that the time was drawing very near, when the Allies were going to strike back very hard at the Germans, and was glad of it. I knew it was close ...'

Indeed she did, for in the first days of June, Nancy noticed something different about the packages she was getting from the heavens. They were *bountiful*. Whereas previously the drops had only been approximations of what she had asked for, and if anything on the low side, now she and her Maquis received everything they wished for immediately. This was not simply arms and money, but now also special basic khaki uniforms and basic black boots. These served the dual purpose of making the Maquis look more like a serious fighting unit when they made attacks in the public arena—which lifted public morale no end—and it simply got them out of the stinking rags most of them had been dressed in. Occasionally, on a good day, Nancy even thought it was worth risking a few deep breaths through *both* nostrils again!

All put together, it was clear that the day they had long planned for, the day when the Allies would launch the invasion to re-take France, and from there push on to Berlin, must be near at hand. In early June, Nancy received a message from London that she had to proceed to a place near Montluçon to pick up a weapons instructor by the code-name of 'Anselm'. The problem was that London assumed that she would know the safe house in the area to which it referred, and the password to gain access, but she didn't. The man who did, Maurice Southgate, had disappeared before he had

had a chance to pass it on. All she knew, was that the woman who had Anselm answered to the name 'Madame Renard'. It was precious little to go on under the circumstances. Orders though, were *orders*—she had at least picked up that much from her training—and there was nothing for it but to head down out of the mountains and make her best endeavours through her other contacts in the area to find where Anselm was secreted. To make the trip to Montluçon, Fournier provided her with a driver and car with a bicycle on top.

'And it was extraordinary,' recounts Nancy. 'The whole area was simply crawling with Germans. Patrols and roadblocks everywhere, and we had to proceed extremely cautiously, taking back roads and sending scouts out ahead of us to make sure that our way was clear.'

At last safely in Montluçon, Nancy began to work through the list of contacts her men had given her, discreetly enquiring about this 'Madame Renard' and if there might have been some 'new arrivals' in the area, until at last she came to a house on the outskirts of town, which she thought a likely candidate to hold her man. She knocked on the door, it opened and there stood before her a distinguished-looking woman she instinctively knew to be Madame Renard. Remembering how successful she had been a lifetime ago when she had fronted the contact in Perpignan for whom she did not have the correct code-word, and simply laid all her cards on the table, she did the same again on this occasion. Something told her this woman was one of them, exactly the woman she wanted, and so Nancy breached her own strict security rules by telling her what she was looking for. There was simply no time to do otherwise, and had she been wrong and the woman had raised the alarm she could have quickly faded into the night anyway.

Initially, the woman simply stared back at her, either dumb-founded, or even more likely giving absolutely nothing away in case this was a trap. But then Nancy had a moment of inspiration. Suddenly remembering a previous snippet of information that this Madame Renard had once been a cook for an ambassador, she suddenly sniffed the air and exclaimed, 'Ahhh, I've heard all about your *Baba au Rhum* cakes and how you used to cook them for the ambassador!'

Clearly no-one who could appreciate her cakes like that could be a double agent, and without another word the woman smiled broadly and bade Nancy enter! No sooner had she crossed the portals than the cupboard door opened and out of it—holding a Colt .45 and ready to kill—stepped the man that Madame Renard knew as 'Anselm' but who Nancy knew as ... René Dusacq! He was the fellow she had met back in her SOE British training camps and who she had become quite close to, the one with whom she'd danced at the Astor Club and who had warmly kissed her goodbye when she'd left for France. The two heartily embraced, laughing and relieved all at once.

Later that night they were heading back to Fournier's Maquis headquarters at Chaudes-Aigues, Dusacq in the back with his gun at the ready, the driver, and Nancy in the front with her preferred arsenal—holding a loaded Sten gun across her lap with the safety catch off, and half a dozen hand-grenades within easy reach. It would be an extremely unfortunate German patrol that tried to stop them that night. Entirely unbeknown to Nancy and Dusacq at that time, strange things were happening elsewhere across Europe on that evening of 5 June, 1944.

In London, a BBC announcer was once again talking apparent gibberish into a microphone, broadcasting his words across France, where over three hundred radio sets in clandestine hideouts were avidly tuned to his words.

'The crocodile is thirsty,' he intoned, albeit in French, before pausing significantly. 'I hope to see you again, darling, twice at the Pont d'Avignon ... You may now shake the trees and gather the pears ... What say, we play a game of *boules* in yonder dark forest? Is Mrs Munchkin ready to play today ...? I wish I was by the seaside at sunrise ...'

So it went for a good hour before he stopped, and no doubt went to have a well-earned cup of tea. Not so the hundreds of partisan leaders and Allied operatives throughout France who now heard the key words they had long been waiting for and were even then marshalling their forces to strike in the night at the targets they had been assigned. By the time the announcer got home that night, the groups were already gathering and moving under cover of darkness towards these targets—there were more than twelve hundred of them across France— taking with them the tons of high explosive they had assembled for just this night.

Out on the English Channel, in the middle of a rough sea, no fewer than five thousand ships, loaded to the gunwales with Allied forces, themselves armed to the teeth, moved south towards the coast of France. A little before two o'clock in the morning, they would have heard above them the roar of their own aeroplane engines—822 planes in all—as US Airborne 82nd and 101st together with the Royal Air Force were on their way, also heading east. At precisely two o'clock in the morning local time the paratroopers dropped just inland from the beaches of Normandy and set about creating havoc behind the coastal defences of the Germans. Other planes—bombers—followed closely behind and in the course of the night dropped over fifteen thousand tons of bombs on selected strategic targets, even as partisans all over France started knocking out their own targets. At 6.30 a.m., through a heavy pounding surf, the first men hit the beaches of Normandy, closely followed by tanks and armoured personnel carriers, as the startled Germans nevertheless concentrated heavy fire upon them. Scramble! Scramble! Scramble! All up, 156,000 men made their way through the frothing and bloody surf that day, of whom around 146,000 were still alive at nightfall.

Dunkirk in reverse, D-Day had arrived.

CHAPTER ELEVEN

Skirmishes

'The greatest and most sincere compliment I ever
heard paid to anyone came from one of the partisans.
After a skirmish with the Germans this man came to
me and said: "Madame Andrée has more guts than
Jacques, and he's the bravest of us all".'

CAPTAIN JOHN FARMER, AKA 'HUBERT'[49]

When she and René arrived back just after dawn at Chaudes-Aigues, Nancy not only learnt that D-Day had come, but that in her absence Hubert had told Fournier, Gaspard and all the other Maquis leaders the designated targets that he had previously memorised, and that they had already begun blowing them up overnight! This time Nancy felt like a month of Christmases had all come on the same day, and yet she had missed the unwrapping of every single present. Already gone were many of the underground telephone cables the Germans had laid in the area, a few railway junctions that were crucial to the German's effective troop movement, and some factories at nearby Clermont-Ferrand and Montluçon.

In the meantime, back on the beaches of Normandy 'Operation Overlord' remained in full swing, while far to the east in Berlin, Adolf Hitler continued to sleep soundly, courtesy of an extra round of sleeping pills taken the night before. When he awoke, it was to find that his High Command had been inundated by reports of the invasion, practically *begging* for support, but initially at least he refused to do anything. Another Churchill plan was working, that is to make the Germans think that the real invasion would be coming at Calais—far and away the closest and most obvious point to attack—so despite the imploring of his senior generals, it was not until nearly four o'clock that afternoon that Hitler ordered the twenty-first Panzer Division to be sent into the middle of the seething throng at Normandy.

Nancy, meantime, had stopped feeling sorry for herself, as there was simply so much work to do. Just as Rome had not been built in a day, France could not be blown up in a night, and there remained many, many targets that had to be hit by Nancy and her crew.

'We were flat out,' Nancy remembers, 'buggering up everything we could. Everything we could blow up! I was blowing things up all day and night—bridges, railway lines, roads—in no fear of the Germans. This was really what we had come here to do, and now it was a positive joy to do it.'

A sign of the growing confidence of the populace was that some of the boldest and/or more remote villages began to display both the French flag and the Union Jack from their town halls—a gesture of open defiance that, while dangerous, was a clear signal. *La France* was on her way back!

The immediate focus of the Maquis was to use everything they had to slow down and harass the Hermann Göring Division of the German Army, which was then based in the south-west of France, and also an entire division of panzers, which was on the Côte d'Azur. Both German groups were urgently mobilising to get to Normandy—two thousand kilometres away—at all possible speed. Both divisions would soon be staggered by the level of hostility directed at them—dodging snipers from all sides; negotiating booby-trapped roads; and trying to cross bridges that simply weren't there any more. All too often they were forced to take back roads to try to continue their progress north, back roads where their vulnerability was all the greater. Nancy's Maquis were in it with the best of them, attacking the local German garrisons wherever they tried to move, and laying the groundwork to stop all massive movements of the other German battalions through their area.

The Germans took terrible reprisals against all French citizens found anywhere near these attacks—burning houses, summarily hanging whoever they caught from lamp-posts and trees, rounding up hostages and shooting them against a wall. It was tragic, but unavoidable.

'This was *war*,' says Nancy, 'and if we were not prepared to withstand their barbarity, Germany would have ruled all of Europe unchallenged.'

One of the many underground newspapers took a similar stance: 'For an eye, both your eyes,' it editorialised, 'and for a tooth, your whole mouthful!'[50]

Who the Germans really wanted, of course, was not the citizens but the Auvergne Maquis themselves; and just four days after D-Day, having re-grouped and fired up, they went hard at them once again. This time with seven thousand crack troops supported by artillery, armoured cars and tanks, the Germans marched to where Gaspard's camp of three thousand Maquis were situated at Mont Mouchet. All of that day, the Germans pressed their attack— in unfamiliar territory, but still confident in their superior numbers and firepower—while Gaspard's men, better armed this time, were guerrillas at their best shooting suddenly and, just as quickly, flitting away again through the deep forest before attacking from a different angle. Their plan was always to avoid as much as possible getting into a full confrontation with the *Boches*, and to instead pick away at the edges and grind them down from there.

Having taken a mauling throughout the day, the Germans withdrew at nightfall but returned at dawn the following morning to redouble their efforts in wiping the Maquis out. Again, Gaspard and all were ready for them, ambushing the first of the nervous convoy that made its way into the forest and taking it from there.

Nancy's own position with the Fournier camp meant that they could hear the sound of the battle raging throughout the day, across the valley on the neighbouring ridge. Still, they were confident that the redoubtable Gaspard and his men were equal to the task and, held back by nearly impassable terrain, held their own position. As it happened, the Fournier camp had its own hands full at this time—of all times—just with trying to cope with the massive influx of new recruits who were streaming into their camp from all corners, demanding to join the Maquis. The nickname for these latecomers among the Maquis was *napthalinés,* the French word for moth-balls, it being said that that is what they smelt of after having hidden in cupboards for most of the war.

Nancy has an explanation for this manifest desire among the domestic locals to join up with one group of Maquis at a time when another group were under a full-blown German attack.

'By this time,' she says, 'it was obvious that the Germans were in serious trouble, that the tide was turning against them and that meant a lot of those people who had been sitting on the fence for the entire duration of the war were now jumping down on our side of it, keen to be with the winners when it all ended. Also, I think a lot of people who had suffered under the Germans for so long, could now see that the time for revenge was at hand, and they wanted to get in on it.'

Over the next days, Nancy continued to organise weapons drops while René Dusacq—or 'Bazooka' as the Maquis had dubbed him because of his love of that particular weapon—continued to train the French in their use. In sum, while the Germans continued to try to kill off the Resistance on Gaspard's hill, new recruits kept streaming in.

Clearly, now with the D-Day landing, the war had moved into another phase ... for at a time when there was a pitched battle between massed forces of German and Maquis on one hill, the need to have top secret night-time drops on the other hill was rather beside the point. In this particular situation, subterfuge and secrecy were no longer the issue rather the catchcry was 'Kill the *Boche!*'—or at the very least do everything in one's power to damage and delay the Germans to prevent them from getting to Normandy. With that in mind it had been arranged with London that just for this special occasion, the next drop would be in broad daylight and this time as well as more weapons, there would also be tons of new British boots and socks to freshly hoof all the Maquis. If it would be going too far to say that this would make them all 'British to their bootstraps', still it was obvious that the wartime command in Britain was delighted with the Maquis fighting force and were keen to support them while their own men continued to storm the beaches of Normandy.

Obviously, Churchill's plan hatched four years previously was working perfectly; for even while myriad German divisions across France were engaged in a mad scramble to get their mixed manpower and firepower to the beaches of Normandy as quickly as possible and so stem the breach to their defences, they were being met by twisted and torn railway lines, blown-up bridges and a possible ambush around ever corner. And many of the factories and power stations that had been central to providing the necessary grunt to keep their war effort going far from home-base were now no more than smoking ruins. What it all meant, later calculations would reveal, was that when the Allies hit the beaches of Normandy, the Germans were deprived of no fewer than fifty of their divisions which had been intended for reinforcement—all were bogged down in far-flung parts of France trying to extricate themselves from Resistance actions and make their way across bridges that were simply no longer there . . .

Meanwhile, Gaspard's Maquisards continued their battle on the ridge across from where Nancy, Hubert and Bazooka were training the new recruits. Eventually the Germans realised that the longer they engaged with this elusive enemy in the forest the more of them would be picked off at the Maquis' leisure, so they withdrew to regroup. Some time later, a triumphant Gaspard arrived, full of bravado about how valiant his men had been in battle; how the Germans had suffered losses at many times their own paltry rate of casualties; how he could not *wait* till the Germans came for them again! And one more thing, he told them. Because it was a firm rule of guerrilla warfare to keep on the move and never let your enemy get a fix on your position, or allow him to adapt to the conditions in which he last fought, he was moving his three thousand back to a plateau very near to Nancy's troupe at Chaudes-Aigues.

'And shortly afterwards,' Nancy recalls, 'they began to arrive, all three thousand of them. There was something different about them this time though. Whereas before they had often had something of a hang-dog look about them, now they were euphoric, positively bubbling over with the excitement of having fought a pitched battle with the Germans and won.'

In the brief lull after that battle was over, Nancy found herself with another problem. One afternoon, after returning from arming a group of Maquis in a distant forest, Nancy was confronted by an outraged local farmer, who was in a *killing* mood specifically targetted at Denden. The way he told it to Nancy, this *éspéce de merde*, this piece of shit who called himself a soldier but who was in fact *un pedé*, a poofter, had made an advance on his own son! The son wasn't happy about it, the father less so, and both it seemed would happily have seen Denden shot for his trouble. Privately, Nancy was in an equally murderous mood when she heard about it, but for the purposes of the exercise at least managed to calm the farmer long enough to promise that really he must be mistaken—Denis was really just 'very, very *theatrical*', she said. She further promised that she would look after the matter herself and Denden would never bother him or his again.

'And he didn't,' Nancy reports, 'but it took Bazooka some time to convince him that this just wasn't on when we were trying to win a war.'

At least Denden was an absolutely first-class radio operator and kept coding messages to London, and decoding messages received from them through all conditions.

Nancy herself at this time, once again became a positive blur of activity, organising drop after drop of armaments, unloading them, degreasing them, handing them out, making sure that when the Germans next attacked every able-bodied Maquisard in the Auvergne would be armed to the teeth with plenty of ammunition. She also continued to hand out money to each group—as much as fifteen million francs a month collectively—which ensured that the Maquis could sustain themselves and buy their provisions from friendly farmers.

Over time, Nancy had built what was essentially a personal band of eighty Maquis seconded from other groups who moved around with her and Denis and Hubert, and who were specifically devoted to preparing the fields, lighting the bonfires, gathering in the parachute drops, unpacking and distributing, and mounting some serious firepower all around while accomplishing all of the above.

'It was a great group to be with,' says Nancy, 'and we had all become not just very close to each other, but also very efficient in the way we did our work.'

Her only real respite from the constant *parachutages* came for the period of ten days or so each month when the moon was too small to generate enough light to see the packages. Good visibility allowed the Maquis to retrieve packages quickly and make good an exit.

The recruits continued to pour in and before long the number of Gaspard's Maquis assembling on the plateau had reached an entirely unwieldy four-to-five thousand. Nancy, Hubert and Fournier all considered this an extremely juicy target for yet another concentrated German attack, but it was in vain though that they tried to convince Gaspard to break the group up into smaller groups. One thing they knew was that they couldn't pull rank on him. For Gaspard, in the catch-as-catch-can Maquis fashion of the time had decided he now had the rank of 'General', to be promulgated after the war, and was less disposed than ever to listen to another view. Nancy countered by saying she was now a 'Field Marshal'—to be promulgated after the war!—but still he would not budge.

In the face of Gaspard's obstinancy, the least the Fournier group could do was to put a moderate distance between themselves and Gaspard. This was on the reckoning that when the day of the next German attack came they would be far enough away to be spared the full brunt of it, and yet still close enough to be able to lend support by attacking one of the German flanks should it come to that. And so it might have proved, but before they could move to the new site several kilometres to the north of their current position, there were two more extremely important *parachutages* that had to be received on successive nights, and they decided to wait until these were completed before moving out. After the second night—a night in which it had positively *rained* parachutes bearing arms—Nancy's troop of Maquis had just returned to their camp as the first rays of the summer sun winked up over the thick mountainous country to the east when they heard it. Gunfire in the distance.

Nancy had just sunk into bed after previously relaxing in the hot natural baths from which Chaudes-Aigues draws its name—trying to soak away the fatigue of the night before—when the first sounds reached her. She was up and dressed in an instant. There was really no need to ask *who* was doing the firing because of course it was the Germans.

What was startling when the first reports came in minutes later was the extraordinary strength of the German numbers. The scouts said the approaches to their mountain top were simply *noir du monde allemagne*, black with the figures of approaching Germans. This was an accurate description of the fifteen thousand crack German troops who had been sent out after the Maquis this time. These troops were supported by a thousand armoured vehicles, heavyweight mobile artillery, and ten planes in the skies above ready to strafe and bomb whoever got in their way. Clearly, this time, it was *on*. '*Once more unto the breach dear friends, once more . . .*'[51]

Throwing everything she could into the car at her disposal, Nancy, with Hubert and Denis Rake at her side, raced to the tiny village of Fridfront at the northern end of the plateau where Gaspard was based, to determine just what his plan of action was. Neither Nancy nor Hubert were in any doubt as to the correct course of action against such overwhelming numbers. Withdrawal. Escape. Live to fight another day. Their game they knew, was always to be hit and run merchants on the Germans, unleash their ambush and then move on, but never *ever* play the enemy on its own terms. It was for this very reason that Nancy had insisted that all the Maquis groups who wanted arms and money from her had prepared escape routes at all times, and she knew for a fact that Gaspard's main group now firing on the approaching Germans had one too.

Now, as the key liaison point with Gaspard, Hubert tried to persuade him to use it. 'Mais, non!' said the recalcitrant Gaspard, clearly shocked at what they were suggesting. This, he suggested, was what it was all about. Yes, the Germans had them in a convenient mass, making a handsome target, but his point was that the Germans *also* were massed! Instead of knocking the *Boche* off in ones and twos or even tens and twenties, the Maquis could kill lots of them, hundreds maybe. In sum, he and his men weren't going anywhere, he said, they were staying put and were going to fight the bastards to the death. It was in vain that Hubert tried to make him understand the folly of this course of action—Gaspard had not risen to be the leader of so many Maquisards by being anything other than strong willed and sure of himself at all times, and he made it absolutely clear that he had made his decision, and that was that.

There was only one thing to do. Inform London of the situation, and see if they could apply leverage via the Free French—the one group to whom Gaspard felt answerable. Nancy coded the message and Rake sent it, after many hours of trying to get through at this unscheduled time. Meanwhile, all around, the sounds of the battle raged, the constant staccato bursts of machine-gun fire mixing with the regular bass drum of the Germans' heavy artillery, the whine of their Junker 88s overhead, the battle-cry commands of the Maquis leaders calling their men forward or back as the situation demanded. The Germans at this point had secured their positions on the slopes leading to the plateau, and were now carefully probing forward, trying to secure a position over the lip through which they could all pour and wipe the Maquis out.

While they waited for London to come back to them, Nancy returned to Strawberry Field and resumed unpacking the crates of arms and ammunition that had been dropped the previous night. Loading her car once again to the gills, she drove around the perimeter of the plateau delivering the fresh supplies of killing material to the men who needed it most. Despite the ongoing roar of the battle, she twice nearly ran off the road because she was actually ... going to sleep.

'I had been getting by on literally two hours sleep a day, often taken in fifteen minute catnaps, and that previous night and morning I hadn't had any at all because of the parachutage and then the Germans; so despite the seriousness of the situation, my body was simply telling me it didn't give a damn about any war, it simply had to stop and have a kip.'

Nancy got the message. War or no war. Germans or no Germans. At that point the Maquis were holding off the Germans pretty well, and London had still not got back to them over Gaspard, so Nancy took the opportunity. Just near where she had been unpacking the weaponry there was an abandoned farmhouse with a bed that Fournier had designated for her as her base, and she was no sooner back to it than she had crawled between the covers and ... and ... was being roughly awakened. It was Fournier, insisting that she not remain there. The house, he pointed out, was an obvious target for the missiles of the Luftwaffe, which continued to hunt along the plateau. Nancy was, frankly, at that point too tired to care and practically slept-walk her way to a tree some hundred metres distance from the farmhouse and lay down there. She was vaguely aware that somewhere behind her as she walked, the house had indeed just been hit, but she barely looked around. The arms of blessed Morpheus awaited ...

Two hours later and partially refreshed, she made her way back to Denis Rake to see what London commanded, and arrived just in time to see him finish decoding the message. As they thought, London was insistent that all the forces withdraw as soon as possible and leave the Germans to it. Just as Dunkirk might have seemed a terrible humiliation at the time but was crucial in preserving a fighting force to fight another day, it was imperative that the Maquis drop all macho notions of fighting it out on the spot and hightail it out of there forthwith on the prepared escape routes.

This was easy for London to say. They weren't actually saying anything that Nancy and Hubert hadn't already told Gaspard, and he hadn't listened to them then, so why would he listen to them now?

'Denden'... said Nancy, with a suddenly shrewd and thoughtful tone in her voice, 'I want you to add something to that message.'

'And what is that, Nancy?'

'Sign it "Koenig".'

If she did say so, herself, it really was a stroke of genius. General Marie Pierre Koenig was one of the fiercest and most respected Generals in de Gaulle's command, and with Gaspard's respect for titles and authority—at least *French* titles and authority—Gaspard would not be able to ignore it. He didn't. Gasping that the great Koenig would even *deign* to be in personal communication with him, Gaspard took the message as holy writ and immediately made plans to withdraw under cover of darkness that evening.

Her job done, Nancy turned her car around and set out for the village of Fridfront, where Fournier's group of Maquis were based. She first became aware that there was a problem when she heard the unmistakably high-pitched whine of a plane screaming in sharp descent. She looked up, and saw it. As they said in the trade: *bandit at 12 o'clock!* It was a Henschel 126, which had peeled off formation and was even then screaming towards her, lining her up for a strafing with its cruel machine-guns spitting hundreds of bullets a second at her. She could see the spurts of sand coming in a line for her, even as she could make out the rough outline of the pilot himself, right down to the brown colour of his goggles.

Nancy reacted, on this occasion, consciously rather than instinctively; that is, she neither braked suddenly, nor sped up towards the oncoming plane, but did the thing the pilot would have least expected, which was to suddenly slow right down, meaning that the pilot had to alter the arc of his descent so that she would still be at its nadir ...

Somehow it was just enough to throw him off, and even as the car paused, the burst of bullets stopped in the road just before her. Not certain that she would be so lucky again if the Henschel came back at her, Nancy sped up looking for some cover, and praying that the pilot would not turn the plane around.

She could see it in her rearview mirror. He was turning around! Lordy, lordy, lordy! *Lordy! Lordy! Lordy!* Not quite sure what to do this time, as it would a far more difficult proposition to evade him when he would be coming at her from behind, she was just contemplating her next move when a young Maquisard she knew appeared by the road ahead, urgently signalling her to stop, to get out of the car and *move!*

Nancy did just that, screeched to a halt, and jumping into the ditch he indicated just as the plane once again screamed overhead, the pilot's aim once again thrown off by the sudden stop. The Maquisard pointed to the woods and shouted '*Vite!*' but Nancy had one more pressing thing to do. Even as she could see the Henschel 126 in the far distance beginning its long loop to come back for one more try, she ducked back into the car, retrieved a package she had previously secreted behind the driver's seat and dived back into the ditch just as the dreadful snarling whine of the Henschel reached its awful climax. This time there would be no mistake ... A sudden roar and terrible blast of heat blowing over the ditch told them that the petrol tank on Nancy's car had exploded.

When they took their hands away from their heads—where they had flown in instinctive self-protection—the Maquisard merely looked at Nancy inquisitively, unable to bring himself to speak. *What*, he seemed to want to know, had been so important back in the car that she had to risk her life to get it?! Nancy felt it only fair, under the circumstances, that she show him: some cosmetics, which were most difficult to come by in war-torn France, some absolutely superb tea which helped keep her sane on bad days, and the red satin cushion she had long treasured. All might be fair in love and war, but it simply would *not* have been fair to let those things go without a fight, and Nancy made no apology as they now raced towards the cover of the thicker woods, and from there back to Fridfront.

By the time they got there, just as darkness was falling, the pull-out had already begun. In situations like this, the plan was for the Maquis to form up into small groups and recede independently of each other, to meet at a pre-arranged rendezvous point in a safer place. Guerrillas in the mist, they would prove a far more elusive quarry for the Germans this way. Thus, while those on the outer limits of the plateau's perimeter kept firing at the Germans double time, groups of fifty and a hundred Maquisards were already on their way along the prepared escape route. Nancy found that Denden had gone with one of them, Hubert with another, while Bazooka, bless his cotton socks, had waited for her. As soon as she arrived, he hustled her into the next group moving out, and they were on their way.

How to escape the tightening circle of Germans though—in much the same way that Hitler had thwarted the previously much vaunted Maginot Line. His success there had been to send his forces through country so rough it had been thought impenetrable, and that is exactly what the Maquis did here. Parts of the German circle were not joined at all, so dense was the forest, so raging the river, and it was precisely here, under the cover of the encroaching darkness, that the French freedom fighters made their way out.

While the Germans controlled all the bridges that led across the Truyére River, and patrolled the shorelines of the shallower parts, they ignored notoriously deep and gushing sections. These were the very areas where, previously, some of the Maquis had expended enormous energy in submerging huge slabs of stone whose tops were now just beneath the surface, allowing the escapees to carefully cross them like invisible stepping stones to safety. Like so many sons of God they walked on water, one after the other in the moonlight made their way through the so-called encirclement, leaving an empty plateau for the Germans to find the following day.

Now out in open country, the seven thousand Maquis headed off in many separate platoons on their own long march to the previously agreed rendezvous at Saint-Santin, a little village near Aurillac, about a hundred kilometres west of their previous position. Of course they did not proceed in that direction straight as the crow flies, for they would inevitably have had to congregate again, but did so in a meandering fashion, criss-crossing the country and making many long detours through thick cover, while frustrated roving German planes looked for them and occasionally descended to drop bombs on any particularly thick bit of foliage they thought *might* be hiding partisans, but which actually never did.

The Nazis had good reason for their anger, having lost no fewer than 1,400 of their crack troops in the whole exercise while the Maquis counted no more than a hundred dead. And, while fifteen thousand of the German troops had been engaged so fruitlessly by the Maquis, the Allied beachhead had now been established at Normandy. The combined American, British and Canadian forces had entrenched themselves and were just beginning to move out from there, even while German forces strove to get there in time to stem the flow. Too late. By the end of June, close to a million men had come ashore in France, along with some 586,000 tons of supplies and 177,000 vehicles.

For Nancy's small group of trekking Maquisards, supplies were a lot thinner. They essentially had to live off the kindness of *paysans*, the poor peasants who worked the country they were walking through. A seemingly paradoxical rule of thumb, Nancy had discovered through the course of the war, was that the less goods people possessed, the more likely they were to share with unfortunate allies, as well as to subject themselves to the risks that went with sheltering escapees.

'I don't know why it was like that,' she says, 'but that's the way it was.'

After three days and three nights of walking, with only intermittent resting along the way, Nancy's group of one hundred and twenty Maquisards came to the approaches of Saint-Santin and inevitably started to meet up with the other groups. Nancy and her crew fell in with Gaspard's group just five kilometres outside the town, and there came a moment that she would treasure for long afterwards. Before she quite knew it had happened, Gaspard himself had fallen in step beside her, linked his arm in hers and said *'Alors, Andrée ...'* before discussing the tumultuous events of the previous few days.

'It was,' she says, 'just a wonderful moment of recognition on his part, the first time he treated me like an equal ... and maybe also his way of acknowledging that we had been right to insist on his departure. For here he was, walking along on a beautiful day, beneath the dappled summer sunlight filtering through the thick green foliage above, *alive* and with his fighting force still intact, instead of lying dead in the forest back on the plateau. He took my arm and that showed that I was on his side, that he had accepted me. And I have never forgotten that.'

It was the beginning of a much closer relationship between the two, and they quickly set themselves up in an isolated house on the outskirts of Saint-Santin, and awaited the rest of the Maquis. For the next few days the fighters kept coming in their groups, all equally elated with their many adventures, and euphoric to still be alive after what they had faced. When Nancy caught up with Denden it was only to find that he had suffered quite a serious leg wound in the battle, and she promptly gave him her treasured bottle of eau de cologne, in the hope that it would be an effective makeshift antiseptic for the wound.

'Next morning,' as the official history of the SOE has it, 'Denis looked much brighter and Nancy asked him whether the eau de cologne had helped. "It definitely did," Denis replied gaily. "I drank the whole bottle . . ."'[52]

But, seriously, Denden was less than euphoric—in fact he was downright devastated. And he had good reason for it. At the height of the battle back on the plateau, when he was absolutely sure the Germans had been about to overrun them, he had taken a particularly desperate measure. That is, he had destroyed his radio codes and had buried the radio itself, petrified lest either or both should fall into the hands of the Nazis. It was the loss of the codes, particularly, which was potentially the most devastating. In Denmark, the Nazis at one point had been able to get a hold of such codes and by continuing to send and receive coded messages in the guise of an agent, were able to garner information that subsequently completely devastated SOE operations there.

Nancy felt sick to the pit of her stomach. The radio was easily the most crucial piece of equipment they possessed. It was what connected them to London, and when they needed it, it gave them access to the Allies' resources, firepower and intelligence. And from London's point of view, she knew, being able to organise and co-ordinate all the Maquis through radio contact was the difference between being able to give the Germans dozens of different pokes in the eye, and many, many smashings with a closed fist—a fist often wrapped around a weapon that London could also provide. There was no point in blaming Denden for any of this of course, he had essentially done the right thing to ensure that the Germans did not get their hands on it, but that did not change their situation.

They simply *had* to get another radio, and be quick about it. The following day, Nancy jumped on a bicycle, and rode over a mountain in an attempt to make contact with a Free French radio operator reputed to be just twenty kilometres away. She arrived exhausted outside a designated bistro where she hoped she could meet the contact, but *hulloa!* what was this? Russell Braddon has previously described what happened next:

> *The patron [of the bistro] rushed out in considerable agitation.*
> *'You must not come in here, Madame Andrée.'*
> *'Why not?'*
> *'There's a communist here. He says he will shoot you.'*
> *Nancy was in no mood to be blackguarded out of a much-needed drink by the threats of a communist. Angrily, she strode into the bistro, head down like a young bull in a manner that had become almost characteristic, flung herself into a chair beside the communist and slammed her revolver down on top of the table.*
> *'I hear,' she announced disagreeably, 'that you are going to shoot me. Well ... you'll need to be very quick on the draw! Patron, a cognac.'*
> *Not for a second, whilst she drank her brandy, did her eyes leave those of the communist. Then she left the bistro ...* [53]

The upshot, finally, was that the contact with the radio had already fled in the face of the swarming German presence now in

the area, so it was a wasted trip anyway. What to do? The only
thing they could do. Try again. Around Gaspard's campfire that
night, they held a veritable council of war. The whole thing was
very much Nancy's responsibility, and her decision, but she was
still interested to have their input, guided by their local knowledge
of the situation.

After much discussion, it was decided that the only chance was
for Nancy to try to ride to Châteauroux, some two hundred
kilometres away along the circuitous route she would have to
follow, where Denden was positive that there was one of their
own—an SOE radio operator who would definitely get Nancy
straight through to London and get them to organise another radio
drop and a new set of codes. True, Denden didn't have the actual
address of this radio operator—spy networks weren't big on
addresses in the first place, and he never had a head for them
anyway—but he had the next best thing. That is, he provided
Nancy with a detailed description of just where exactly the
operator could be found, right down to a drawing of the brasserie
opposite his home.

This plan did not meet with the universal accord of the leaders
in the group. Some thought it was simply beyond Nancy's physical
capabilities to cycle a round trip of four hundred kilometres over
mountainous terrain; others thought it crazy for her to spend that
long a time defenseless on a bike, without proper identity papers,
amid Germans looking for people just like her. None, however,
could mount a serious argument against Nancy's two central
points. First, that without a radio the sad truth was that they
weren't too far north of being just a bunch of French ferals in the
forest. Secondly, that she was the one who had the best, if not the
only, chance of getting through. For though her situation on this
bike ride would be precarious in the extreme, they all knew her
very sex would be an enormous advantage.

Nancy's past experience had taught her that not only does sexual
attraction not recognise national borders nor political divisions—
meaning she had often been ogled by the very guards meant to
check her—but the innate warmth and intimacy of that attraction

was a great soother of possible suspicions. If she got it right, it had to seem beyond the range of possibilities for the Germans between her and her destination, that such an attractive young woman could be on a mission specifically devoted to bringing them carnage and destruction in the very near future. That, at least, is the factor Nancy intended to play to the hilt and she spent the twenty-four hours before departure rustling up the most attractive outfit she could get, and though it was an enormous effort to do so, the final result—after she also used judiciously some of the very last of the cosmetics she'd treasured all this time—looked pretty damn good, even if she did say so herself.

There is an old French joke about the Gypsy recipe for chicken soup: 'First, steal a chicken ...'. In much the same fashion, it was Laurent who first realised that while they had all been discussing the pros and cons of Nancy's bike ride, they didn't actually have a bike good enough for her to make such a long journey (her previous bike being adjudged inadequate for the task). He personally put that in order very quickly by heading off into Montluçon and stealing a particularly sturdy one. Laurent also took charge of sending word to every Maquis contact in the villages she would pass through so that they might look out for her and give her information about German checkpoints and troop movements in the area. Nancy took no weaponry whatsoever, it being decided that the advantages of having a gun were clearly outweighed by the possibility of bluffing her way out if she got into any trouble.

At least for the first part of the journey, to Montluçon, she would be accompanied by a strapping Maquisard who was going to the town to visit his heavily pregnant wife, but after that she would be on her own. And the beginning of the trip really was easy. Mostly they stuck to the little back roads that criss-crossed the countryside and where the Germans rarely ventured for fear of ambush. On those occasions when they were obliged to take the main road, they pushed their bikes instead of riding them, on the reckoning that if they saw the distant silhouette of any German cars approaching, they could simply dive off the road and into one of the roadside culverts.

On the outskirts of Montluçon, Nancy took leave of her companion as night began to fall, and continued alone on the road to Saint-Armand. It was an extremely lonely venture she was engaged in, riding solo in the twilight with the fear of a German checkpoint around every corner, but there was simply nothing else she could do. One thing she was feeling more than a little, was a bone-crushing, soul-destroying fatigue. Still only forty kilometres into her planned journey, and already her legs were feeling like hot lead.

'I just concentrated on doing one more turn, one more turn, one more turn,' she explains, 'as the miles slipped by.'

After traversing some extremely hilly country, Nancy stopped in a bistro halfway between Montluçon and Saint-Armand both for much needed refreshment *and* to get information. Dining quietly, but with her ears straining to hear every snatch of conversation of her fellow patrons—as always focused on the activities of the *Boche*—she gathered that mostly it was all quiet on the western front. Armed with that information, she headed off again, pausing only to have a brief kip in a roadside barn shortly afterwards— being sure to sleep only in her underwear so that her skirt wouldn't get crushed. Whatever happened, she must look like someone who had spent the night in her own bed nearby.

Rolling, rolling, rolling. Riding, riding, riding. Straining and pushing at the pedals. Trying *not* to focus on just how tired she felt. Finally in Saint-Armand, she stopped for coffee and ascertained that the nearby town of Bourges had felt the German heat the day before. With some trepidation, thus, she continued on her way into Bourges to find everything quiet again ... maybe a little *too* quiet; for if there weren't tumbleweeds rolling down the street like she'd sometimes seen in those American cowboy movies, there should have been. There was no-one on the streets, all the shutters were closed, and a heavy air of great sadness hung over the place. And for good reason. Nancy later learnt that the Germans, taking revenge for partisan activity in the area in the previous few days, had shot hostages in Bourges that very morning. The town she was passing through was partly in mourning, partly cowering in terror. The only activity Nancy saw on the streets were groups of German soldiers marching off to parts unknown, but as they let her pass unhindered Nancy kept doing what she'd been doing all that day—pedalling.

Her next port of call was the tiny burg of Issoudon, where she stopped at a local black market restaurant she knew of, for refreshment and this time for a major break to clean herself up in the ladies' room.

'It was absolutely imperative,' she insists, 'that even though I was exhausted and windblown from travelling so far, I not *look* that way. Whatever German patrols saw me had to think I was simply a young housewife tootling along home or to the village, who was not worth bothering with, but *not* someone doing a major trip.'

It was for this reason that she went to the local markets at Issoudon and purchased some vegetables to put in the string bag she had bought for that very purpose. Just a local housewife off shopping ...

Sometimes, if trucks of passing German soldiers waved at her and called something out, she would wave back in a demure fashion even though, as she says, 'I longed to break their fucking necks'. Ditto, when she cycled past a series of German checkpoints. If even one had asked for her papers she would have been forced to try to bluff her way through, saying she had left them at home, but fortunately it never came to that.

'I would just look over to the officer, flutter my eyelashes and say 'Do you want to search *moi*?' and they would laugh flirtatiously, 'No Mademoiselle, you carry on'.'

Back at Saint-Santin, around the campfire, Gaspard, Laurent, Fournier, Denden, Hubert and the others talked in low growls and wondered with no little trepidation just how Madame Andrée was getting on. Had they sent this brave woman to her death? Had she been arrested and tortured, in which case their own position was extremely vulnerable? On one thing they could at least agree. Even if Andrée *was* tortured, they felt sure she would never talk. All they could do for the moment though, was wait, and hope that she was all right.

Similar emotions were felt in London, at SOE headquarters at 65 Baker Street, where Colonel Buckmaster and his closest staff wondered why 'Hélène' had gone so strangely quiet—they feared the worst. They already knew that there had been a major German attack on the plateau at Montluçon, and they had heard absolutely nothing since. What were they meant to think? All they could do was wait.

Out on the road to Châteauroux Nancy cycled on, up hill, down dale—though seemingly a lot more of the former than the latter. As she came within fifty kilometres of Châteauroux the road was simply too crowded with Germans to be safe—not least from their big bloody trucks which kept roaring past her flimsy bicycle—and she decided to come at the town indirectly, making a long loop to come into the town from the north-west instead of directly due south. On the outskirts of the town there was still one more German checkpoint, but when Nancy made as if she were quite happy to stop and show them her papers, they waved her on in a bored manner.

Is it possible? She'd actually made it. She had covered over two hundred kilometres in just over a day-and-a-half through enemy lines and, had she paused to consider her feat, she would have been extremely satisfied with her performance thus far. But she simply could not stop yet. While it was one thing to have actually made it this far, it was all worse than useless if she didn't find the SOE radio operator in question. With that in mind she continued to cycle her way around the town, looking for the bistro that Denden had described, fairly fruitlessly, as it turned out, for after two hours of searching she still had not located it. Wondering just what to do and where to go from here, and feeling *extremely* alone with Germans all around, she suddenly saw not just a *friendly* face, but a familiar one!

A man was smiling at her and she recognised him instantly as

Bernard, a Maquisard, who, just like she, was a long way from home—a bloke she'd met in passing in Brive-La-Gaillard several weeks before in the *département* of *la Corrèze*. The two embraced and compared notes, only to find that they were pursuing almost identical tasks. As with her group, their own radio had been knocked out in a battle with the Germans—their operator being killed—and he was up here looking for a Free French radio operator who was meant to be operating in these parts. They decided to join forces and, shortly afterwards, *hey presto!* there was the very bistro she was looking for. It just had to be!

Alas, when she finally found the man who she had come all this way to see, he point-blank refused to help her on the grounds that she did not have the required password and, for all he knew, she might be working for the Gestapo. Nancy pleaded, pointing out that if she were working for the Gestapo he already would have been either arrested or shot, but nothing moved him. She left, disgusted, and rejoined Bernard who had been waiting for her in the bistro. It was time to try to find *his* contact and see if they had any better luck in that quarter. They pedalled on to another part of the town only to find the area crawling with Germans. One of Bernard's contacts informed them, crucially, that although the Free French operator had made good his escape, the Gestapo was even then waiting inside the apartment for just such callers as they were to arrive. It was time to leave and take another tack. Nancy and Bernard arranged to meet at a designated point on the other side of town, going by separate routes, where they would play their last card. The Briviste said he knew of a group of Maquis in the *département* of *le Creuse* who might still have a radio in operation and they should try their luck there.

On yer bike, Nancy. Always on the bloody bike. Over the last two days, she had grabbed only about five hours' sleep and she was entirely spent, but still the two joined up on the other side of town, and proceeded to the forest where this band of Maquis could be found. And indeed they had a radio! And an operator! True, this band of Maquis were aligned to the Free French in Algiers and previously had had nothing to do with the SOE, but thankfully their leader agreed to pass a message on to Algiers, asking them in turn to pass it on to Colonel Buckmaster in London—telling him what was needed and where to drop it. The Maquisard would do all that, he promised, on the morrow when the radio operator returned.

'If my radio operator says okay, then okay.'

Nancy could not wait to see if the message got through.

'I had to get back,' she remembers, 'and simply trust to luck that he would do what he had said he would do.'

Nancy had passed 'exhaustion' about a hundred and fifty kilometres back along the road and 'complete collapse' seemed as if it were just around the next bend, so she decided to head back to Saint-Santin by the most direct route and to hell with the Germans.

'I really didn't have the energy to do anything else,' she says simply, 'so it was a relatively simple decision. Every time I turned the pedals I was racked by pain, so I wanted to turn those damn pedals the very least I could. Many times, I wanted to stop and have a pee, but I thought if I do I'll never get on again, so I had to pee my pants. Fortunately I didn't have to do the other, because I don't know what I would have done then.'

Refusing to give in to exhaustion, she kept moving, her face oozing with the greasy kind of sweat which comes when the body barely has anything left to give. Yet if fortune favours the brave it also must be said that the brave seem to be able to draw on more energy than the meek, and a combination of good luck and great energy saw Nancy keep moving through the night, fighting off cramps all the while. She had a momentary scare on the outskirts of Montluçon when a figure suddenly emerged onto the road in front of her, but it proved to be the same Maquisard who three days' previously had accompanied her along the first part of her journey on his way to visit his wife. 'C'est un garcon!' he cried by way of greeting. It's a boy! The proud father had guessed which road she would be returning on, had waited for her and now figuratively rode shotgun for her all the way back to their encampment at Saint-Santin.

Of all the things she accomplished during the war, Nancy is most proud of this marathon ride, having completed just over four hundred kilometres in seventy-two hours.

'I got back and they said "how are you?" I cried. I couldn't stand up, I couldn't sit down. I couldn't do anything. I just cried. For the next few days and nights I could barely move as all the skin had been rubbed away from the insides of my thighs, so I really just had to lie there while the village doctor applied dressings and then spend a few days immobile till I could walk again.' For the record, fifty-four years on from that journey, Nancy still hasn't been back on a bike. 'Not once,' she says with some feeling.

But the job had been done.

Within forty-eight hours, a wonderfully familiar drone came from the west by the moonlight, and a package emerged floating down gracefully on the end of a parachute. A brand spanking new radio! Being carried by a new radio operator! He was a nineteen-year-old from Ohio by the name of Roger, and he proved to be excellent back-up to Denden who got on well with him from the first. From that point on, Roger essentially became Nancy's personal radio operator, while Denis Rake stuck more with Hubert.

They were back in business, with still plenty of business to get through . . .

CHAPTER TWELVE

'Le Jour de Gloire est Arrivé'

'War is too important to be left to the generals.'
FRENCH PRESIDENT, GEORGES CLEMENCEAU, 1917 [54]

'My philosophy was eat, drink, and be merry, for
tomorrow we die.'

NANCY WAKE [55]

Up and about at last, Nancy noticed that there had been an addition to the group. He was a Frenchman of rather pompous air who'd arrived from Clermont-Ferrand and who presented himself as a full-blown colonel of the regular French army. The whole manner of the man got up Nancy's nose from the beginning, this infernal air he had about him that while the amateurs might have done well for themselves to this point, it was a good thing that the professionals had arrived to get them organised. She thought him nought but a pompous twit, as overblown in body as he was in ego.

At one point, the fellow even dared to make a speech to the assembled gathering to the effect that he would be taking over control of the group from this point, and he looked forward to working with them all. To Nancy's mind at least it seemed as if this conceited bastard was directing the speech at her—to gauge just what sort of reaction the woman with the weaponry wand would have to his assuming control—and she did not disappoint ...

'All your plans sound fine, *Monsieur le Colonel*,' she returned, before coming to the point. 'But just what will you be using for weapons, ammunition and money, because there will be none coming from *moi*.'

Gotcha. Aces high, jacks low, clubs are trumps and in these conditions a *chef du parachutage* beat a *Monsieur le Colonel* every time! Hubert cheered and clapped Nancy's ringing declaration while the said colonel—whose rather pretentious moustache seemed instantly to droop—was left gasping for an appropriate response. What could he say, after all? Still, rather than engage in a turf war, Nancy and her bevy of SOE operatives and personal band of Maquis (now about a hundred strong) decided to decamp, move north, and stay near their old friend Henri Tardivat in the *département* of the Allier—the same Tardivat of course who had first greeted them when they landed.

This time, it really was a match made in heaven. Nancy and her band decided to set up their independent camp just a couple of valleys over from 'Tardi', near one of the fields they had been using for air drops, about ten kilometres outside the town of Ygrande. Fortuitously, as it would turn out, they were also close to a camp of six Spanish Maquis, who were anti-Fascist refugees from Franco's administration.[56] The key thing at the time for Nancy though, was that they were close to Tardivat.

From the first, Nancy had adored the good-looking and extremely charismatic former teacher. He had an easy charm, a quick wit, and was a natural born leader. Highly trained by this time to judge the battle readiness of a band of Maquis by just having a quick look around their camp, Nancy could see at a glance that Tardivat's was among the best she'd seen. The band were well fed, well shod—always an important factor when fighting in this terrain—looked happy, and were deferential to Tardivat's lead without a hint of the useless bowing and scraping that she'd seen around so many other tin-pot 'Generals'.

'And they laughed a lot,' Nancy says. 'It wasn't that they were frivolous by any means, they did more damage to the Germans than any of them, but they enjoyed being with each other in the forest and were fighting my kind of war.'

In these early days with Tardivat, a lot of their energies were focused on accompanying him on ambushes of German convoys heading for the Normandy front, ambushes having long been one of Tardi's specialties, even if he did say so himself. The country they were operating in was perfect for the task, with many roads pushing through the thickly wooded terrain that towered over them.

'We mostly did these ambushes when we could find the time,' Nancy says. 'We used to pick a nice high point so we could see, and then we'd place these bombs covered with plants by the side of the road, and we'd run a long piece of string from the trigger up to our hiding place and then wait for the convoy ...'

Presently, the low rumble in the distance would indicate that the convoy was getting close—confirmed by a look-out secreted at a point further up the road, who would flash a mirror—and the ambushers would crouch down in their hiding places, simply peeking out to await the right moment. Rumble (getting close now). Ten trucks, two armoured escort vehicles, one at the front, and one at the back. Lots of grim-faced Germans with helmets on, looking out, wondering if the thick forest held just such as Tardi & Co. Waiting. Waiting. Waiting, and ... NOW!

At the precise moment when the first bombs exploded, the Maquis would themselves explode into action. Often from both sides of the road, they would pour sustained fire on the stunned Germans who, superbly trained, would be rallying to return fire as quickly as they could.

Even as she was firing her own Bren gun or hurling grenades for good measure, Nancy would shake her head in wonderment at the ferocity with which her partisans engaged the Germans in battle. Their passion and pure fearlessness, often running up close to throw petrol bombs right upon the *Boche*, continued to stagger her.

While she was fighting against an ideology, these partisans were fighting against invaders who dared to occupy sacred French territory. They fought thus, with *l'ésprit de clocher*, the French notion of 'the spirit of the churchbells'—the innate knowledge that you are always stronger when you can at least metaphorically hear the sound of your own village churchbells in the near distance. They fought against the men who—to their eyes—had been personally responsible for the deaths and disappearances of their friends.

Careful though. An astute commander such as Tardivat would never let the action continue for too long. The Maquis were hit and run merchants, and must avoid at all costs a serious tangle. At Tardi's signal, they would start to pull back, melting into the forest while four or five chosen especially for the task kept the fire up on the Germans. Another signal, and those who had pulled back to a selected vantage point would start to fire allowing the others to withdraw . . . and so on.

'He and his Maquis were very, very good at it,' Nancy says admiringly. 'The best I'd seen. I loved fighting with them, and did everything I could so that London would give them absolutely everything they needed.'

At least to a point she did. When, a week after their first ambush together, Tardivat requested that Nancy provide a full load of Bren guns for his men, she said she would provide them on one condition. She wanted an improvement in her sleeping arrangements. After months of sleeping on the forest floor, it wasn't just the rustic charms of nature that had worn thin with her. So had her patience with bloody pine needles, wetness and bumpy ground. She hungered to sleep in something solid, with a roof, and preferably something that could still be moved—something like a bus!—and Tardivat proved equal to the task.

The process was quite simple. Taking fifty of his best men, he simply set up a blockade across the road and stopped every bus that came their way. All the passengers were invited to get out while Tardivat went to the back of the bus and inspected the back section to see if it had what Nancy specifically required—two seats facing each other where she could place her big mattress.

So it went, throughout the morning, with bus after bus rejected and the relieved passengers allowed back on, until precisely the right kind of bus turned up and those passengers had to walk the rest of the way. That left only the mattress to be found, and a local shopkeeper soon proved happy to oblige. The job was done.

From early July of 1944, let the record show, Madame Andrée was retiring at night to the very lap of luxury, on a large mattress covered with the silky sheets of the parachutes, while robed in a frilly nightie that she'd managed to bring with her all the way from London. This, she felt instinctively, was the *right* way to fight a war.

For his part, Tardivat had a band of Maquis who were soon positively *awash* in Bren guns. This was as well, for they were certainly going to need them. And, as it turned out, the bus was much more than Nancy's bedroom and entertaining area. It became an able workhorse when the time came for the Tardivat Maquis to move camp, which was often. To minimise the chances of the Germans ever locating them in the forest, their policy was to move to another site every few days, and when that happened Nancy's bus would be loaded to the gills and they would move out. It was as well, too, that Nancy's security policy of always having a well-established escape route was strictly adhered to, for when at one point they were warned that three thousand Germans were on their way to attack them, they simply loaded up the bus and left— leaving the Germans once again no solid thing they could strike at.

At this stage of the war, in early August, 1944, the Allies began sending something new with their weaponry. Manpower. Now that SOE operatives were well-established all over Europe, and there was an aerial pipeline along which weapons could be funnelled, it was decided that the next stage was to bolster trained Allied manpower on the ground to better organise the big battles with the Germans that were certainly to come.

The evening after the day in which the *Boches* had attacked an abandoned campsite, Nancy went to one of her fields to pick up two American weapons instructors who were parachuted in. With the numbers of Maquis in their area continuing to swell, the need to train them up was paramount, and these instructors were particularly welcome additions to their crew. Their reception went without a hitch, and they soon found the two men, Captain Reeve

Schley and Captain John Alsop, to be hearty companions just itching to get into it. Nancy took them back to one of the Maquis encampments near Tardivat—a place where they had some rooms in a farmhouse—and with a few others they all sat around in her bus drinking. At one point, Schley asked whether they were ever attacked by the Germans, and seemed a little nonplussed when Nancy casually replied that as a matter of fact they had been attacked that very day, but that she felt they would probably not be attacked the following day! Schley took another drink, and, indeed, they all drank heavily until four in the morning.

One can only imagine, then, what the Americans made of the pounding in their temples the following morning—only a few hours later. Was this a hangover to beat all hangovers? No. It was in fact the Germans coming right at them—finally having located their camp at last—and firing hard as they headed up the hill. Birds, alarmed at all the noise, were flying every which way above them away from the shooting as Nancy made an instant assessment. At this point in her camp there were only some eighty Maquis, plus thirty untrained fresh recruits, plus the two Americans, plus Denis Rake and herself. She estimated the Germans were attacking with around five hundred crack troops.

What to do against such superior numbers? Try superior weaponry! As it happened, in the previous evening's drop, the Americans had brought with them a full load of bazookas complete with ammunition, and though none of the Maquis knew how to aim and fire the bazookas, the Americans certainly did. No matter that they didn't speak French worth a damn, Nancy did! In short order it worked like this ... while the most hard-bitten of the Maquis held off the worst of the cautious German attack—they had no idea, after all, just how many Maquis they were up against— Nancy, Alsop and Schley began to move towards the battle with their band of volunteers, some of whom were *napthalinés*, new recruits, to a position where they were in bazooka range of the attackers. All around was the sound of machine-gun fire, grenades and the occasional scream. There was also a steady flow of injured Maquis coming back from the battlefront.

To get to the point where they could launch their bazooka-led counterattack, Nancy insisted they keep to the cover of the thick wood, and not take the easy route down the track. In the confusion of battle, some twenty of the newly joined Maquis became separated from them and took the track, perhaps thinking it was simply easier. This was a deadly mistake.

'We were in the woods,' Nancy remembers, 'carrying the bazookas forward when, just over to our right and quite close to us, there was this sustained burst of machine-gun fire followed by a lot of screaming.'

Nancy suspected what it meant, but would only be able to confirm it later. It was the recruits, in full view on the open road, being cut to pieces by German machine-guns. Seven lay dead or dying where they fell, thirteen made it back to the camp, shattered but alive.

Nancy and the Americans, with another fifteen Maquisards, did the only thing they could do, they kept pressing forward. At last they were in range, ready to exact some revenge. The men settled the bazookas on their shoulders and began firing on the forward German positions, as the Americans moved along the line and Nancy ran from one gun crew to another translating operating instructions. *Now* they could have a fair fight. FFFFWUMP!! FFFFWUMP!! FFFFFWUMP!!

It worked, after a fashion. With the Germans suddenly realising they were up against more than mere rifles—and seemingly not keen to take over the positions that had just been knocked out—they declined to press their attack. No matter that the bazookas were soon out of ammunition, they had introduced doubt into their enemies' minds and, in the momentary respite, Nancy and her men were able to make their way back to their original encampment.

They had bought themselves some time. Now, what to do with it? That, too, was obvious. They needed to get a message to Tardivat to attack the Germans from their rear and so provide the diversion necessary for them to get away on their escape route. Nancy adjudged that the best way to do this was to crawl to the Spaniards' camp, situated about two kilometres away, and get them to try to reach Tardi. Not wanting to trust such an errand to anyone else, particularly after what had happened to the recruits, Nancy and a courageous young Maquisard she admired crawled in a snake-like fashion across several fields—at one point under German fire—until they reached a forward outpost of the Spanish Maquis and could ask them to send to Tardi for help.

As Nancy details in her autobiography, 'When I returned to our camp, Schley said he didn't want the Germans to smoke the Havana cigars his father had given him back in New York, so the three of us sat down and puffed away as if we didn't have a care in the world. Suddenly we heard the sound of Bren guns and mortars to the rear of the Germans. I yelled out to everyone: "Tardivat, let's go!" He gave us time to retreat, then retreated himself, leaving the Germans to conquer a deserted campsite.

'Tardivat and his men had been sitting down to lunch when he received my SOS. I was amazed that Frenchmen would leave their meal, and said so flippantly. All he said was, "Aren't you glad you gave me all those Bren guns?" However, he had saved our lives.'[57]

What remained, was what always remained after such a battle. Cleaning up and burying their dead. The wounded had already been ferried to a quiet religious hospital nearby, but dealing with the dead was the worst of the worst. The following day when the Germans had departed, Nancy returned to where the seven bodies of the young Frenchmen had been laid out by their surviving comrades, in a barn of the farmhouse where the Americans had been staying. To enter into the darkness of that barn, with its deathly evil atmosphere and cloying smell—and then to try to accustom her eyes to what they were about to see—was truly wretched, but it simply had to be done.

Feeling somewhat responsible for their deaths—though it had in no way been her fault—Nancy insisted on bathing and dressing the corpses herself, trying to return to form bodies and faces that had in some cases been nearly blown away. The Germans had come along shortly after their ambush and had shot bullets at point-blank range into the foreheads of those who were initially wounded. Certainly, it did not necessarily make a whole lot of sense for Nancy to make such an effort on men who would very shortly be beneath the sod anyway, but she knew it was the right thing to do.

'I know it might sound absurd,' she says, 'but I felt in a way I was caring for their broken bodies on behalf of their mothers who weren't there, but would have wanted them looked after like that.'

Perhaps with that in mind still, Nancy equally insisted that this time they were not going to simply bury their dead in some nameless mound in the forest. Instead, she declared, they would go in full force to the local cemetery with their colours flying, and inter them there where they could be honoured for perpetuity; and where, after the war was over, a tombstone would be erected above them on which their names would be written with a simple acclamation: *Morts Pour La France*—Died for France. So many times in the past they'd just had to bury their fallen where they lay—if they had time to recover and bury the bodies at all—but this time it would be different. This time they *had* time, and they would do it properly.

With the dressing done, Nancy, with her band of Maquisards and the two Americans in tow, swept into the local village, placed some armed guards on the gate and conducted a funeral and burial service with all the trappings, including the local priest who had been rounded up for the occasion.

'It was right,' Nancy says simply. 'It was what their mothers would have wanted.'

A parenthesis. Although through all such events, Nancy's relationship with Hubert remained quite awkward, he was clearly quietly growing in his admiration for her. Shortly after the war in France was over, the British major was quoted in the London *Daily Telegraph* newspaper:

'She was magnificent, and incredibly popular with the Maquis. The partisans, many of them pretty tough boys, worshipped her, and were all a little scared of her. They could never really get used to calling a spade a spade. After one night in August, she became almost a legend in Maquis country. The Germans found our camp and attacked. There were only eighty of us. Nancy, armed with a small Colt automatic which she always carried, and a bazooka, led a section of ten men against a German machine-gun post, knocked it out, and led the section safely back.

'Another [time, our] camp was attacked and broken up and forty of us had to walk one hundred and fifty miles through the mountains to escape. It was her courage and humour which helped us through. The greatest and most sincere compliment I ever heard paid to anyone came from one of the partisans. After a skirmish with the Germans this man came to me and said: Madame Andrée has more guts than Jacques, and he's the bravest of us all'.[58] Close parenthesis.

After this tragic episode with the new recruits, Nancy and her troop made their next move, deep into the nearby forest of Tronçais, where it was judged the Germans would have an even harder time finding them, let alone attacking them. Not least of the pleasures of this place was that it was near a large pond big enough to bathe in, meaning that they would not have to wash out of buckets, which was their usual fate when not near the warm natural springs of Chaudes-Aigues. It was from such small things that great joy was generated during war-time conditions. It was only shortly after settling in there—in late July, 1944—that word came to Nancy that she was not, after all, the only woman living among the seven thousand Maquis. She was told that a nearby band of Maquis with whom she had had little contact to that point had captured three women who they said were spies, and they were abusing them sexually. Well, she'd be damned if such a thing was going to happen on *her* watch, whatever it was they were guilty of.

'Bring these women to me,' she commanded, a modern-day Boadicea whose word was law. Thy will be done, gone the sun. And it was. The following day, around breakfast-time, three bedraggled women in rags were ushered into her presence in the campfire before the bus. Though all had clearly once been attractive, they looked like nothing so much at this minute as haunted, hollow-eyed, and horrified with their lot.

The claim of the Maquis concerned was that they were all working for the Germans, and that one of them actually was a German. Nancy decided to interview them one by one to see if she could determine for herself just what the situation was. The young French girl, perhaps seventeen-years-old, was first—and it all came pouring out. She most certainly was *not* a spy, she said, and would never do such a thing *contre la France*. As far as Nancy could determine, the one reason this girl had been captured by a particularly reprehensible band of outlaw Maquisards was because of her extraordinarily voluptuous body. This was confirmed with subsequent enquiries, and the girl was not only instantly set free, but extreme disciplinary action was soon to be taken against those Maquisards who had so sullied their collective honour.

As to the older, perhaps thirty-year-old Frenchwoman, the reason for her capture was a little more complex. She had simply fallen in love with a man she shouldn't have, a *Milicien*—and the Maquis had had their revenge on her. Nevertheless, Nancy equally came to the conclusion that the woman presented no danger and assured her that her nightmare was over—that while Nancy couldn't approve of her ever sharing her charms with a man who was co-operating with the Nazis, she would no longer be subjected to the hideous treatment she had been and she was free to go.

The third woman, however, was entirely different. She *proudly* supported the Nazis and was open about the fact that she saw it as her duty to do everything she could to advance their cause. It was as unthinkable to release her as it was to set her back in the clutches of the same feral bunch of Maquis who had so ill-used her—or to send her to any other band of Maquis for that matter. That left only one option, and as Nancy looked at the thin woman with the straggly blonde hair and yet piercing blue eyes glaring straight back at her, she had no hesitation in making it happen.

'I am sorry,' she told the woman, 'but we cannot release you, and we do not have the facilities to keep you. This is war and you must have known the penalties for spying on the Maquis and reporting their movements to the Germans before you began to do it. You will have to be shot immediately, and I would like you to prepare for that.'

There might possibly have been some danger in telling such a woman such a thing—even though twenty armed men were within thirty metres of them both right then—but still, she was somehow not surprised when the young woman merely glared and nodded without fear, as if she were expecting that all along. She projected an air which was a curious mix of acceptance *and* defiance. Certainly there was nothing she could do about her fate, but she was not going to give her captors the satisfaction of thinking that they scared her.

'So I got a dress for her,' Nancy recalls, 'as she was practically naked, dressed in rags, while I went to organise the firing squad.'

Therein lay a problem. While a certain section of the Maquis clearly had no problem with keeping three women against their will as sexual vassals and lining up to abuse them without end, they drew the line at executing one of them in cold blood, and initially they outright refused to do so.

'If you don't, I *will*,' Nancy threatened, and meant it.

Shamed at the possibility that a woman was prepared to do something they weren't—even shoot another woman—they reluctantly agreed. Nancy sat down under a tree to have her usual breakfast of stale croissants and coffee brewed hot over the fire.

Usually in firing squads at this time, the one to be executed was put up against the corner of a building so that any missed shots were guaranteed to ricochet away from the execution squad, but in this case there was no need. Trees would absorb the bullets, and only a few minutes later the woman—now attired in one of Nancy's dresses—was led to stand in front of a massive pine tree while the firing squad formed up. Having refused a blindfold she simply stared imperiously straight back at her executioners and ... And wait, for there was, after all, one more thing she wanted to do.

Ready ...

Now averting her gaze to stare straight at Nancy sitting beneath a nearby tree, she first spat in her direction, ripped off her dress and threw it at her feet before lifting her arm in the classic Nazi salute ...

Aim ...

'*Sieg heil!*'

FIRE!

The sounds of the dozen shots rang around the forest as the now shattered and naked body of the woman was thrown back against the tree with the force and then crashed to the ground where it moved no more.

For a moment, as the last of the echoes faded away, there was a near total stillness. Nancy kept eating her croissant and sipping her coffee. What was done was done, and more importantly, what was done had *had* to be done.

'I was not a very nice person,' she says. 'And it didn't put me off my breakfast. After all, she had an easy death. She didn't suffer. I knew her death was a lot better than the one I would have got. And if I hadn't done it, and she had got away and reported to the Germans what the Maquis were up to, how could I have ever faced the families of the Maquisards we lost because of it? It was definitely the right thing to do.'

The final upshot of the episode was that the 17-year-old girl who Nancy had set free, begged that she be allowed to stay and look after Nancy's affairs in the bus—she simply had no family and nowhere to go to, she explained—and Nancy agreed. The young girl was not the equal of her young maid back in Marseille, Claire, but she wasn't bad.

For Nancy, these were the busiest days of the war, and her province of operations seemed to be continually expanding as London insisted she travel from her base further and further afield to assess the needs of more bands of Maquis and then organise the *parachutage*. If being the bearer of such largesse inevitably increased her popularity with those who received her beneficence, the downside was that it made her extremely unpopular with those bands of Maquis whom she declined to support—by reason of the fact that she simply didn't think they were deserving. To wit, by this time even the very term 'Maquis' to denote a single body of fighters was something of a misnomer, because there were now so many groups pursuing so many—often political—agendas. There were socialist and communist Maquis, secret army and regular army Maquis, ex-Vichyiste and ex-Milicien Maquis, even a Maquis for civil servants! While Nancy was interested in helping only those Maquis whose sole focus was beating the Germans, she had no desire to help groups whose chief interest seemed to be in manoeuvring for political advantage once the war was over, and on occasion she cut some groups dead completely.

On one occasion when she was on her appointed rounds driving in her car, unbeknown to her, a plan was being hatched by a disaffected Maquisard to kill her. He was a drunkard to beat all drunkards, and one day he announced to all and sundry in a bar where he was drinking, that the reason his band of communist Maquis had not received any money was because this so-called Madame Andrée had been spending it all herself, and he was personally going to administer summary justice—having been informed by an accomplice that she would shortly be visiting that very bar. (In fact, as Nancy recalls, the reasons she would not give his group of Maquis money was not simply because they were communists, but also because they were a slovenly ramshackle organisation who she thought could never be turned into an effective fighting force, no matter how much money and matériel London afforded them.)

'And when I came along,' Nancy recounts, 'this man had had way too much drink, and when he came out to throw the grenade at me he forgot to throw it in time, and took the pin out and blew himself up. And all I knew was, I was sitting in the car and bits of flesh were going all over the place, landing on the bonnet and on the windscreen.'

A happy ending, perhaps, for all but the Maquisard who'd come to such a grisly end, but for the other Maquisards—Tardivat, first and foremost—it was too much. To think that their beloved Andrée, their friend, comrade in arms, and provider of so much that was so valuable, had almost been lost to them, was too much. Tardivat stepped in and insisted that from that point on Nancy would travel only with a bodyguard, and a powerful bodyguard at that. And he knew where he would get that bodyguard from, too. At a previous point he had said to Colonel Paishing, the leader of the Spanish Maquis, on the subject of Nancy—'She is the most feminine woman I know ... until the fighting starts! Then she is like five men!'[59]—but now he went back to the same man, and told him that Nancy needed some extra armed grunt, and that they were the men who'd provide it.

Colonel Paishing and his Maquis, already admirers themselves, agreed with alacrity and from that point on Nancy travelled in a convoy of three cars, each one fully loaded with heavily armed Spaniards who were just *itching* for a fight.

'In the beginning,' Nancy recalls, 'they had me in the middle car, with one in front and one behind, but that was no good, because it was all dusty. So then I sat in the front car, and everything was fine.'

While even with her newfound firepower she tried to keep to the back roads to avoid the roadblocks, sometimes the Germans or the wretched Milice were there too.

'Twice,' Nancy says, 'we just had to shoot our way out. As we pulled up, we'd just have to suddenly point our Bren guns out of the window and start firing into them and then stamp on the accelerator.'

As she recollects, she never felt any qualms at the time, or remorse afterwards, over such cold-blooded killing of fellow humans.

'I loathed them,' she says flatly, 'I *loathed* them.'

On those occasions when she was not busy with her formal SOE work, she put a lot of her energies into fighting side by side with Tardivat, who always seemed glad to have her along. At this point in the war, late July of 1944, they all sensed that the Germans were beginning to reel under the combined onslaught of partisans all over France. Tardivat was keen to heighten this German sense of vulnerability by doing some daring courageous act that would demonstrate to the *Boche* that they were *never* safe, wherever they happened to be. Why not, he wondered out loud one evening around the campfire, launch an attack on the Gestapo headquarters at Montluçon!

What a splendid idea! For the next few days, Tardivat organised his men within the town to surreptitiously note down exactly what kind of defences both the Gestapo and the German garrison had set up there: how many sentries, where they marched, what time they changed shifts, and where their machine-gun nests were set up. When all this information was collated, a plan was formed.

What was clearly needed was a lightning strike on the Gestapo HQ, followed by a very quick getaway that would take the Maquis well away from the barracks of the soldiers. They would strike, it was decided, at 12.25 p.m., just before the Gestapo men had their lunch, at a time when they would be knocking back their usual luncheon aperitif of schnapps or the like. At this point they would be at their least vigilant, their attention distracted both by the alcohol and the meal to come. As usual with Tardivat he liked to have two bands—one to do the job and the other to provide support and help with the getaway. With that in mind, one band would make the attack while the other would position itself along the escape route to take out any pursuers or—even more importantly—attack any who would seek to block their exits.

Nancy, to her infinite delight, found that just as she had hoped, she would be with Tardivat in his attack group. He was that rarest of all leaders, as intelligent as he was brave, and she couldn't have asked for better. Watching him give orders like this, calmly organising his fighters in this life-and-death action to maximise both their own chances of survival *and* do damage to the Germans, Nancy realised all over again just how highly she regarded him.

'I loved him,' she says simply, 'and we were soul-mates. I never loved him sexually, but I loved the man, and I loved fighting with him.'

It was settled then. Just after midday, Tardivat, Nancy, and fourteen others of the first band made their way as unobtrusively as possible into the outskirts of Montluçon in four cars, all of them dressed to look like common workers coming into town for a bit of lunch.

Ready? Ready! *Maintenant! Vite! Vite! Vite!*

At 12.25 p.m. exactly, the cars roared up to the back entrance of the one-time town hall and now Nazi HQ—which the Gestapo, in rare organisational laxness, had left substantially unguarded—

and the Maquisards poured out of the cars and through the gate, Nancy staying just behind Tardivat. Bren guns and grenades at the ready, they stormed up the stairs, firing as they went, and along the top corridor where they knew the top brass would be gathered. Grenade pin out, NOW, Nancy turned the handle on her assigned door, put her shoulder on it, and threw open the door.

'I just saw Germans in uniforms looking up at me, startled,' she recalls, 'and then I threw my grenades at them, shut the door, and ran like hell.'

All of the marauding Maquis had been doing the same, and by the time the raiders were all back on the stairs again the air was split, *screaming split*, with the sounds of the grenades going off in the enclosed quarters, followed by the inevitable shrieks of the mortally wounded. Thirty-eight Germans were right then either dead or dying.

Vite! Vite! Vite!

It hadn't, of course, been only the rest of the Gestapo headquarters who had been alerted by the noise of the attack, and by the time they were back in their cars trying to make good their getaway, the roads were suddenly blocked. Not by Germans, as it turned out, but by the cheering people of Montluçon, who mistakenly thought they were being liberated and wanted to embrace their liberators! The cheers fell on ears still ringing from the sounds of grenades exploding too close to them, but there was no time even to rub them.

'We leaned on the horns, we threatened, we told them to go back to their homes, we did what we could,' Nancy says, 'but it was all we could do to get out and away.'

All up, the operation had been a colossal success and, emboldened by it, Tardivat, Nancy and all the rest decided to go to Cosne-d'Allier immediately to stop a train. Not to blow it up, or disable it, merely to stop it at the station to show they could. All passengers were required to disembark and present their papers to show that they were proceeding on business that had nothing to do with helping the Germans.

'It was more a signal than anything,' states Nancy, 'a signal to show to the populace that the Maquis was growing in strength, and that we too could stop trains and ask people their business. It was no longer the Germans who were solely in charge. We wanted to send a message that *la France*, the real France, was coming back.'

Time out for a moment. Things were going well and it was time, Tardivat decided, to celebrate, for several reasons. They had yet to properly welcome the Americans, who had been such wonderful weapons instructors to the Maquis and who were very likeable to boot. They had yet to rejoice that Madame Andrée had survived the outrageous attack on her. More than all of those, however, they had yet to toast three times through and once more for good measure that *la France* was on her way back!

Why not have a big dinner to celebrate everything put together, to which all of the Maquis in the most immediate of the nearby forests would be invited? Within a week, it was done. Literally out of the fields emerged bottle after bottle of France's best champagne, bubbly that some of the local farmers had buried in their fields against the day that the *Boches* would be gone from their lives and when they no longer risked having their cellars raided—and were now happy to share with the Maquis.

Makeshift tables were fashioned out of long logs on which old sheets and real borrowed tablecloths and parachutes were draped. A superb chef from a nearby village was appointed to prepare an eight-course meal with his entire staff on the stoves in his hotel, and then on the morning of the big day he was 'kidnapped' at gun-point and brought into the forest with those supplies—the kidnapping to forestall any possible repercussions from Germans or *Miliciens* if it was discovered that he had co-operated with the Maquis. All the invitees, and there were perhaps two hundred of them, were instructed to dress themselves to the *neufs*, and all did. The Americans wore their uniforms, with the brass and leather polished to a mirror-like state. Nancy wore a lovely dress that she had had fashioned out of the very parachute which had first borne her from the skies and into the arms of all these wonderful men!

And so it began, in the early evening, around seven o'clock. At that summery time of year the twilight went until about ten pm, but even so Hubert and Denis had somehow managed to rig lights up to some batteries, giving the whole dinner the superb effect of a forested fairyland. If perchance German planes came over, those lights could be doused at a moment's notice, but in the meantime it was magic.

'And it was just the most wonderful meal I have ever had,' Nancy says. 'Not just because the food itself was superb, but because we were celebrating such wonderful things—like the fact that despite everything, we were still *alive!*'

As Nancy has previously written, 'We toasted everyone and everything. We swore our eternal allegiance and love to France, Great Britain and the United States of America. When we couldn't think of anything else to toast we swayed to our feet and toasted the Germans and the Allied Forces for not having interrupted our gala dinner.'[60]

At one point in the festivities a visitor arrived from another Maquis group bringing a message from his leader. Invited to join them he stared goggle-eyed at the detritus of the four courses already gone, the empty wine and champagne bottles scattered around, and couldn't help himself . . .

'Do you eat like this *every* night?' he asked.

'Yes, of course, don't you?'

Waiter! More wine! And so it went until a storm in the early hours of the morning sent everyone scurrying back to their bases. Not to worry, the mood couldn't be broken, the feeling that the end was near for the Germans . . .

This, of course, was not merely because of all the good work done by the partisans. While across France they had been busily going about their work, so too had the formal forces of the Allies been making good headway up in the north-west, where the armies under the overall control of General 'Ike' Eisenhower were continuing to break out from their Normandy landing site to formally liberate Occupied France mile by bloody mile. If there remained a problem with this, it was that the Germans were still able to concentrate their defensive forces on just the one breach. It had long been planned to open a second front against the Germans in France, by launching an invasion along the Mediterranean coast, and it was at this time that Nancy's group got word that they were to prepare for such an eventuality.

Just as immediately prior to D-Day, the *parachutages* had come thick and fast, so too now. Every night, for nearly the entire night, she was engaged in organising the drops and then distributing the arms to the men. While Nancy still used Tardivat's camp as her base, many of her activities now came to be concentrated on the southern sector of her vast domain, as this was where the retreating Germans would be coming through, and this meant that she had to travel vast distances through territory still infested with an enemy who would shoot her and her guard on the spot if they had even one *whiff* of what they were up to.

'We had no choice,' she says. 'Sometimes I requested and London did. Other times, like now, London commanded, and I did. They were now insisting that I organise to arm the Maquis in the southern section and that's what I had to do.'

Across France, across Europe, the battle raged. On 15 August, 1944, the Allies did indeed up the ante another notch. Just after dawn on that morning, they launched Operation Dragoon on France's Mediterranean coast, with the Seventh US Army, under the command of Lieutenant General Alexander M. Patch, bolstered by three US divisions, an airborne strike force and a body of French commandos hitting the beaches between Toulon and Cannes together. The German defending force—both literally and figuratively shell-shocked—receded quickly under the onslaught, and after only twelve hours the Allies had 86,000 men and 12,000 vehicles on shore and ready to fight the good fight of liberation. The following day a fully French force, launched from the Free French in Algeria, themselves landed and quickly liberated Toulon and Marseille.

Clearly, for the remaining Germans, the game had changed for the worse, and unless they got out quickly they would be cut off by the liberating forces from the north-west and south joining up. With that fate before them if they didn't act, they did the only sensible thing and began to withdraw, harried and hassled all the way by the Allies behind and partisans in front.

Nancy—beside herself with joy that Marseille was now free and with it, she hoped, Henri—followed such events as well as she could from the scattered reports that were available, as did all those in her band. Now that the Allies had landed in the south, she and her band of Maquis set about knocking over specific factories, depots, bridges and the like as they had been instructed from London.

For Nancy and Hubert, though, there was one key difference from this point on. Both wore their full-kit military uniforms—just as many SOE operatives did around France. It was a signal to the populace that the Allies were already well on their way to liberating France, already active, and it was time for them to get with the strength. As to the Maquisards, they too loved seeing Madame Andrée strutting around with a military cap on her head, real pips on her shoulder, khaki tie, crisp shirt, army slacks and shiny boots. More than ever, it looked like she meant business, serious military business, and thenceforth they began to salute her when she gave an order.

The Germans, under assault from all sides and in the face of a population that was rising as one against them, continued to try to withdraw from the southern part of France. The Maquis, now that the hour of vengeance was fully upon them, continued to try to kill them off, until the last Nazi foot had left French soil.

Paradoxically, though, a large part of the Maquis' energies at this time were specifically designed to *slow* the German movement out of France ...

'*There,*' said Tardivat, putting his finger on the Michelin map on the tiny town of Cosne-d'Allier beside the Allier River, the same town she and Hubert had first been taken to. 'We must take out those bridges.'

It was nought but common sense. Intelligence had told them

many German divisions were even then heading their way and were trying to escape the pincers coming at them from the south and west by heading through the French geographical feature called the Belfort Gap, to get back to Germany and re-group. Essentially a gap in the mountains which allowed passage from west to east, the Belfort Gap had the Allier River standing guard on its western approaches and if the bridges across it could be blown, the Germans would be isolated.

Happily, the Maquis had a huge cache of explosives stashed away for just such an operation, Nancy having previously ordered it from London. They quickly retrieved the explosives from a cave near one of the parachute fields where she had hidden them several weeks earlier. Under normal circumstances they would have waited until the dead of night to carry out such an operation, but on this occasion there was simply no time.

'We knew we just had to go and take it out immediately,' Nancy remembers.

With explosives in hand, Nancy and Tardivat, plus Alsop and Schley and Nancy's ever-present band of Spanish Maquis bodyguards, simply sailed into the town, bold as brass, and after establishing that there were no Germans or Milice there that they would have to take out first, they drove to the road bridge. With several men posted at each end to thwart or at least delay any attacks that might come, they unloaded their explosives and got to work.

'The trick to blowing up a bridge,' Nancy explains, 'is finding its weakest point and then getting the explosive placed in just such a way on this point that it will do the most damage.' Unfortunately this weak point is rarely in the most accessible of places, and it typically involves attaching one end of a rope to a fixed point and the other around your person before climbing down to it, but ... 'But like so much of what I did during the war,' Nancy says, 'there was simply no other way, so with the explosives strapped to us, Tardi and I and some of my bodyguards started climbing down the struts of the bridge towards the point we had selected and set the explosives in place.'

Job done, they set the timers for five minutes and climbed back up to the top of the bridge to discover a problem.

The residents of Cosne-d'Allier. Alerted by the posting of the Maquis sentries that something was up, the townsfolk had turned out in force and were streaming all over the bridge. This was not, mind, in an effort to stop them blowing up the bridge, but to see if they could help!

'It was extraordinary,' Nancy says. 'They were jumping up and down, screaming with joy, even though what we were about to do was obviously going to seriously inconvenience them for a long time to come. They didn't care about that though, what they cared about was that we were going to stop the Germans! When the people saw that there really was hope, everybody got into the act and helped us.'

In this instance, the enthusiasm was almost too much as it was all Nancy and the others could do to clear them off the bridge before it blew up. But finally it was clear. There was a massive explosion, a screaming, searing screech as newly broken metal took the strain of weight it was never going to be able to bear and before their very eyes the entire bridge tumbled into the river below. They did the same to the railway bridge, and then skedaddled. Shortly afterwards, several German divisions trying to get back to the safety of the Fatherland, found only an impassable culvert where there had once been free passage. Over coming days they would be harassed and harried from all sides by other partisans and would end up losing a large number of their forces before finally surrendering.[61]

The effort of the Maquis in this operation was admirable, but there was another action to the south of them at that time which was even more courageous. A panzer corps was even then heading towards the town of Eure to cross the last remaining bridge on the Evreux River. Somehow or other this bridge was the last one left standing from all the RAF attacks. At the personal behest of the man who had risen to the very top of Allied military forces in Europe, Supreme Commander General 'Ike' Eisenhower, the SOE was assigned the task of taking out the bridge within the next twenty-four hours, even though the Germans had it heavily guarded.

As he details in his book, Buckmaster sent an urgent message to their best man on site, a Frenchman by the name of Hervé. The message read: 'BRIDGE AT EVREUX MUST REPEAT MUST BE DESTROYED NORMANDY BATTLE HINGES ON IT HAVE YOU EXPLOSIVES FOR JOB REPLY MOST URGENT MESSAGE ENDS.' Late that night, the redoubtable Hervé replied: 'MESSAGE RECEIVED AND UNDERSTOOD WILL DO IMMEDIATELY EXPLOSIVES AVAILABLE VIVE LA FRANCE VIVE L'ANGLETERRE.'

What happened immediately afterwards was never possible to tie down exactly under the circumstances, but its essence was clear. Hervé borrowed a bicycle from a local postman and filled its saddlebags and satchel with explosive.

'Then,' as Buckmaster writes, 'he cycled boldly up to the bridge and past the guards who controlled it. As he reached the centre of it, before the guards could do anything to stop him, he flung the bike and himself to the ground and pressed the instantaneous detonators on the charges he was carrying, so blowing the bridge and himself to pieces.'[62]

The bridge was blown, and the panzers stranded and left as easy targets for a squadron of RAF anti-tank planes that flew to wipe them out the following afternoon. On such acts of selfless heroism would the war be won.

One of the other places Nancy's Maquis hit was an armaments and munitions store in the Mont Mouchet area which, because of its strategic importance, the Germans had ensured was heavily guarded. It was going to be tricky. Stealthily in darkness, Tardivat assigned each of the band a gate that they were to try to breach at the appointed time, after first making sure that they had taken out the two sentries that were guarding them. After the sentries had been overpowered and secured, the rest of the band of fourteen would force the entrances, set their charges, and scarper like there was no tomorrow—for there wouldn't be one if they didn't get away quickly enough. This far into her career with the Maquis, Nancy was not surprised, but still a little honoured, to be given command of the band that was to neutralise the two sentries on the western side. By way of security, the Germans had cleared the surrounding low scrub to a distance of ten metres around the store, and it was in this space that the two SS sentries patrolled, back and forth, forth and back, back and forth.

From the safety of the bushes some hundred metres away, Nancy could see them, two ram-rod silhouettes discernible only because they were just that little bit blacker than the near blackness all around—all such establishments having doused external lights for fear of bombing. It was time. She gave the signal to her band of four and together, softly, oh so softly, they crept forward on their bellies trying to get close enough to strike. Mercifully, a recent rain had ensured that the leaves they were crawling through didn't rustle. Half an hour later, Nancy and her crew were so near they could hear the ceaseless *tramp, tramp, tramp* of the Germans' jackboots on the wet gravel beneath their feet, could see the shape of their helmets and even the rough contours of their noses and chins.

Nancy's heart pounded, her mouth dry. She was not afraid, simply aware that she and her band were now in an absolute life-and-death situation. Whatever else, they were about to 'play for keeps', as they used to call it back in the playground at Neutral Bay. The plan at this point was for the Maquis to wait till the two sentries met in front of the gate, about-turned and headed back on their appointed course and then when they were far enough apart to be no help to each other the attackers would leap out of the darkness and overpower them, before waving on the second band to do their stuff. That, at least, was the plan ...

The moment came. Nancy gave the signal to *move!* and was herself stealthily running towards her own target—hoping that she and her accomplice could be upon the sentry and knock him out before he knew what hit him—but the German heard them when they were still perhaps five paces away. In terms of the actual mechanics, Nancy could never be absolutely sure what happened in the next couple of moments but what she remembers is the stunned look on the face of the German as he saw them coming, his gleaming bayonet slicing up through the night as he tried to bring his gun to bear, and her own almighty leap upon him. Acting out of instinct pure—yet an instinct that had been trained and nurtured—she formed her right hand into a karate-like axe, and brought it crashing into the German's neck just two inches below the ear. Whatever cry had been just about to come out of his throat died with him as he fell like a sack of spuds at the stunned Nancy's feet, even as the other two partisans of her band signalled that they had the other sentry secured.

'I was glad to find the method worked all right,' Nancy remembers of her initial reaction to the knowledge that some mother's son lay dead at her feet, 'but was also conscious of the fact that I'd been hurt, and maybe badly hurt.'

She was that—the German's bayonet somehow having sliced along her right arm as she brought her right hand onto his neck. Reeling, and suddenly feeling faint, she was still able to signal to the rest of the band that the job had been done and that they could storm the entrance and place their explosives, before she herself passed out.

'Fortunately though,' she recalls, 'we had a friendly doctor available in a nearby village who could establish that it was really only a deep wound, and could stitch me up. Otherwise I think I would have died of blood loss or maybe gangrene.'

Afterwards, when it was all over, and she was safely back in her quarters with her arm heavily bandaged, and all the others—after assuring themselves that she was quite all right—had gone to celebrate the destruction of the armament store, she of course reflected on what had happened. The way she remembers it, she was not unduly troubled, in fact not at all . . .

'How had I become so aggressive?' she asks rhetorically. 'I remembered Vienna, Berlin and what the Germans had done to the Jews. I remembered seeing that poor French woman seven months pregnant, tied to a stake and bayoneted, criss-cross, in the stomach by the German soldier. I remembered how her screaming two-year-old held her hand and she was left to die with her unborn child as the German officer stood by. I remembered my friend in the escape route network who was beheaded with an axe after he had been captured by the Gestapo. *That's* how I had become so aggressive.

No, I did not weep for that sentry. It was him or me, and by that time I had the attitude anyway that the only good German was a dead one.'

It was raining again. It was a strange thing, Nancy reflected, how two weeks of rain could seem like two months, while two weeks of sun could pass like two days. And now, as a matter of fact, it seemed like it had been raining in l'Auvergne for as long as she could remember. Buckets of it. *Chats et chiens*. Cats and dogs. As a young girl, one of her principal pleasures had been to lie on her bed beneath the corrugated iron roof and listen to the rain thundering down just above her head while she was all curled up as snug as a bug in a rug ... but here that was not a possibility.

She and her men remained deep in a forest of quagmire, completely mired in quag, if that was what all this mud was called. Her bus was nestled in up to its axles, pools of water lay all around, a campfire of any sort was out of the question, and the only real shelter for a lot of them was in her bus, which was chock-a-block. The only upside of the whole thing was that it was so wet it seemed that even the Germans were staying indoors.

Or was it that, really, enough of the Germans had scarpered that the game had now changed? Maybe, the feeling grew, it was time to come out of the forest! Maybe, Nancy and Hubert discussed, it really was time to move in to some serious digs. Digs with walls, a floor and, most particularly, a *roof!* There was a place they'd heard of that seemed absolutely ideal, a sprawling and semi-abandoned chateau called 'Fragne' in an isolated spot about ten kilometres out of Montluçon. They went over and cased it out. It had no electricity or running water—and as a matter of fact it was so old it had never had either—but it was solid, well away from roads frequented by German patrols and the caretaker who lived in a small cottage at the gate was a patriot, just as the owner proved to be when contacted. The upshot was that they were in like Flynn!

On 20 August, 1944, the whole lot of them moved in, throwing mattresses on the floors and hanging up their clothes to dry in front of the roaring fires, as the rain continued to pelt down outside. And

Nancy, after having spent most of the previous four months organising death and destruction to Germans by use of Sten and Bren, now organised her Maquis to wield mops and brooms to thoroughly clean the place out. They got their water from a deep well at the rear of the chateau, they raided the cellar for some of the wine that was still there, chopped up some nearby dead trees as fuel for the fire, and when they were done after one full day of settling in, they wouldn't have called the king their uncle!

'It was wonderful,' remembers Nancy, 'absolutely wonderful, just to be in a solid structure again. It wasn't the Ritz, but it felt like it, after what we had been through.'

One of the best things about their new situation was that the grounds of the chateau were so extensive that they could be used as a site for drops from London. This was no small thing given that these drops were continuing flat out, as the Allies remained keen to press the advantage they felt they had already gained over a German army on the run. From then on, while Nancy still made one or two trips with her Spanish bodyguards to far-flung fields of distant Maquis, most of the drops fell right here in the grounds of the chateau.

But, first, a pause for great celebration. *Two* celebrations in fact ... Just a short while after they had moved into the chateau, the splendid news came through. Paris had been liberated! For the previous few days as the Allied armies had pressed closer, the men and women of the French Resistance Movement had begun to rise as one, joined by more and more of the citizens, and it quickly reached a point where they were collectively strong enough to openly fight the Germans in the streets of the capital. It had turned into a massive popular uprising, the kind at which Paris has always been rather adept—see 14 July, 1789, and a prison called *la Bastille* —and the Germans had had little stomach left for the fight.

On 25 August, a column of American and Free French troops entered the city to find only a few shattered Germans remaining, and the people literally dancing in the streets to meet them. As soon as the following day, Colonel Buckmaster himself landed in Paris to survey the ground and co-ordinate from on site the rest of

SOE's activities. He records a wonderful episode in his book, *They Fought Alone*:

'I remember very clearly,' he writes, 'on 26 August, 1944, when I entered Paris for the first time since the war began, a small boy of six or seven walked solemnly up to me as I crossed the almost deserted Champs Elysées. "Permit me," he said in faultless English, "to shake hands with a gentleman. We have not seen any gentlemen for four years".'[63]

Down in the chateau outside Montluçon they toasted the wonderful news three times three into the night, by the light of the flames in the enormous fireplaces.

Then to the celebration that Nancy would cherish every single moment since.

On her thirty-second birthday—30 August, 1944—Nancy came back from organising a drop at a distant airfield to find that a surprise luncheon had been organised in her honour. Similar in calibre and tone to the one held at night-time in the forest a few weeks previously—with hidden champagne and wine once again suddenly emerging from scattered burial dumps and many Maquis in the area invited—this one yet had a difference.

Before it began, Tardivat invited Nancy to follow him to the rear steps of the chateau where he presented to her a huge bouquet of flowers. She held them in her left arm, but was obliged to do something else entirely with her right arm. That was, she was obliged to stand ram-rod straight, flanked by her fellow officers, and salute as corps after corps of smartly dressed Maquis marched past saluting her. Even as she was standing there, Nancy remembers being amazed at the sheer *numbers* of men who kept on coming and coming and coming and coming. How on earth were they going to feed them all? Then she twigged.

'I recognised one of the beaming men saluting as one who I had already saluted in one of the front ranks! Those that had marched out of sight were quickly doubling round the chateau to come round and march again! They were a wonderful group of fighters, of *men*, and I was privileged to serve with them.'

Laughing herself silly—it was after all the thought that

counted—Nancy gave a very unmilitary hug to Tardivat for his thoughtfulness and the honour he had done her, and then the whole lot of them went inside for a lunch of more toasts and celebrations. After that, came another special pleasure.

'Everyone brought me some little gift,' Nancy once wrote. 'They must have been searching in the villages for ages as at that time everything was in short supply. My Spaniards, who had absolutely no money, had gathered all the wildflowers they could find in the forest and wrapped them in a Spanish flag, and one of the bodyguards had written me a poem. It was all very touching. The party continued until the early hours of the morning. It was a great success and the talk of the Allier for some time.'[64]

Only shortly after this party, Nancy was awoken one morning by the shout of the American, John Alsop, telling her that she had to wake up because 'the entire German army's coming up the drive!'[65]

Nancy looked out the window from her second-floor bedroom, and it was clear that Alsop was right. At the very least there was an enormous convoy of German vehicles passing by their front gate, a convoy that seemed to go on without end. Far from an aggressive force, however, it was clearly the German garrison pulling out of Montluçon. Happily, while Madame Andrée gave orders for everyone to lie low and not make any move to attract attention, the Germans continued to roll on past the chateau, grim-faced and barely giving it a glance. In the mood they seemed to be in—which was to get out, out, *out*—it is by no means sure they would have wanted a fight with the Maquis even if they'd known they were massed there. Surely they'd all had enough of the Maquis for one lifetime . . .

Just a few days later, the German garrison in Vichy itself took the same decision—or maybe even followed the same orders—and pulled out. Marshall Pétain had already fled two weeks before, being taken to the safety of Germany. Not only was the Wehrmachts' situation in this part of France now deemed hopeless, but it was getting time for every able-bodied German soldier still standing to get back and defend what was left of the Fatherland. The way things were going, not even Berlin was considered safe.

With the German departure, there was a race to formally liberate Vichy, and as Nancy's Maquis were only a hundred kilometres away, they were among the first to arrive and were granted a similar reception to the first Allied troops that had entered Paris.

The German philosopher Nietzsche once wrote of 'the melancholy of all things completed', but appropriately enough on this most un-German of all days, Nancy didn't feel it. Rather, she shone like a Sunday morning. Arriving in Vichy with her band of Maquis was the veritable end of a long campaign for her, as for so many, but her paramount emotion was joy. *Light-hearted* joy and *savage* joy both, the former for the looks on the faces of the Vichy people who were now liberated from the yoke of German occupation, the latter for the looks on the faces of the few captured Germans themselves, the persecutors now persecuted.

Many captured Germans were instantly shot or hanged in these tumultuous days by a vengeful populace, as were a large number of *Milicien* and collaborators who were now made to pay the price for their folly. By one authoritative account, 'during the weeks before and after the liberation, at least eleven thousand collaborators were summarily executed.'[66] French women who were known to have slept with Germans were often shaved bald and paraded in public squares.

Overall, though, the mood on this particular morning—as the victorious Resistance fighters drove through the crowded and celebrating streets—was one of liberation, not just of the city itself, but of collective emotions too long contained.

'People were cheering us, jumping up and down, singing, embracing us,' Nancy recalls, 'and this went long, long into the night.'

Which was fitting in a way, as between all the *parachutages* and raids, evacuations and celebrations, Nancy calculates she only averaged four hours' sleep a day, if that, for the whole time she was in France on her mission.

The morning after Nancy's arrival in Vichy, a ceremony was organised at the Cenotaph—the memorial for all those locals who had given their lives during the Great War. This was essentially a ceremony of thanksgiving that France had come through the war with her territories intact, while the invaders had for the most part been sent packing back to a Berlin that would surely soon be burning. Many of the citizens were in their finery, bearing wreaths to honour those who had fallen in this war; the Maquis themselves were in their pomp, still bearing the arms of victory, and Nancy was in the best of all possible moods when she saw a face she recognised.

She instantly started waving and calling out her name. It was a woman she had known from her Marseille days, the receptionist at the Hôtel du Louvre et Paix. Nancy embraced her warmly, and though the woman returned the warmth, there was horror to come in her next words.

'What are you going to do now?' she asked Nancy.

'I'm going back to Marseille.'

'Why are you going there?'

'To see Henri.'

'Oh no, Nancy, don't you know? He's dead.'

Nancy burst into tears, and nearly collapsed. To hear such a thing, on such a day, in such a way, was simply more than she could stand. She pressed the girl for more details, but there were none. All the young woman could say for sure was that Henri was dead, and the Germans did it because he would not co-operate with them. Nancy just couldn't believe it. Dear, sweet, wonderful, laughing Henri. Dead. All through her activities in France, she hadn't dared contact her husband for fear of compromising either him or herself, even at the point when she had walked within one hundred metres of the front door of their penthouse. But she hadn't dared doubt that he was still alive. Henri was just like that—so full of life and love that it was simply inconceivable that he could ever lie there lifeless, his body shattered by bullets ... She howled, the thought of it simply too horrifying. Denis, good ol' Denis, took her by the arm and led her away, the better to compose herself, while Hubert also moved to comfort her.

'Anyone would have been torn apart by the news,' he says, 'but in Nancy it seemed so much worse, because she was always such a happy, joyous soul. This was the only time I ever saw her, seriously, seriously distressed.'

As soon as that afternoon, Nancy was heading south, south to Marseille in a car with Hubert, Denden, John Alsop and a Maquis doctor by the name of Pierre Vellat. Her closest friends had insisted on accompanying her on such a dangerous mission, for going to Marseille at that time was not simply a matter of heading the car south and following the bonnet bauble till the distinctive silhouette of the famous port city appeared on the far horizon. Not only were many of the roads closed because the hulking wrecks of burnt-out German vehicles still blocked them, but many key bridges had also been blown up—either by the Allies bombing from the sky, or ironically enough, by the Resistance taking out their designated targets to hamper German movement in the face of the Allied advance. In short, it was a long trip, with many dead ends, and searching for alternative back roads—against a constant flood of movement coming the other way—with Nancy sitting stoically in the front, barely speaking, as quiet as they'd ever known her to be.

At last, they reached Marseille. Nancy's first port of call was her butcher's shop. It had clearly not been damaged since she'd last seen it, but it was closed. She went around the back in the hope that the butcher and his wife would be there. And they were. The look in their eyes when they saw her almost made her weep aloud anew. Their eyes said: *We know what happened to Henri ... but do you?*

Nancy nodded that, yes, she knew her husband was no more, that it was all right. She had accepted it, but now she wanted to know what more they knew of the terrible event.

It would take some time to get the full story, and when it came it was very ugly indeed. As near as she could work it out, O'Leary had been arrested by the Gestapo in March 1943 and had been taken to their dreaded headquarters at 425 La Rue Paradis, before shortly thereafter finding himself in a cell at Saint-Pierre prison.

He had been sent to rot in gaol. Somehow or other he had come across information in this gaol which he needed to pass on to the Resistance and he chose Henri as his point of contact. To relay the message in early May he had told a prisoner who was about to be released Henri's address, the password with which Henri would know he was 'one of them', and the password with which Henri would reply. It all happened according to plan, yet no sooner had Henri given the incriminating password in reply than he was arrested by the Gestapo and taken away to a cell. The 'prisoner' who had been released, was in fact a double agent in the service of the Gestapo. From there, it got even uglier.

Much later, a French protestant pastor who had survived in the same Gestapo prison as Henri, would tell Nancy what had happened next. The Gestapo, realising they had got a big one— quickly working out that Monsieur Fiocca's absent wife must have been the White Mouse they had been looking for—had subjected him to daily beatings and torture. Putting it all together, Nancy realised that while she had been gallivanting and drinking in Gibraltar waiting to get on her convoy in May of the previous year, her husband was being tortured at the hands of sadistic Nazi brutes who were surely doing to him what they truly wanted to be doing to her.

'They beat him so much that eventually his back just caved in,' Nancy has previously recalled. 'By the time they had finished with him his kidneys were hanging out of his body.'[67]

One other story that the priest told Nancy would never leave her. That is that the Germans, desperate to break Henri, had approached his father and made it absolutely clear that the only way his son could save his life was by co-operating with them and giving them some clue as to where they could find his wife. With this in mind—and more firmly convinced than ever that his daughter-in-law was simply a human manifestation of catastrophe as he had always said she was—the father had gone to see the son and had tried to convince him that he had only one hope of salvation, which was to give over all information that might lead to the arrest of Nancy. Through shattered teeth and bloodied lips from that morning's attempt at persuasion by the Germans, Henri had told his father to *never again* speak to him of such things or he would no longer call himself his son.

He would not co-operate with the Nazis, and that was the end of it.

And that really was the end of it. Henri had been taken from his cell and shot at dawn on 16 October, 1943.

'I blamed myself for the death of that wonderful man,' Nancy says, 'and I always will.'

Nancy was, of course, not the only one completely devastated by the loss of Henri. On the streets of Marseille perhaps three days after returning, and still lost in a haze of grief, she nearly ran into him, her father-in-law. Upon seeing her his face froze, and then pulling himself up to his full hauteur, he spat it out.

'*Vous avez assassiné mon fils!*' he roared. You have assassinated my son.

What happened next was as instinctive as it was sudden. Before even she knew it had happened, Nancy had drawn her arm back and slapped him across the face as hard as she could—which was very hard indeed.

Shocked, Monsieur Fiocca made a motion to return serve, but was held back by his companion, hissing urgently '*Dédé, ne fait pas l'imbécile!*'.

And it would indeed have been an imbecilic thing to do, for even as he had drawn his own arm back to strike his daughter-in-law, Nancy's four companions had moved forward and would have struck him senseless if he had hit her. And there the matter rested, uncomfortably, for ever afterwards.

An old friend she met in a Marseille restaurant told Nancy another thing about Henri's last months that she would never forget.

'After you left Marseille,' she said, 'he would come to our house sometimes, other times he would just stay at home. But all the time, at our home or his, every night, he just sat and played patience. He wouldn't go out to meet people. Not anyone. All the time—just patience. And whenever we tried to shake him out of it, he would look at us and say: "I'm all right. I just want to wait till Nancy gets home". I thought you would want to know.'[68]

The one bright spot in an otherwise extremely unhappy return was that she was reunited with Picon, her beloved dog. He had

been cared for by friends, and from the moment she had knocked
on their door and called out, the little terrier had joyously barked
up a storm. She was back.

*Home is the sailor, home from the sea, and the hunter home
from the hill.*[69]

In fact, though, Marseille would never again be a home to her.
Without Henri she simply did not want to stay there any more.
When she returned to their apartment it was to find that while the
walls were still standing, near everything else of her furniture and
personal effects had disappeared, was ruined, or reduced to the
detritus of her old life, lying around on the floor. Whoever had
been staying there after Henri's arrest and execution had clearly
pulled out with the German forces, and she wept some more to
think of her and Henri's home having been used by Nazi
sympathisers or worse. (She would later find out it had been taken
over by three female Gestapo agents.)

Seemingly, only one artefact from her old life had survived more
or less intact, and she found it in their cellar. All the wine had of
course been consumed or taken, but there on the floor beneath all
the rubbish she found it.

'It was my copy of *Anne of Green Gables*,' she says, 'and I
rejoiced to find it. Somehow, through everything I had been
through, it was still there for me.'

She sat right there on the floor, turned to the opening page, and
began to read:

> *The good stars met in your horoscope,*
> *Made you of spirit and fire and dew.*

Still more tears . . .

It had been a long war. While the fighting would go on for
several months, her own active part in it—in terms of actually
firing the bullets—was all but over. The safe deposit box in the
Marseille bank in which Henri had left her money as insurance,
even after he was gone, was empty, the entire bank having been
raided and looted in the last days before the Germans left. She
would have to start over anew.

After tying up more loose ends and saying many many goodbyes, Nancy, with Picon in tow, returned to the chateau in l'Auvergne where the rest of her Maquis were continuing their own mopping-up operations. The last of these was to quite literally mop up the chateau to ensure that it was in good order before handing it back to the owner who had so very kindly let them use it. Between times, they all attended endless lunches and dinners put on in many of the newly liberated towns around them, to thank the Maquis for everything they had done.

Finally the day came to say goodbye: to l'Auvergne, to the Maquis, to the intense life they had all lived together. On a shining morning in late September of 1944, with a car happily idling at the bottom of the chateau's steps, Nancy embraced Tardivat first and foremost, and those of his fellow-fighters who had not yet returned to their villages. There were tears, vows that they would all meet again soon, that they would never forget each other, that they would all write to each other regularly, and yet more last embraces and kisses on both cheeks.

'And then,' Nancy says, 'I just had to turn, and walk away. Get into the car and go. It had to end sometime, and that is when it ended.'

Nancy, Hubert and Denden drove north to Paris where the SOE had set up a headquarters to greet and liase with all their agents across France—most of whom were similarly gathering in the newly liberated City of Lights once their own areas of operation had been rid of all Germans. Along their route towards the French capital they encountered cheering crowds as the entire nation seemed to have re-emerged from beneath the Nazi jackboot and were both rejoicing at their newfound freedom, and expressing their thanks to all those in military uniforms who were clearly the liberating forces. In Paris they had an emotional reunion with Colonel Buckmaster, who was lavish in his praise for what they had achieved; and then began weeks of partying, dancing and drinking as they continued to celebrate.

Not that *everything* was all sweetness and light. While she and a female friend were taking their time to order in a restaurant which had been reserved for British officers, Nancy overheard a French waiter muttering that he much preferred to serve forthright Germans than the dithering English. Well she never! Using some of the best epithets she had learned over the previous decade, Nancy told the waiter *exactly* what she thought of him and his likely parentage and, by way of emphasis only, felled him with a single blow. The man fell at her feet unconscious while other waiters fluttered around nervously, yet she noticed with satisfaction that all were extremely careful to remain just out of her range. Then the *maître d'hôtel* arrived with a glass of his finest brandy, intended to revive the still felled waiter. Nancy grabbed it from his hand, and downed it with a single swig.

'It was my favourite brandy,' she explains, 'Bisquet Dubouche, and I didn't want it to be wasted on that nincompoop.'

She then returned to the table, where her friend had been waiting patiently, and they went on with their meal. The next waiter made no comment at all on the time they took to make their selections. While they enjoyed their meal in a liberated Paris, to the east the war continued as the Germans grimly held on.

But the result of the war was now clear to all, and, on 16 October, 1944 Nancy flew back to London, mission accomplished.

Nancy was more fortunate than she knew at the time to be able to fly back relatively unscathed from her mission, as many of her fellow agents had not survived at all, many coming to grisly ends. Just under one hundred of the 469 SOE operatives in the French Section had been killed in action, and as many again were severely wounded. There had been thirty-nine women who had been given missions and of these a dozen had been killed outright, while three had been imprisoned and tortured at the infamous Ravensbruck concentration camp, though had at least survived to tell the tale.

EPILOGUE

'It was dreadful, because you've been so busy and
then it all just fizzles out.'

NANCY WAKE
The Australian, 25 April, 1983

And then?
Exactly. After the war was over, Nancy was not quite sure
what she wanted to do. Whereas in the previous six years she had
always had a bright star by which to steer—to rid France and
Europe of the Nazis—it was not nearly so easy to find a satisfying
direction now that the Nazis' destruction had indeed been
accomplished.

'After everything that had happened it was out of the question
to return and live in Marseille,' she says, 'I simply couldn't bear to
be there without Henri, and nor did I want to return to Australia.
By this time I had become sort of European-ised.'

This was all understandable, but feeling European and being
able to afford to continue to live there were two entirely different
things. With Nancy and Henri's wealth now effectively gone, what
she most urgently needed was a stable job. Immediately after the
war ended, Nancy had managed to secure some clerical work in
Paris with British Military Intelligence, but when that job petered
out after just three months she really was at a loose end.

'It was tough for a little while when the office closed,' she
recalls, 'and I didn't know what I was going to do. But then out of
the blue Denden came to see me with some good news. He had
been given a job in Paris, in the British Passport Control Office,
and advised me to go post-haste to see the same Miss Southam
who had interviewed him.'

In short order Nancy herself had secured a job there. The work itself didn't thrill her, but it at least allowed her to remain in her beloved Paris, meaning she could be with her many French friends, as well as see the many British service people whom she had come to know during the course of the war and who had stayed on. One person she saw regularly was her old friend Tardivat. In the final months of the war, 'Tardi' had joined the suddenly reformed and revitalised French army who were pursuing the Germans back to their borders. Terribly, in the fighting at Belfort Gap, he had sustained a serious injury to his left leg, causing its amputation, but he had quickly made the best of his situation. After the Germans had finally surrendered, he had moved to Paris to begin a business career, had married his childhood sweetheart, and together they had a little girl whom they christened Nancy after her godmother.

'It was one of the proudest moments of my life,' Nancy remembers warmly, 'when Tardi made me godmother to that beautiful little baby.'

Tardi went on to prove himself a great success in the world of business, so much so that he was able to employ a doorkeeper at his office block for well over three decades—a man who was now as singularly devoted to the former Resistance leader as he had once been to Nancy. For this doorkeeper was none other than Colonel Paishing of the Spanish Maquis who had been Nancy's bodyguard—and the opportunity to see the Spaniard was yet another reason that Nancy so often delighted in going to see Tardi.

Another whom Nancy saw a lot of was Micheline, who had settled in Paris with her husband Tom Kenny, and who was busy raising their three children. Though Nancy was not formally a godmother to those children, she was a frequent dinner guest at their apartment and an always available babysitter.

In a way thus, her life in Paris was a slightly tamer version of what it had been ten years previously, except that instead of working as a journalist she was sorting out British visas and passports, and instead of nightclubbing till all hours she was more likely to be dining till late with friends either at their place or hers. It was fun, sort of, but she still was far from content.

'I missed Henri,' she remembers, 'sometimes terribly, and hadn't really met anyone else, but in those situations there is nothing you can do but keep going and that is what I did.'

She was at least thrilled to receive a lot of recognition for her wartime achievements from Britain, France and the United States of America—and the medals bestowed upon her soon made her one of the most decorated of all those who had fought in the Second World War. While the Australian government awarded her no honours—on the simple reckoning that she had not fought for any of the Australian services—France awarded her the *Croix de Guerre* with Palm and Bar; the *Croix de Guerre* with Star; and the highly coveted *Medaille de la Resistance*—rarely awarded to the French themselves, let alone to a foreigner, and the *Chevalier de Legion d'Honneur*. The Americans awarded Nancy the Medal of Freedom with Bronze Palm, with the citation concluding: 'Her inspiring leadership, bravery, and exemplary devotion to duty contributed materially to the success of the war effort and merit the praise and recognition of the United States'.

It was the award from Britain that touched her most though. On 21 April, 1948, at a cocktail party held at the British Embassy—attended by her nearest and dearest in the French capital—the British Ambassador Sir Oliver Harvey presented Nancy with Britain's highly coveted George Medal, 'for brave conduct in hazardous circumstances'.

None of the above, however, stilled the sense within her that she wanted much more from life than processing passport and visa applications. This dissatisfaction is clear in a small article which appeared in the British newspaper *The Star*, the day after Nancy was awarded the George Medal.

Bored Heroine
Over the phone from Paris today a musically girlish voice asked me: 'Can you get me an exciting job? I'm so bored...' Owner of the voice was Mrs Nancy Fiocca, wartime heroine who has just been presented with the George Medal for exploits in France in 1944.

You would think she had seen her full quota of thrills ...
But Mrs Fiocca assured me today she is ready for more.
('I'll do anything and go anywhere—to the North Pole if
possible.')

At the moment, grey-eyed, dark-haired Mrs Fiocca works
in the Visa section of the British Embassy. She has a
furnished flat, gives dinner parties and goes to occasional
cinemas and theatres. But all the time she hankers after life
with the partisans ...'[70]

Nancy sounded a similar theme when an Australian newspaper interviewed her about her medals shortly afterwards and, after the writer had skimmed briefly over the stupendous nature of her life and times with the Maquis, had finished with a quote from Nancy: 'Now,' she grumbles, 'I'm sitting in a so-and-so office'.[71]

This growing restlessness finally propelled Nancy to leave that so-and-so office—even if it was in Paris—to return to Australia to see if she might be more contented there. To overcome the ongoing money problem, she actually worked her passage home as a nurse on a ship called *Svalbard* which brought 899 displaced refugees from the British and American zones of Germany. She sailed through the Heads of Sydney Harbour on the bright sparkling morning of 16 January, 1949. It had been seventeen years since she had left—effectively a lifetime ago, it seemed to her. The most obvious difference was that when she had left Sydney in 1932, she had been as anonymous as a wrong number, but now Nancy was amazed to find that she was something very close to famous!

'Six Medal Heroine Returns', ran the headline in the *Sunday Sun* on the day she landed—and from that point on she seemed to be hailed far and wide wherever she went.[72] Old school friends and teachers looked her up; mere acquaintances claimed her as a warm friend; she was stopped by strangers in the street and had her hand warmly pumped. 'Good on yer, Nancy!' they enthused.

Happily, Nancy's family, including her mother, had also welcomed their heroine warmly. The last time Mrs Wake had seen Nancy she had been a slip of a girl disappearing through the window as she ran away from home, but both mother and daughter were conscious that of course things were different now. Now, they were two grown women. Accordingly, Mrs Wake made no attempts to control her 37-year-old daughter's behaviour in even the tiniest manner, and for her part Nancy had matured enough to realise that she might have been too hard in her previous assessments of her mother.

'I realised more than ever,' Nancy says, 'that life had not been kind to my mother, and that I should be.' While there would still remain something between a niggle of a strain and a strain of niggle in their relationship, the two were more or less reconciled two decades on from their falling out. Beyond that, Nancy was absolutely delighted to see her favourite sibling, Stanley Herbert Kitchener. He was a lot thinner than she remembered. He had spent most of the war as a prisoner of war in the infamous Changi Prison Camp—he had been captured by the Japanese after his ship had sunk—and had still not quite recovered. But it was still her Stanley all right. The two talked for days, for weeks, catching up with what each other had been up to and during the war ... and considering just what Nancy might do now that she was home.

For the same problem beckoned. Changing her address had not really changed her situation. Where to head? What to do? How to pay the rent? The medals she had been awarded had been a great honour, but they were far from legal currency. She was just beginning to wonder whether she should have remained in Europe when an interesting offer came her way.

Why not, a senior Liberal Party official asked her, use all her fame for the good cause of running for the Federal seat of Barton against none other than the then Deputy Prime Minister, Dr Clive Evatt? Why not indeed? Nancy agreed and when she did indeed win preselection for the electorate—centred on Hurstville and Kogarah in Sydney's southern suburbs—the Liberal Party sent Dr Evatt a telegram: 'Nancy Wake, Liberal candidate, parachuted into Barton tonight'.

Nancy's move into politics prompted another round of headlines—'Maquis Heroine Tries Politics',[73] 'War Heroine's Lib

Selection'[74]—and she spent most days thereafter travelling from her tiny apartment at Kirribilli by ferry across to Circular Quay and from there by train to her electorate, where she pounded the pavement, knocked on doors and addressed meetings.

'I wasn't sure if it would be my sort of thing when I started,' she says, 'but the more I did it, the more I liked it.'

Not that there weren't problems for all that. The Liberal Party was a deeply conservative organisation with very firm ideas about how a woman should behave, and many local members looked askance at 'the Nancy Way', for it was hardly a perfect match. She, for example, never wore stockings or a hat, and was quite happy to cross her legs while sitting on a public platform if she felt like it. And, if she wanted to have a drink in a beer garden she did so, and she simply did not give a damn if some in the party thought that this was too unladylike for their proposed representative.

'What did I care about trying to be a lady?' she asks rhetorically. 'After what I had been through, the thought that I would worry about whether or not I wore stockings or a hat was completely ludicrous. If any of them ever wanted to chip me about it, I told them off in the strongest possible language.'

In the media, the language Nancy used to promote her bid was also very forthright, bordering on extreme.

'At first,' she told the *Sydney Morning Herald*, in an article explaining why she had gone into politics, 'I didn't realise what was happening in Australia. Then I came down to earth, seeing exactly the same sort of things happening here as caused all the trouble in Germany and Europe: a gradual gathering together of controls, centralisation of power in the hands of a few power-hungry fanatics. A few people have actually set out to rule the country without Parliament, certainly without taking proper notice of the Opposition. That is why I decided to take up politics.'[75]

With all her fame, and the energy she was clearly putting in to winning the seat, the Labor Party wheeled in its biggest of all big guns. None other than the Prime Minister himself, Ben Chifley, came to exhort the electors of Barton to return Dr Evatt to Canberra, though he was careful not to utter one word of criticism of Nancy Wake. It seems that this was more than simply a polite public stance, for when, by pure chance, the Labor Prime Minister happened to come face to face with the Liberal candidate in the corridor of a hotel in the Barton electorate on a day when they were both campaigning, the Prime Minister removed the pipe from his mouth, bowed deeply, and moved on.

'He was a lovely man,' Nancy recalls warmly, 'a true gentleman.'

In the end, it was very close. Going into the election, Dr Evatt had a margin of 11,112; coming out of it that margin had been cut to just 2,644. At least, to Nancy's satisfaction, he was no longer Deputy Prime Minister as the Labor government had been defeated.

'I never liked Dr Evatt,' Nancy says, 'and I was glad I at least gave him a fright.'

Undaunted, Nancy decided then and there to stand against Dr Evatt in the next election, and spent much of her time subsequently speaking to women's groups, Rotary Clubs, at fundraisers for various community groups, Liberal Party gatherings, and the like.

'I had got so close in my first attempt,' she says, 'I thought I would have to be a very good chance the second time.'

Between times she paid her rent by working as an Appeals Officer for Legacy—an organisation devoted to helping the families of the fallen from the war—deciding to whom their precious resources could best be allocated.

In the interim, Nancy had a wonderful surprise and a most pleasant break when, in the winter of 1950, her beloved 'Denden', Denis Rake, turned up in Sydney as a steward on a luxury cruiser. Nancy welcomed him by standing on her Kirribilli lawn and, in a pre-arranged signal, waved a big white sheet as the cruiser arrived. Denis had also been recognised for his wartime feats with a Military Cross, *Croix de Guerre* and Distinguished Service Order, and for the four days he was in town the two barely slept—talking late into the night about old friends, past exploits, and the extraordinary times they had known together. If they shared the tiniest measure of pathos between them that only such a short while after the two had been so actively involved in a project as grand as ridding Europe of the Nazis, the world only now required one of them to serve coffee to rich tourists and the other to work the telephone for Legacy ... it mostly went unacknowledged.

'I think,' Nancy says, 'we both knew that each of us had experienced far better times, but it wasn't the sort of thing we wanted to dwell on. It was just really good to see him.'

In 1951, another Federal election was called, and Nancy went after the prize even harder than the first time. Referring to the fact that as a King's Counsel, barrister Dr Evatt had won a famous legal victory in the High Court by successfully arguing that the Communist Party Dissolution Act was invalid, Nancy went in with all guns a'blazing—as of course, she was wont to do.

'I am the defender of freedom,' she told the press. 'Dr Evatt is the defender of communism.'[76]

This time, sensing that Candidate Wake really had a great chance of victory, the Prime Minister again came to speak, but this time the Prime Minister was the Liberal leader Robert Menzies, telling the electors that they must send her to Canberra! In the final wash-up they very nearly did, as after all the counting had finished Nancy finished just 127 votes behind Dr Evatt. This time, though, she had had enough. Just two months after this defeat, the Liberal Youth Party from Nancy's electorate gathered in her cabin on the good ship *Oronsay* to wish her farewell. She was leaving, heading back to London.

'I really just decided that I wasn't happy in Australia after all, and would be better off back in Europe,' she says.

Australia had not offered her the stability or sense of direction she desperately needed. At least in London things got off to a better start and really did work out better.

'As soon as I unpacked my trunks and settled into the little flat I had rented I felt a great load had been lifted from my shoulders. It was just wonderful to be back there.' Through her many contacts and her extraordinary reputation she was soon able to secure a job on the staff of the Air Ministry in Whitehall in the Department of the Assistant Chief of Air Staff (Intelligence). One of the many tasks she had was to lecture Reserve Units on techniques of evasion and escape while in enemy territory, and she also devoted herself to writing a manual of combat survival, endeavouring to commit to paper the techniques she had used to stay alive during the war.

In the meantime, the well-known Australian writer Russell Braddon had begun to interview Nancy for a book he wanted to write about her exploits. Many nights after work, Braddon would sit with Nancy till late taking notes and trying to sort out just exactly what happened and when. They got on very well.

'He was far and away the nicest biographer I've ever had,' Nancy says, 'and we got on like a house on fire. A lovely man.'

Even while the process of writing the book was underway, Nancy's name still occasionally showed up in newspaper articles, such as a series in 1956 that the London *Daily Express* did on war heroes, entitled *What Happened to the Heroes?*.

Reading that particular piece on Nancy was one of her old acquaintants, Flight Lieutenant John Forward, a tall fair-haired bomber pilot who had flown with the RAF during the war, until he was shot down in 1942 and was then obliged to stay as a POW in Stalag Three in the heartland of Germany for the rest of the war. Once hostilities were over and he was released, he had immediately re-joined the RAF and, on a brief posting to Paris, had met Nancy before their ways again parted. Reading about her now, he was reminded how much he liked her and decided to call in on her unannounced at her flat in Dolphin Square. At the time Nancy was just getting ready to go out on a dinner date with a work colleague when the doorbell rang.

'And I opened the door,' she remembers and there he was. 'In a way, he never left again,' she says; for she really liked Forward, and he liked her. The big fellow liked a joke, loved a drink, was hearty and bluff just the way she liked her men. She adored the way his huge moustache twitched at both ends every time he roared with laughter, which was often. They made a good pair, even if he was four years younger than she. Before long the two were keeping company, and as soon as the following year—in mid-December, 1957—they were married in a London Registry Office.

By this time Braddon's biography, *Nancy Wake, The Story of a*

Very Brave Woman, had been published and such a celebrity did Nancy instantly become that it was almost a relief when John took her back to Malta, where he was posted with the RAF, so she could get away from it all.

'To have a book like that written about me was a big thrill,' Nancy says, 'and I was very happy that it made the bestseller lists, but really all I wanted to do was spend happy time with John.'

The two remained in Malta until John retired in 1959, and it was in fact at his behest that they moved back to Australia almost immediately afterwards, hitching a ride there with John Forward's superior officer, Air Chief Marshal Sir Theodore McEvoy, who was going there on a trip and who was happy to take them.

'I still really wanted to live in Europe on our savings and combined pensions,' Nancy says, 'but John said he had always wanted to live in Australia, and he also thought our money would go further there and that he could get a good job.'

John decided that he was going to like Australia very much from the moment they landed in the town of Pearce in Western Australia and, as part of Air Chief Marshal McEvoy's entourage, they were taken to inspect an orange orchard in the nearby countryside. Through a misunderstanding, the orchardist was not there to greet them, but this presented no problem at all.

'Never mind,' said their guide as he opened the unlocked front door himself and walked right up to the refrigerator, 'Joe would be very annoyed if we didn't all have a beer.'

Once in Sydney, the two moved into an apartment in Crows Nest on the city's lower North Shore not far from where Nancy had grown up, and settled down to live quietly—or at least as quietly as Nancy could manage. Now in her fifties, she was as energetic a woman as ever, and only ever a hair-trigger away from hilarious laughter or high-octane indignation. She did what she wanted, said what she felt, and let the devil take the hind-most.

'That is the way I've always been,' Nancy says, 'and John never seemed to mind.'

The couple were not well off enough to retire yet, so John began working as a mid-ranking executive in a textile firm, while Nancy figuratively and literally kept the home fires burning. It was a curious thing all these years on to be living as a simple homemaker, and to Nancy's surprise she found she actually quite liked it.

Still, despite this apparent contentment, no-one was surprised, least of all John, with Nancy's announcement in early 1966.

'I'm taking another stab at politics,' Nancy told the press. 'In the 1951 elections I took nine hundred votes from Dr Evatt—if I can do that with Danny Curtin at Kingsford Smith, I'll be in for life.'

John quickly installed himself as her campaign manager and supported her to the hilt. But, despite tremendous energy on both parts, Nancy lost. This time, it really was the end of politics for her. 'Bugger the lot of them,' she said to John then, and she meant it. She had been willing to do her bit to go to Canberra to help Australia, but if the electors didn't want her, then she for one wasn't going to be begging them. Besides, she just didn't need that kind of hassle in her life. Some time later, as shown in her autobiography, Nancy's feelings had greatly hardened on the whole exercise, even since the time of her crushing disappointment.

'Without a doubt,' she wrote, 'the most stupid thing I ever did was to join the Liberal Party of NSW and become involved with politics. They used me in the same manner in which they used several men who had distinguished war records.'[77]

Despite this political disappointment, she and John were generally very happy together. In a series of articles published in the *Sydney Morning Herald* in 1968 on the spouses of famous people, John Forward waxed lyrical:

'What does it feel like to be married to a famous Australian?' he said. 'I admire, and always will, her record and decorations, but I must confess that I selfishly think of her as the best cook in Australia. She is a real Cordon Bleu—not just the product of a three-week wonder course in London, or at some restaurant.'[78]

Nancy also played a good round of golf, while John enjoyed going to the pub. When he retired completely from business in 1970 the two often went for long drives together, doing nought but chatting and enjoying the pleasure of each other's company. Not surprisingly, their experiences in the war were never far away for either of them. It was, after all, the foundation stone of their commonality, the thing that had at least initially brought them together—and the two often reminisced with each other.

They also noticed that it seemed that every succeeding generation of the French and Australians would discover Nancy's story, and she would be in the news again for one reason or another. In 1970, Nancy was deeply honoured for the French government to award her the *Chevalier de la Legion d'Honneur* to add to her collection, and if there was still no sign of any recognition from the Australian government, then so be it.

'It didn't matter at all,' Nancy says firmly. 'I hadn't fought for medals in any case. I had fought for freedom.'

Throughout the seventies, John and Nancy lived happily, very occasionally managing to afford to return for a few weeks to their friends in Europe and in the meantime living a life of friends, cooking, drinking, golf and long drives mixed in with regular gatherings at Anzac Day and the Royal Escaping Society—an association for those Australians who had successfully fled the Germans in the Second World War. Journalists would still come to talk to Nancy about her life and times, and she threatened repeatedly to write her autobiography to finally set the record straight on a number of things that journalists often asked about, but often seemed to get wrong.

In the early eighties she actually began to write the book, and in 1985 it appeared. *Nancy Wake: The White Mouse* was in the end so successful that it prompted the Australian television network Channel Seven to commission a mini-series about Nancy's wartime experiences, with the well-known Australian actress Noni Hazlehurst playing Nancy's role. Again, the production was well-received and helped introduce Nancy's story to a new generation of Australians.

It was around this time that Nancy was invited to Port Macquarie on New South Wales's mid-North Coast to open an air show, so she and John took the opportunity to explore the picturesque town. John, particularly, liked what he saw and suggested that it was the perfect place for them to live out their twilight years. And so they moved, settling into a second-floor apartment about a kilometre to the east of the town centre. John liked the lassitude in the air of Port Macquarie and settled in happily—meeting and making friends at the local RSL club where he and his wife would often go for a drink—while Nancy still hungered for the hustle and bustle of Sydney, or better still London and Paris. Sometimes it almost seemed like she was a schoolgirl again, looking out through the window and wondering what those places were like. Had it all been a dream?

Yes, it had all been long ago, but she was certainly not forgotten in the land where she had forged her fame. In 1988, the French Defence Minister, Andre Giraud, awarded Nancy yet another decoration from his country, this time bestowing upon her the *Croix d'Officier de la Legion d'Honneur* aboard the French ship *Jeanne D'Arc*. This award is the second highest French honour that can be bestowed on a foreigner.

With absolutely typical bluntness, Nancy used the opportunity to publicly pour scorn on those who would attack France over their nuclear testing at Muroroa Atoll, saying that if Australia didn't like it they should declare war on France, or otherwise shut the hell up. She also said, curiously, that all those women involved in the worldwide peace movement would be better off staying home and baking biscuits, which attracted enormous fire from feminists, who pointed out that in her day she had done no such thing.

Nancy didn't care. There was a part of her that simply enjoyed a good scrap and she developed good instincts on just what would most likely provoke a storm.

It was in the same year, for example, that while addressing an RSL conference in Victoria she unburdened herself of the view that Vietnamese immigration into Australia had gone way too far—as had Japanese investment—and that if it were up to her, seventy-five per cent of the Vietnamese would be sent home. This prompted a rebuke from the Australian Prime Minister, Bob Hawke, something else Nancy took as a badge of honour. If she was getting rebuked by a Labor prime minister she felt she really must be doing something right.

'I am not a racist,' she says, 'and hate racism, but that is what I felt at the time, and that is what I said. The Japanese were responsible for worse atrocities during the war than the Germans, some of them against friends of mine, and I just didn't think it right that we always had such a shining economic welcome mat out for them.'

In 1994, after a long discussion with John, Nancy sold her medals at a Sotheby's auction. They were bought by the Australian RSL, for some 165,000 dollars, and are now permanently on show at the Australian War Memorial in Canberra. If it might seem strange that Nancy would put on the block something that had been so hard won, Nancy has an answer.

'I can't take them with me,' she says, 'I don't have children, and they might melt in the place that I am going. So why wouldn't I sell them?'

Such straightforward practical common sense had always stood her in good stead.

In 1997, Nancy was widowed for the second time when, at the age of eighty-one, John Forward died peacefully in his sleep. The days since have been long for Nancy, and sometimes lonely, though at least regularly interspersed with visitors from near and far. Still, oft-times the hours yawn. She watches a bit of television, turns it off, has a beer, turns it on again, has another beer. Every now and then she will go on a shopping expedition, and is a well-known sight around the streets of the town. She has a particular affection for the Port Macquarie taxi drivers and they for her. It is not uncommon for one taxi driver with a passenger to spy Nancy starting out on the slight incline that leads from the town centre back to her home, and call for another taxi driver to come and pick her up, mostly at no charge.

'They are adorable to me,' Nancy says, 'and I appreciate it.'

Her health is so-so. She has had a couple of minor strokes in the last three years, but all things considered—now on the edge of her ninetieth year—she is doing all right. A doctor recently told her that he thought she had every chance of receiving a telegram from the Queen for her one-hundredth birthday. That would be nice, but in the here and now Nancy hungers after one thing. She wants to leave Australia and spend the remaining years of her life either in Britain or France where her surviving friends are.

'I only want one room,' she told her second biographer at their first meeting, 'a bathroom and a small kitchen, anywhere over there. The people of Port Macquarie have been wonderful to me, as have most individual Australians I've met, but I just feel the need to go to where I am appreciated.'

An example of the 'appreciation' she receives in France is that when she is wearing the rosette of her *Officier de Legion d'Honneur*, all the gendarmes salute her, and even stop the traffic so she may cross the road. The Australian Government recently made contact to see if she would accept having her achievements acknowledged by their awarding her an Australian medal, but she knocked them back outright.

'No,' she says flatly. 'The last time there was a suggestion of that I told the government they could stick their medals where the monkey stuck his nuts. The thing is if they gave me a medal now, it wouldn't be given with love so I don't want anything from them.'

In the calendar of her life, the one day of the year she looks forward to above and beyond all others is Anzac Day.

'It means first of all,' she says, 'remembering Australia's contribution during the First World War, where our men were so terrific. Back then, Australian men were men, and they were loyal to their country, and I think we must always honour what they achieved.'

Often Nancy will spend Anzac Day up at Dorrigo, just inland from Coffs Harbour, where she is a patron of the local RSL sub-branch. Though she now finds it too hard to get herself up and about in time for the dawn service, she usually takes part in the rest of the day's activities, with all the other returned servicemen and women in the region.

This she thoroughly enjoys, but it is still not where she most wants to be—in Europe.

'I'm not sure,' she says, 'whether I will be able to raise the money to get back to Europe, but whatever happens, I know what I want to happen to my body when I'm gone.'

And what is that?

'I want to be cremated,' she says, with the timbre of barely controlled emotion creeping into her voice. 'And I want my ashes to be scattered over the mountains where I fought with the Resistance. That will be good enough for me.'

APPENDIX ONE

B ecause of her efforts, Nancy Grace Augusta Wake, became one of the most highly decorated heroes of the Second World War. The Americans awarded her their Medal of Freedom, the British the George Medal, and the French two *Croix de Guerre* with Palm, the *Croix de Guerre* with Star, and the *Medaille de la Resistance*. In 1988, they awarded her the *Chevalier de Legion d'Honneur*.

She has yet to receive official recognition from Australia, though as this book goes to press, that is under discussion.

Ensign Nancy Grace Augusta Wake, FANY
George Medal Citation

Presented to her on Wednesday 21 April, 1948, by Sir Oliver Harvey, the British Ambassador in Paris.

This officer was parachuted into France on the 1st March 1944 as assistant to an organiser who was taking over the direction of an important circuit in Central France. The day after their arrival she and her chief found themselves stranded and without directions, through the arrest of their contact, but ultimately reached their rendezvous by their own initiative.

Ensign Wake worked for several months helping to train and instruct Maquis groups. She took part in several engagements with the enemy, and showed the utmost bravery under fire. During a German attack, due to the arrival by parachute of two American officers to help in the Maquis, Ensign Wake personally took command of a section of ten men whose leader was demoralized. She led them to within point-blank range of the enemy, directed their fire, rescued the two American officers and withdrew in good order. She showed exceptional courage and coolness in the face of enemy fire.

When the Maquis group with which she was working was broken up by large-scale German attacks, and W/T contact was lost, Ensign Wake went alone to find a wireless operator through whom she could contact London. She covered some 200 kilometres. On foot, and by remarkable steadfastness and perseverance succeeded in getting a message through to London, giving the particulars of a ground where a new W/T plan and further stores could be dropped. It was largely due to these efforts that the circuit was able to work again.

Ensign Wake's organizing ability, endurance, courage and complete disregard for her own safety earned her the respect and admiration of all with whom she came in contact. The Maquis troop, most of them rough and difficult to handle, accepted orders from her, and treated her as one of their own male officers. Ensign Wake contributed in a large degree to the success of the groups with which she worked, and it is strongly recommended that she be awarded the George Medal.

Citation for the American Medal of Freedom With Bronze Palm

Ensign Nancy Wake, British National, FANY, for exceptionally meritorious achievement which aided the United States in the prosecution of the war against the enemy in Continental Europe, from March 1944. After having been parachuted into the Allier Department of France for the purpose of co-ordinating Resistance activities she immediately assumed her duties as second-in-command to the organizer of the circuit. Despite numerous difficulties and personal danger she, through her remarkable courage, initiative and coolness succeeded in accomplishing her objective. Her daring conduct in the course of an enemy engagement safeguarded the lives of two American officers under her command. Her inspiring leadership, bravery, and exemplary devotion to duty contributed materially to the success of the war effort and merit the praise and recognition of the United States.

GO 3. Hq USFET, 9 January 1947.[79]

APPENDIX TWO

·‒

The following letter was written by Colonel Maurice Buckmaster, as a reference for Nancy.

72 Pelham Court,
London
1st March, 1946.

To Whom It May Concern

Mrs Nancy Fiocca was employed by my department for about a year, during which time she volunteered for a special and most dangerous mission in enemy occupied territory. She accomplished this task with outstanding success and displayed great qualities of personal bravery, endurance and determination. Her strong personality gave her the undisputed leadership of a large number of French patriots, whom she organised, with great tact and savoir-faire, to attack the enemy. Under continuous fire from superior forces she showed exemplary courage.

She has much shrewdness and common sense, and has accomplished an outstanding important task with unqualified success.

Maurice Buckmaster.
Colonel G.S.
(Demobilized July 1945)

BIBLIOGRAPHY

Braddon, Russell *Nancy Wake: The Story of a Very Brave Woman.* W.W. Norton & Company, London, 1957.

Buckmaster, Colonel Maurice *They Fought Alone: The Story of British Agents in France.* Odhams Press Limited, Long Acre London, 1958.

Cookridge, E.H. *Inside SOE.* Arthur Barker Limited, London, 1966.

Cookridge, E.H. *They Came From the Sky.* Corgi, London, 1976.

Foot, M.R.D. *SOE in France.* University Publications of America, Inc., Maryland, 1984.

Foot, M.R.D. *SOE, An Outline History of the Special Operations Executive 1940–46.* The British Broadcasting Corporation, London, 1984.

Jackson, Robert *Heroines of World War II.* Arthur Barker Limited, London, 1976.

Laffin, John *Australians at War. Special and Secret.* Time-Life Books Australia, Sydney, 1990.

Miller, Russell *The Resistance, World War II.* Time-Life Books, Alexandria, Virginia, 1979.

Wake, Nancy *The White Mouse.* Sun Books, South Melbourne, 1985.

Woods, Rex *A Talent to Survive. The Wartime Exploits of Lt. Col. Richard Broad, MC.* London, 1982.

ENDNOTES

1 *Sydney Morning Herald,* April 25, 1918.

2 Quoted in *Time Magazine* (Australian edition), July 31, 2000, p. 47.

3 This staggering passage was brought to my attention by Wallaby coach, Rod Macqueen, who read it as the last thing the Wallabies heard from him before they went out to play, and win, in the final of the Rugby World Cup, 1999, at the Millennium Stadium in Cardiff, Wales.

4 Although Nancy did not know it at the time, it later emerged that Mussolini had been intimately involved at every stage of planning the assassination of the Yugoslav king—one of the first examples of state-sponsored terrorism. Mussolini had personally promised 500,000 lire to the man who killed him.

5 Nancy Wake, *The White Mouse*, Sun Books, 1985, p. 25.

6 Habitués of this famous health resort were known in England at the time as 'Champney Chumps'!

7 William Shakespeare *Julius Caesar*. Act 3, Sc. 1, l. 273.

8 Nancy Wake, 1985, pp 32–33.

9 This editorial appeared in the *New York Times* in early June 1940, and was subsequently reprinted in a Ninth Division News Sheet in Egypt in 1942, where it was read, and subsequently memorised, by the author's late father, Lieutenant Peter McCloy FitzSimons, who was serving with the Ninth Division of the Australian Infantry Forces at the time.

10 E.H. Cookridge, *Inside SOE*, Arthur Barker, London, 1966, p. 96.

11 E.H. Cookridge, 1966, p. 98.

12 Acknowledgement to Russell Miller, *The Resistance, World War II*, Time Life Books, Alexandria, Virginia, 1979, pp. 10–16 for information about this informal resistance.

13 *The Sun*, November 21, 1949.

14 Nancy Wake, 1985, p. 67.

15 *Woman's Day and Home*, June 4, 1951.

16 President Roosevelt's famous phraseology was uttered in his address to Congress on 8 December, 1941.

17 This human traffic across the Pyrenees, often along old smuggling routes, was in fact a reverse of the traffic during the worst of the Spanish Civil War during the late 1930s when thousands of Spaniards fleeing Franco went north to Perpignan. The French held them in camps and sent many hundreds on to Spanish-speaking South American countries.

18 Russell Miller, 1979, p. 127.

19 *Woman's Day*, June 11, 1951.

20 This information drawn from Russell Miller, 1979, p. 110.

21 Russell Braddon, *Nancy Wake: The Story of a Very Brave Woman*, W.W. Norton, 1957, p. 66.

22 Russell Miller, 1979, p. 180.

23 Based on the account in Robert Jackson's *Heroines of World War II*, Arthur Barker, London, 1976, p. 100.

24 *Daily Telegraph*, 31 October, 1987.

25 Russell Miller, 1979, p. 113.

26 E.H. Cookridge, *They Came From the Sky*, Corgi, London, 1976, p. 56.

27 Happily, O'Leary was not only one of the very few who survived the terrible privations of Dachau, he was also awarded by Britain the George Cross for his service, and rose to the rank of Major-General, becoming the Belgian Army's senior medical officer.

28 Russell Braddon, 1957, p. 86.

29 The name was, correctly, Olga Pullofsky and comes from an old song about the eponymous Olga the Spy, a spy so beautiful that the firing squad can't bring themselves to shoot her; it was misspelt in Nancy Wake's autobiography, 1985, p. 97.

30 E.H. Cookridge, 1966, p. 6.

31 E.H. Cookridge, 1966, p. 3.

32 Maurice Buckmaster, *They Fought Alone: The Story of British Agents in France*, Odhams Press, London, 1958, p. 66.

33 As described by Russell Braddon, 1957, p. 110.

34 Maurice Buckmaster, 1958, p. 49.

35 Robert Jackson, 1976, p. 104.

36 Maurice Buckmaster, 1958, p. 49.

37 Maurice Buckmaster, 1958, p. 49.

38 *Times of Malta*, 25 January, 1959.

39 Maurice Buckmaster, 1958, p. 127.

40 *TV Times*, 2 November, 1956.

41 M.R.D. Foot, Introduction to *S.O.E. In France*, University Publications, Maryland, 1984, p xvii.

42 E.H. Cookridge, 1976, p. 43.

43 Maurice Buckmaster, 1958, p 123.

44 This imagined conversation is based on a passage in Maurice Buckmaster, 1958, p. 67.

45 Private communication with John Farmer, 18 January, 2000.

46 *Woman's Day and Home*, 4 June, 1951.

47 E.H. Cookridge, 1976, p. 44.

48 Maurice Buckmaster, 1958, p. 53.

49 *London Daily Telegraph*, July 15, 1945.

50 Russell Miller, 1979, p. 116.

51 William Shakespeare, *Henry V* (Part II), Act 3, Sc. 1, l.1

52 E.H. Cookridge, 1966, p. 362.

53 Russell Braddon, 1957, p. 164.

54 Quoted by A.M. Thomson, *Here I Lie,* 1937, (cited in *The Wit and Wisdom of the 20th Century*), 1980, p. 374.

55 Nancy Wake, 1985, p. 47.

56 Russell Braddon, 1957, p. 177.

57 Nancy Wake, 1985, pp. 140–141.

58 London *Daily Telegraph*, July 15, 1945.

59 Russell Braddon, 1957, p. 179.

60 Nancy Wake, 1985, p. 147.

61 John Laffin *Australians at War. Special and Secret*, Sydney, Time Life, 1990, p. 17.

62 Maurice Buckmaster, 1958, p. 241.

63 Maurice Buckmaster, 1958, p. 238.

64 Nancy Wake, 1985, p. 152.

65 Russell Braddon, 1957, p. 218.

66 Russell Miller, 1979, p. 194.

67 *Sunday Telegraph*, 29 March, 1971.

68 Russell Braddon, 1957, p. 232.

69 Robert Louis Stevenson *Requiem*, 1887.

70 *The Star*, 22 April, 1948.

71 Newspaper clipping from Nancy's personal scrapbook. Neither the date, nor the name of the newspaper is clear.

72 *Sunday Sun*, 16 January, 1949.

73 *The Sydney Morning Herald*, 30 March, 1949.

74 *The Daily Mirror*, 1 April, 1949.

75 *The Sydney Morning Herald*, 30 March, 1949.

76 *Sunday Sun*, 15 April, 1951.

77 Nancy Wake, 1985, p. 175.

78 *The Sydney Morning Herald*, 18 March, 1968.

79 Russell Braddon, 1957, pp. 253–4.

INDEX